big earth

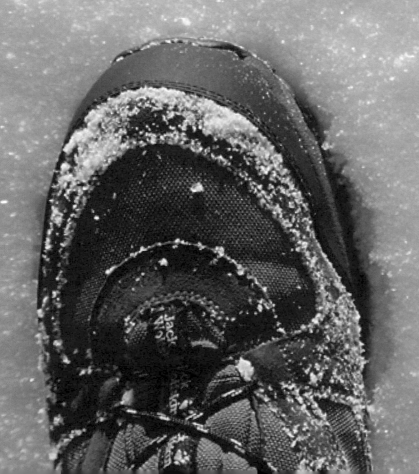

This book is dedicated to my amazing family
who not only let me go off to do these amazing
adventures but who sometimes joined me, too!
Thanks to Mum and Dad (Jill and Tony),
my daughter (Emily) and my girlfriend (Victoria),
and of course a special thanks
to Ewan and Charley.

big earth

101 AMAZING ADVENTURES

Russ Malkin

BANTAM PRESS

LONDON · TORONTO · SYDNEY · AUCKLAND · JOHANNESBURG

I always wanted to experience the thrill of a grand travelling adventure, and to do it on the back of a motorcycle. In a simple way, travelling opens up the soul in a manner that's hard to describe, and I'd encourage anyone to go and take a plunge into the unknown.

The world is your oyster, in terms of where to go and how long for, and you can achieve a huge amount if all your prep is done correctly. That's how my relationship with Russ started, in the visa application quagmire and the Carne list exasperations. How many spare tubes does a journey of 20,000 miles, mostly off-road, require? Dried food or fresh? Can our American team members really not get into Libya? Routes, maps, spares, timetables, weather, temperatures, wild animals, risks . . . the planning is seemingly endless, but it's also exciting and fun.

Behind it all is the dream of what's to come, and if the prep is done well then you're free to live the dream and experience the landscape and the people to the full. Raising awareness, and even cash, for charities as you pass through countries is also wonderful. It's a way to leave something behind as you go along and it's beneficial to all, but finding out how to do this is often confusing and difficult. Russ has enormous experience in this and has boiled down all he knows so that we might all get more out of our trips. Bon voyage to you all, whether you're planning a day trip to Brighton or a polar challenge on ice skates.

I hope to see you on the road.

Travel safe . . . don't leave rubbish!

Ewan McGregor

Ewan and I were excited to be asked to write the forewords for Russ's book. Russ had been involved from the early stages in planning our first joint project, *Long Way Round*. That project was born out of a dream that I'm sure many people have, to travel around the world. In our case, the dream was to travel by motorcycle, and since Russ had a similar passion for two wheels, and also had experience in planning and executing major projects, it seemed like the ideal combination. It was funny, though – at the outset when I mentioned I was going with Ewan McGregor, Russ looked at me doubtfully, and it was only when he saw Ewan pull up outside his flat in Battersea that he believed me.

An adventure can change your life – Ewan and I agree on that – but probably the most difficult part is making the decision to do it. After that, planning and research are crucial. Yes, we would all like to just get up and go – and I bet you'd have a real laugh doing it this way, because you would be on the seat of your pants every day trying to find places to stay, manage your money, organize border crossings, and so on – but the truth is that to get the most out of an adventure it is better to plan ahead. Believe me, enough unexpected stuff will happen to you on the road.

As well as choosing where to go and when, think about how you want to travel. Do you want to travel on your own or in a crowd, to touristy places or remote locations? As I've discovered with Russ, when you travel with other people there will be times of stress and arguments, but the bond you create will last for ever.

Big Earth: 101 Amazing Adventures is a great book to read, and, like Ted Simon's *Jupiter's Travels*, which Ewan read, and which provided the inspiration for *Long Way Round*, this book is your cue to pull out an atlas. Take ideas from this book and then go and have some fun. Do it our way or do it your way. Whatever you do, go. I would certainly recommend to anybody that they break out at least once in their lives, do something different, something off the beaten track, something wild, something wonderful, something amazing!

Good travels.

Charley Boorman

Introduction

I was standing next to Ewan at the side of the road in far eastern Russia, staring out over mile after mile of empty steppe. We were in the middle of absolutely nowhere, on a road that had been washed away in numerous places by flooding rivers. We had no idea if we could make it through to our destination, and no idea if we could make it safely back in the direction we'd come. All around us were clouds of aggressive mosquitoes, and there was the constant awareness of bears and treacherous road conditions. There was no doubt that this was deeply hazardous territory, and yet, at the same time, I'd never felt more alive.

I often think back to that moment. If I'm stressed out, frantically running between meetings in London, exhausted after a long week of business, friends and other commitments associated with day-to-day life, then picturing that distant road is like taking a deep breath of fresh air. At the time it was uncomfortable and dangerous, but there was also an overwhelming sense of freedom, of self-reliance and of being a world away from ordinary life. In short, it's a moment that for me sums up the appeal and the importance of adventure.

Working with Ewan and Charley on the *Long Way Round*, *Long Way Down* and *By Any Means* programmes has left me with a passion for travelling, and

convinced me of how valuable it can be to get out there and be adventurous. People kept asking me how we were inspired to produce those television expeditions, and often inspiration comes from reading a book by someone who taps into your idea of adventure. For this book, the more I thought about it, the more I realized that an adventure doesn't have to be a three-and-a-half-month, round-the-world epic. An adventure could take a year or just a weekend; it could be a life-threatening challenge or something that's pure fun. So I decided to come up with 101 adventures that would both inspire others and convey my understanding of what 'adventure' really means. Those I have chosen range from the hardcore, such as the Dakar rally or surviving in a tropical rainforest, to the relaxed, like sailing a narrowboat on the Llangollen canal.

For me, whether something qualifies as an adventure isn't to do with how tough it is. It's not about proving something to someone else, and it's certainly not about ticking boxes. It's about having an experience that takes you outside your normal life, beyond your comfort zone, and in doing so gives you some space to think and feel. I think part of the attraction is that an adventure brings back associations of childhood – the sense of exploring somewhere that's new to you, experiencing fresh things, feeling independent, and being free of the day-to-day worries of adult life.

Some of the adventures in this book are famous challenges, like taking on the Cresta Run or riding the Isle of Man TT circuit. Others are far more obscure, like getting a taste of life on board a trawler boat in the Irish Sea or living with a team of cowboys in Guyana. But all of them are escapes from the humdrum.

Often the best adventures are the result of a personal interest. I travelled to Bolivia to pursue my fascination with the film *Butch Cassidy and the Sundance Kid*, and in Australia I got to live out my ambition of riding on the footplate of a steam train. Unusual choices, perhaps, but to me they were fabulous experiences. Crucially, this book isn't intended as a 'tick-list' for people to work their way through. The whole point about adventure is that you are free to do what you want, to make your own decisions and discoveries, rather than to slavishly follow someone else's instructions. Of course, if you like the look of any of the adventures in the book, then go for it, but really they are there to give you a sense of what is possible, and to inspire you to create your own trip.

There are three stages with any adventure. First is the planning, working out what your own objectives will be and committing yourself to go (in itself, a very exciting moment). The second stage is enjoying the event, heading off, however briefly, to occupy a new and different life, whether it be in the wilds of Dartmoor or sitting on a train across India. Enjoying the moment is fundamental.

But almost as important is the third aspect – the memories. If you have recorded the trip in a diary and with photos or film, you will always have something to look back on, even a legacy to pass on to your children. Your trip can go on informing your life long after you get back. Very rarely do you meet somebody who regrets having gone off on an adventure. In fact, it's often the experiences that seem worst at the time that prove the most worthwhile in retrospect. I can clearly remember being high up in the rigging of the tall ship *Soren Larsen*, so afraid that I was utterly frozen, gripping on to the mast with white knuckles, unable to go up or down. And then there was the night in the South American jungle, when the howler monkeys were making their blood-curdling screeches, our fire had gone out and it seemed like dawn would never come. At the time I kept asking myself why I was putting myself through these ordeals when I could be sitting on a beach with a cocktail in my hand. But these are the experiences you never forget, the ones you feel proud of coming through, which can put a smile on your face years later, on even the wettest and windiest of British afternoons.

So use these ideas, adapt them to your own interests or treat them as the starting point for dreaming up your own journeys. I hope you enjoy the book but, more importantly, I hope it spurs you into setting out on your own adventure. Don't leave it too long, and have fun!

Once in a Lifetime

The journey locator

The journeys

1 Into the Abyss

Why	For a geological marvel where there's peace underground
Where	Brazil	**Duration**	Two days

We were walking through the forest in the middle of nowhere when a man's head popped out of the ground. He was overweight and sweating profusely, gasping for breath and swearing in Portuguese. He clambered out of a gap in the earth a couple of feet across, then collapsed on his back, exhausted but with a broad smile on his face. '*Assombroso . . .*' he said quietly to himself. 'Amazing.'

Back in the late 1970s, a fire ripped through this area, around fifteen miles from the town of Bonito in the western Brazilian state of Mato Grosso. With the vegetation stripped away, a local farmer noticed a narrow crack in the ground, stuck his head in and saw a breathtaking sight – a lake far below.

It wasn't until 1984 that the cave was properly explored, by an expedition which found that the narrow hole opened up like the neck of a wine bottle, and the lake, 72 metres below ground, was the size of a football pitch. In 1996, divers from another expedition reached the bottom of the lake for the first time, 80 metres below the water's surface. Then, in 1999, the cavern was opened up to tourists.

Even today, though, few foreigners have been down into the cave, the Abismo Anhumas (meaning 'Abyss of the Anhumas region'), because it is limited to an absolute maximum of sixteen visitors per day. Partly this is to preserve the cavern's ecology, but mainly because there is only one way into

> *Because there are only ever a tiny number of people in the cave, you really get a sense of its peace and otherworldliness*

Dangling 70 metres on a rope was a dramatic moment — and I had to climb back up!

the cave and one way out – abseiling 72 metres down a rope to enter, then climbing that same rope to get back out.

Our adventure had begun the previous day at a climbing wall in Bonito. There, anyone who wants to go into the cavern has to undergo a short course in abseiling and rope-climbing. And while the guides are showing you how to use the harnesses and climbing equipment, they are also assessing your fitness and mental state. This is vital to ensure safety – if someone were to start freaking out halfway up the rope, or found they weren't fit enough to climb all the way out, those left at the bottom could be in trouble.

And now we were ready. At the top of the Abismo, I inched towards the edge of the crack and looked down into the bowels of the earth. One thing was abundantly clear – if you have even the slightest sense of vertigo, this isn't an adventure for you. In case the figure of 72 metres doesn't convey very much, think of it as the equivalent of a 30-storey office block, and you start to get a sense of the scale.

With a helmet and harness on, I clipped myself on to the rope and prepared to descend. You use a device that looks a bit like a metal handle, which clamps to the rope. Squeeze a lever in the handle and it releases its grip on the rope, so you slide downwards. Release the lever and the handle clamps on again, bringing you to a halt.

I gingerly squeezed the lever, and dropped – all of six inches. It seemed to work, so I squeezed again, this time a bit harder and more purposefully, and lurched down a couple of feet before a self-preservation reflex kicked in, making me release the lever and shudder to a halt once more. A couple more false starts, then a big squeeze, and

I was three metres into the hole.

At this point the walls of the cavern are close enough to touch on both sides, and this gives a sense of perspective, and somehow comfort. But another few metres down, the walls disappear off into the darkness and you find yourself hanging in a vast open space. The only light is the shaft of sunlight from the hole you have just come through, and it's down this shaft of light that you must keep descending to reach the bottom. I stopped and hung there for a few moments, taking it all in.

'Come on!' shouted the guides at the bottom, and I looked down to see two tiny faces far below. With more confidence, I started descending quickly towards the lake. As I neared the bottom, the two guides yanked the end of the rope so that, rather than dropping into the water, I landed beside them on a wooden pontoon. I unclipped myself from the rope, stepped back and then turned in circles, taking in the subterranean cathedral around me.

After exploring the lake in a small inflatable dinghy, gawping at the stalactites hanging from the ceiling, some thick as pillars, others like delicate icicles, it was time to get into the water.

I put on my wetsuit and snorkel and lowered myself off the pontoon, shivering as I waited for the suit to warm up. Adjusting my mask, I looked down and got a shock. Filtered through the rocks, the water here is so clean and clear that you can see right to the bottom of the lake, where dramatic cone stalagmites, some of them 20 metres tall, reach upwards towards you. You can scuba-dive here, but there's no need. The water is so clear you almost forget it's there, leaving you with a bizarre sense of floating in mid-air high above a rocky canyon or a submerged city, the cones like skyscrapers. In some ways it is more vertigo-inducing than the abseiling.

The nice thing is that because there are only ever a tiny number of people in the cave, you really get a sense of its peace and otherworldliness. I lay motionless on my front in the water for 15 minutes, looking at the rocks far below, then turned and floated on my back for another 15 minutes, looking up at the stalactites that have

taken millions of years to form. It was like a grand, natural version of the flotation tanks you get in smart city gyms. My wetsuit hood dulled any sound, and I found it relaxing to be able to turn off my brain for a bit, immersed in water, deep under the ground.

I was there for so long that someone came down to nudge me and check I was all right. But there was no rush to leave. Climbing the rope up out of the cave can take people up to an hour and a half, so I knew it would be a while before the others in the group got out and it was my turn to leave.

Climbing out isn't easy. Using the rope-clamping device in reverse, and with your feet in a sling attached to the rope, the idea is to use your leg muscles rather than your arms to gradually push yourself up. You stand up on the sling, slide up the clamp with your arms, bend your knees to your chest – and repeat, for what feels like a thousand times. Experts can ensure all their effort goes into pushing upwards, and no weight goes on the arms, but novices find themselves swinging from side to side, hauling themselves up with their arms and upper body. After 15 minutes my biceps were on fire. I looked down and saw I was only 20 metres from the pontoon. Looking up, the dazzling shaft of light seemed to go on for ever.

After 45 minutes, I made it up into the narrow neck of the cave, and the guides at the top all started shouting: 'Go on, Russ! You can do it! You're nearly there!' And with a final push, my head popped back out into the real world.

Five hours after descending below the surface, I clambered out of the hole and lay wheezing on the ground, staring up as the clouds swept across the deep blue sky. Now I understood exactly what had been going through that fat Brazilian man's mind. I smiled and soundlessly mouthed the word, 'Amazing . . .'

Now do it . . .

Tours for the Abismo Anhumas can be organized through Pure Brasil (www.purebrasil.net). For more information, visit the official website (www.abismoanhumas.com.br).

2 Exploring the Aral Sea

Why	To combine bizarre sights with environmental awareness
Where	Eastern Kazakhstan	**Duration**	One week

Many of the adventures in this book are about escaping into wilderness environments where there is no sign of human activity, but this trip is the absolute opposite, a sort of cautionary tale, a journey on which you can witness just how extreme the effects of man's actions on the natural world can be.

In 1960, the Aral Sea was the fourth largest lake in the world, covering 26,000 square miles between Kazakhstan and Uzbekistan. It supported 40,000 fishermen, and produced a sixth of the entire Soviet Union's fish catch.

Back then the town of Muynak was a bustling port at the southern end of the sea, and the centre of Uzbekistan's fishing industry. Go there today, walk out along the long pier, and you are confronted by a bizarre, shocking sight – the sea has simply disappeared. Instead, the pier stretches out over a grey expanse of desert, a few mangy camels wander around, and dotted around in the sand are the rusting hulks of the stranded fishing boats.

The reason is entirely man-made. In the 1940s, the Soviet government started to divert the two rivers that fed the Aral Sea, the Amu Darya and

> **You are confronted by a bizarre, shocking sight – the sea has simply disappeared**

the Syr Darya, into irrigation channels to create vast new cotton plantations. Their scheme worked and Uzbekistan is now one of the world's largest producers of cotton. But the sea began to shrink.

By 2007 it had shrunk to a tenth of its original size and split into three separate lakes – the North Aral Sea, now entirely in Kazakhstan, and the east and west basins of the South Aral Sea. By 2009 the eastern lake had disappeared altogether.

With no water, the fishing industry collapsed and the inhabitants of the once vibrant towns around the coast drifted away, leaving scores of ghost towns. Those that have stayed have been affected by high levels of cancer and other diseases, the result of toxic dust storms that whip across the salty seabed, picking up the residues from decades of pesticides and fertilizers from the farms upstream.

'It is clearly one of the worst environmental disasters of the world,' said Ban Ki-Moon, secretary-general of the United Nations, when he visited in 2010.

We camped on the banks of the Aral Sea, then in the morning drove out across it to look at the fishing boats. You need to be careful as many are unstable and so very dangerous, but it's absolutely fascinating. You can walk right up to them, climb in through the holes left by salvage teams removing the engines, then explore the cabins and bridge. Standing on the deck, looking out over the perfectly flat, totally dry, desert is an eerie and chastening experience.

There is a glimmer of hope for the region. Oil-rich Kazakhstan has decided to save the North Aral Sea, and in 2005 completed a dam which should lead to the lake refilling completely, and a second

It was very eerie seeing rusting hulks sitting in a sea of sand.

dam is now under construction. Already the water level has risen and the salinity decreased, enough for the fish to return in numbers that can support commercial fishing. The sea, which had retreated sixty-two miles from the port city of Aral, at the northern end of the lake, is coming back – by 2010 it was only sixteen miles away.

For the South Aral Sea, however, the outlook is very different. It seems the last remnants will soon vanish altogether, leaving more boats high and dry on a sea of sand, bizarre warning signs of what can happen when man meddles with nature.

Now do it . . .
Silk Off Road (www.silkoffroad.kz) not only offer 4x4 hire, but also various tours in the region.

3

The Road of Bones

Why	For remote wilderness and epic landscapes
Where	Far Eastern Russia	**Duration**	Two weeks +

From the very beginning of the planning process for *Long Way Round*, a TV show which saw Ewan McGregor, Charley Boorman, David Alexanian and I travel round the globe from London to New York on motorbikes, Charley was adamant that whatever we did, we must ride the Road of Bones. As a route for an expedition it seemed to have all the right ingredients – it was steeped in mystery, it was remote and considered very dangerous, few people had ever been there and, perhaps most importantly, everyone was telling us not to go.

The road stretches 1,270 miles across Kolyma, beyond Siberia in Russia's Far East. It's officially called the M56, but locals know it as the Trassa, which means simply 'the route' – no other designation is needed because this is the only road passing through an area almost as big as the USA.

The history of the road makes it more forbidding still. It was built between 1932 and 1953 by prisoners of Stalin's gulags, many of them guilty of nothing more than refusing to collaborate with the regime by informing on their colleagues. The prisoners were told to build a road all the way from Yakutsk to the far eastern port of Magadan and to make it smooth enough so that when the officer in charge drove along it with a glass of vodka on the bonnet of his car, not a drop would spill. If it did, the guards would shoot every tenth prisoner. The ground to the side of the road is frozen solid in winter, and an impassable quagmire in summer, so the victims were buried in the road itself – hence the name.

In fact, many of the prisoners died of exposure, not from the shooting. Two towns on the route, Tomtor and Oymyakon, both claim the world's coldest recorded temperature outside Antarctica, –71°C. The *average* temperature in Oymyakon in January is –41°C.

The isolation and the elements would make this route a challenge in itself, but that's only the start of it. On top of that, the road isn't maintained by the government, which means it is full of potholes and in a terrible state, and in the summer when the snow melts, rivers sweep across it, washing away sections and leaving it all but impassable.

We arrived in Yakutsk in June, having travelled overland from London, but you can fly in via Moscow on Aeroflot. If you fly in you should be able to find someone to take you to Magadan in a truck, which would probably

TOMTOR
KURANAKH-SALA
KADYKCHAN
KHANDYGA
ADYGALAKH
MATTA
YAKUTSK
KARAMKEN
MAGADAN

SEA OF OKHOTSK

JOHN O' GROATS TO CAPE TOWN

LONG
way down
EXPLORE!
Mac Tools
SONIC
NOKIA
6110
Navigator

' The isolation and the elements would make this route a challenge in itself, but that's only the start of it '

cost around $1,000, but many people want to ride the road by bike. The road has been successfully ridden by only a handful of people, some solo, some in groups. Despite the cold, the consensus is that it's easier to ride the road in winter when the rivers, rubble and potholes are frozen solid. Unfortunately, the scheduling of the rest of our round-the-world trip meant that we had no choice but to take it on in the summer. We started on bikes, but soon realized that at this time of year we'd need the back-up of a couple of trucks to stand a chance of reaching Magadan.

We began by taking a ferry from Yakutsk across the Lena River, then spent a sketchy few hours riding across deep gravel before the road surface improved and we began to pick up speed and enjoy ourselves. The scenery was fantastic, starkly beautiful, if almost completely monochrome – black mountains with white snow caps, grey dirt beneath the wheels and dark rocks lining the road. We climbed several mountain passes, where the road narrowed to a precarious single track, with big drops to the side, then passed an ominous sign: 'Magadan 1430km'.

We were doing fine until about five days in, when we came to a river that was so fast and deep there was no way we could cross it. It was probably only 15 metres across, but might as well have been 1,000. The meltwater and heavy rains washing down from the mountains had swept away a section of road, leaving cliffs where the road fell away into the water. No car, let alone bike, could get through, and even the big Russian trucks we had with us, a Ural and a Kamaz, didn't stand a chance.

We spent a fretful night camped at the side of the road—the thought of turning back, abandoning the whole round-the-world adventure, didn't bear thinking about, but going forward didn't look very inviting either. Ewan McGregor was adamant. 'This journey simply isn't important enough to risk someone drowning in a freezing rapid,' he said. 'I

'The scenery was fantastic, starkly beautiful, if almost completely monochrome'

couldn't forgive myself if anything went wrong.' He was right, too. When you watch an adventure like that on television, you know everyone's going to be all right, but when you're out there doing it, you haven't a clue what will happen next.

The next morning the water level had fallen by a foot or so, and we came up with a plan. We started to hammer big metal spikes into the edge of the road, levering off chunks of stone and rubble and then using spades to pack them down into a ramp that vehicles could use to drive in and out of the water.

The first to use our home-made ramp were four enormous Russian logging trucks that were coming in the opposite direction. They had tried to cross the night before but they'd nearly turned over in the rapids so had retreated. Now they revved their engines for another try.

As they charged down into the river, fumes pouring from their exhausts, it was like watching a scene from an action movie. The wheels of the first truck clawed at our ramp for a few seconds, but it held and the mammoth vehicle lurched back on to dry land. The others followed and the drivers were so pleased that they insisted on cracking open the vodka. With glasses that were full of mosquitoes we toasted each other's health. And then it was our turn.

As we loaded the bikes into our own vans, it occurred to me that if there was a problem, the only way out would be by Russian helicopter flying from Magadan, and the likelihood of that getting to us in time to help in a real emergency was remote . . .

Our first truck inched down the ramp, then eased slowly across, the driver's knuckles white from gripping the steering wheel so tight, then scrambled up the far bank. Ewan whooped with delight. The other trucks followed safely and we celebrated on the other side. Building the ramp and getting across had been hard work – in the rain, with mosquitoes buzzing around – but it had also been a total team effort.

A week, and many more river crossings later, we came around a hill and saw Magadan before us. Everyone was elated – we'd crossed Europe and now Asia. Magadan has a grim history – it was here where the prisoners were unloaded from ships and marched off to the gulags – but today it's a pretty place with pastel-painted wooden houses, not to mention a nightclub complete with a helicopter on the dancefloor.

Sitting in the hotel bar, looking back at our journey, I was surprised none of us had got hurt. But the felling of trees, ramp-building and pick-axe work, the chatting in the open backs of the trucks, the camping, cooking and drinking vodka had made it a real boys' own adventure. I was exhausted but I've never felt more alive in my life.

Now do it . . .

Compass Expeditions (www.compassexpeditions. com) lends BMW vehicles for great treks all over the world, including London to Magadan. The Russian National Tourist Office can help with visas and accommodation (www.visitrussia.org.uk).

'The felling of trees, ramp-building and pick-axe work, the chatting in the open backs of the trucks, the camping, cooking and drinking vodka had made it a real boys' own adventure'

4

Sailing the English Channel

Why	For an iconic sailing trip and a personal challenge
Where	English Channel	**Duration**	One day

LONG WEEKEND

When Charley Boorman and I embarked on *By Any Means* in 2008, we were attempting to travel to Sydney using as many means of transport as we could, and for each to be appropriate to the country we were travelling through. We used tuk tuks in India, elephants in Nepal, a Citroën DS in France and a vaporetto in Venice. When it came to crossing the English Channel, there seemed only one fitting option – to sail.

To be honest, we didn't think it through. As a child I'd sailed a lot with my dad, but hadn't come near a dinghy for thirty years. We did a one-day refresher course beforehand, during which I managed to capsize, and then we set off from the slipway in Dover in our Laser dinghy. It's only about twenty-five miles across the channel but this is the world's busiest shipping lane, so when you leave the protection of the harbour and start staring up at the waves from a 13-foot dinghy, it brings home the seriousness of the situation pretty quickly.

This certainly isn't something to attempt without a motorized support boat with some experienced crew on it, and you need to understand the international rules of the shipping lanes you'll be crossing. Get them wrong and you can be fined, or, far worse, be hit by a big ship. This does occasionally happen – often with fatal consequences.

If you don't have access to a support boat and crew, there is still a way of doing it. Every summer, the Royal Yachting Association (RYA) runs what it calls a 'Sail Cruise' in which amateur yachtsmen come together to form a small fleet to sail across the channel and on to the Channel Islands, taking six days in all. There is safety in numbers, of course, but also RYA professionals on hand to give advice and support. You are still in charge of your boat, but there are briefings each morning and evening, and the fleet remains in VHF radio contact with each other during the crossing, so help is at hand should you run into difficulties.

They normally only accept boats between nine and twelve metres, but sometimes make exceptions if you contact them in advance. Our boat was far smaller than that – barely over four metres – and I was soon wishing we were in something bigger.

The boat was dancing from side to side as each squall hit us, the team on our support boat were screaming instructions, and I could feel capsize getting closer and closer. On one occasion the left-hand side of the boat was in the water and we had no choice but to let all the ropes go. The sails

'You can do something in a single day that you will remember for ever'

I must admit to being nervous as we passed in front of tankers!

flapped free, stopping the boat in its tracks so it sprang upright and almost threw us out the other side. Then the wind got up, and we started making real progress. Soon we were halfway there and with the French coast in sight we started to think we might succeed. We'd thought it might take ten hours to get across, but after just five we were nearing France.

Sailing into Calais harbour would have added another hour or more, so we headed straight for the first beach we saw. I felt a real sense of elation jumping out on to French soil. It showed me that you don't have to go to the other side of the world to have an adventure, and you can do something in a single day that you will remember for ever.

There was just one house near by, so I walked up and knocked on the door. A woman answered

and peered at me suspiciously (well, I was wearing a rubber suit). 'Toilette, s'il vous plaît, madame?' I said, with my best smile.

'Non,' she replied, and shut the door in my face.

Now do it . . .

For more information on sailing and boating, contact the national body for boating, the RYA (www.rya.org.uk).

5 Motorbiking across Cambodia

Why | To start your engine and ride, leaving stress behind

Where | Cambodia | **Duration** | Three days +

I was standing on the top of a ruined and overgrown temple in the Cambodian jungle, when I dropped my lens cap. It slowly bounced down the worn steps and into a dark doorway. I followed and knelt down to reach it, stopping with a sudden jerk when I spotted, inches from my nose, a spider the size of my face sitting on its web. I decided I could live without the lens cap.

The spider may not have been dangerous, but there wouldn't have been anyone around to help me out if it had been. Beyond the world-famous temples of Angkor Wat and the capital Phnom Penh, Cambodia is only just opening up to tourists, and in great swathes of the country it's possible to feel as if you're exploring and discovering for yourself, rather than following a backpacker trail. We were at Beng Mealea, a twelfth-century temple only about 30 miles from the tourist hotspot of Angkor Wat, but we had the whole place to ourselves.

Of course, during the dark years of the Khmer Rouge and the civil war that followed, the entire country was off-limits to travellers. The communist Khmer Rouge seized power in 1975 and set about trying to return the country to the Middle Ages, forcing the people out of the cities, destroying anything considered Western and killing an estimated 2 million Cambodians. Years of factional in-fighting followed and it wasn't until 1991 that a peace settlement was agreed and 1993 that the monarchy was restored.

This journey was one of the be[st] rides I've ever had.

Since then tourists have begun to trickle back, and today Cambodia is getting a reputation as one of the most interesting countries of South East Asia and, in particular, as one of the best destinations in the world for an off-road motorbike adventure. In much of the country there are only dirt roads, so you get to test your riding skills on rough, muddy terrain, while also accessing remote villages and hidden temples that are almost impossible to reach by conventional buses or cars.

You can either rent bikes yourself in Phnom Penh or Siem Reap, or else join one of the many group biking tours that have sprung up in recent years. Cambo Enduro, for example, is a two-week group ride set up in 2010 by the organizers of the well-established Enduro Himalayas ride through northern India. It runs four times a year and, after a blessing from Buddhist monks, takes riders from Phnom Penh to Ratanakiri, a little-visited province in the north-east of the country, then on to Siem Reap. There are river crossings by dug-out canoes, the chance to visit remote hill-tribes, see the spectacular

Riding between idyllic villages.

*Cambodia has a really strong
spiritual feel to it.*

In great swathes of the country
it's possible to feel as if you're
exploring ... rather than following
a backpacker trail

Bou Sra waterfalls and swim in Yaklom, a volcanic crater lake. The roads are so challenging you'll average less than a hundred miles a day.

Alternatively, you can arrange a trip via a Cambodian-based company like Red Raid, which has offices in Siem Reap and Phnom Penh. It offers trips from two to nine days, taking you all over the country. Highlights include seeing the rare Irrawaddy river dolphins in the Mekong, and exploring the hills and traditional villages of the eastern Mondulkiri province.

I only scratched the surface of Cambodia, starting at Voen Kham on the Laos border in the north-east, and spending a couple of days travelling west across the country to Poipet, where we crossed into Thailand. Even that was enough to make me desperate to return – few other countries seem as exotic and unspoilt.

The roads may be rough, but that isn't to say travelling in Cambodia is difficult. In fact, there are guesthouses in most villages so you can always find somewhere to stay, or you can do what we did and camp. Don't be tempted to rent a conventional roadbike though. If you're heading anywhere in the countryside you need a proper off-road machine. We rode 250 trailbikes, and had an absolute blast.

The most memorable thing about Cambodia is how friendly it is. It seems that after enduring all those years of horrors, the people are keen to welcome outsiders with open arms. Everywhere we went we'd be invited into people's houses for cups of tea. I remember at one point riding through a farming village and getting caught up in the midst of a herd of cattle walking along the road. We were surrounded by cows, inching along, when the whole village came out of their houses to wave at us. It was a wonderful moment.

Now do it . . .

The Bike Shop (www.motorcyclecambodia.com) offer motorcycle tours and rental throughout the whole country. For information on Cambodia itself, visit Tourism Cambodia (www.tourismcambodia.com).

Mountain biking in El Salvador

Why	For coffee plantations, jungle and challenging tracks
Where	El Salvador	**Duration**	One day

In 1993, El Salvador was a nation in shock, reeling from twelve years of civil war that had left 75,000 people dead. But gradually, stability and confidence have returned, helped by a small but growing tourism industry.

Of course, at its worst, tourism is guilty of causing great harm and rampant over-development, but it can also be a force for good, particularly in countries scarred by recent conflict. In Rwanda, Cambodia and Vietnam, the influx of the tourists, usually led by an advance guard of adventure seekers, has brought foreign currency, jobs and self-respect.

Today in El Salvador, small-scale eco-tourism projects are flourishing, particularly in the mountainous west of the country where the hillsides are covered in coffee plantations. The so-called Ruta de las Flores (route of the flowers) winds its way through the Ahuachapán region, connecting the pretty colonial towns of Salcoatitán and Juayúa, where art galleries and eco-lodges are springing up, and passing the flanks of the numerous volcanoes that dot the region.

We'd come to El Portezuelo, a coffee farm four miles from Juayúa in the Ilamatepec mountains.

It's owned and run by Julio Vega, a Salvadorean who was living in Baltimore but decided to move back and get involved in the nascent eco-tourism industry here. There's a cosy lodge, a campsite and activities from horseback riding to hiking, birdwatching to paragliding. We were here to mountain bike through the coffee plantations.

But this wasn't a straightforward bike ride. We started on horseback, climbing up from the campsite at Portezuelo to the Cerro Cuyanunsul, a peak 1,900 metres up. There we switched to bikes, kitted up in helmets and protective pads, and set off, swooping along the red-earth trails built for the coffee-pickers to get around. The climate up here in the hills is warm and sunny, without the humidity of the jungles down by the coast. Pounding the pedals, though, I was soon drenched in sweat.

The beauty of this ride was that it was more or less downhill all the way to Juayúa, our destination. For fifteen miles we flew down over grass, gravel and mud, knuckles white from gripping so tightly. On one fast corner I lost my back wheel and ended up tangled in a bush, but better a bush than a rock.

After three hours we reached Juayúa and collapsed into chairs outside a café in the beautiful

Today in El Salvador, small-scale eco-tourism projects are flourishing

colonial square, before chilling out with a cup of locally grown coffee. We'd only had a taste of the opportunities for adventure in the area, but it's easy to see that it's somewhere with a bright future.

Coffee plantations — it's always good to learn about a country's economy.

I like the style!

All the gear but no idea!

Now do it . . .

Mayan Escapes (www.mayanescapes.com) are your best contact to plan your own biking adventure. For more information, contact El Salvador Tourism Board (www.elsalvador.travel) and Journey Latin America (www.journeylatinamerica.co.uk). For information on Central America go to www.visitcentroamerica.com

Heliskiing in the midnight sun

LONG WEEKEND

Why	To conquer this thrillseekers' 'must-do'
Where	Scandinavia	**Duration**	One day

Pull back the curtains in the nightclub at Riksgränsen and you are in for a rather strange sight. For a start it's broad daylight, even at midnight. Weirder still is that just outside the windows is a helipad, and if you keep looking for half an hour or so, you'll see a helicopter swoop down to pick up skiers, drowning out the DJ as it does so.

Riksgränsen is the most northerly ski resort in the world, a collection of a few wooden buildings on the border between Sweden and Norway, 125 miles north of the Arctic Circle. Its latitude means that the ski season continues here long after the lifts in the rest of Europe have closed. Most alpine resorts wind down in early April, when the season here is only really getting going. Riksgränsen's lifts usually run until late June, and by May the sun never really sets, allowing the lifts to stay open until after 1 a.m. and the helicopter to fly into the night.

Perhaps the strangest thing about Riksgränsen is that although, as you would expect in Scandinavia, the drinks in the club are ruinously expensive, the heliskiing is some of the best value in the world. You can sign up for as many lifts in the helicopter as you like, and they work out at about £75 each. Midnight heliskiing is slightly more expensive – a three-lift package costs around £275. But it's worth it.

You set off at 10 p.m., lifting up above the roof of the throbbing nightclub and heading out into the silence of the mountains. The sun hangs low on the horizon, turning the snow pink. It's like that magical moment just before the sun disappears on a summer's day, except here it's prolonged, lasting for hours as the sun circles along the horizon.

In the Alps heliskiing is heavily restricted and pilots can only land in a few permitted spots. Here, the pilot and guide have more than a hundred peaks to choose from. At the summit, the skiers pile out, crouch low in the snow and wait for the chopper to fly off. And then the fun begins – descents of up to 1,000 metres on snow that is completely untracked.

There's everything from hardcore steeps to mellow cruising runs, and you may well get to ski past reindeer. But really it's all about the scenery – the Arctic wilderness stretches for as far as the eye can see in every direction. There's no sign of human life, just endless glaciers, peaks, snowfields and fjords, glittering in the midnight sun.

Now do it . . .
Visit Riksgränsen (www.riksgransen.nu) or VisitSweden (www.visitsweden.com) for further details. Elemental Adventure (www.eaheliskiing.com) can arrange packages.

| **Why** | For exploring space and cosmic adventures |
| **Where** | Chile | **Duration** | One night |

If you really want to romance your partner under the stars, try taking them to the remote Elqui Valley of northern Chile.

It's an area renowned for being one of the best in the world for stargazing, thanks to its exceptionally clear, dark skies. So good are the conditions that universities and governments from Europe and North America have set up vast observatories here, and many of the largest telescopes in existence are clustered around the region.

In fact, the European Union is in the process of building a £700 million telescope just to the north of the Elqui Valley. It will house a mirror 42 metres wide and powerful enough to seek out distant planets capable of supporting life. It's being designed by some of the most brilliant scientific minds, but they seem to be less good at thinking up snappy names – it is called the European Extremely Large Telescope. They were going to build an even bigger one, the Overwhelmingly Large Telescope (seriously!), but it was too expensive.

Anyway, back to the bedroom. A couple of hours' drive from La Serena, the nearest airport, is the Elqui Domos hotel. Each of the seven rooms is a geodesic dome – like a more angular version of an igloo – with a double bed on stilts inside. Wait for nightfall, get into bed, then reach up and throw open the roof to reveal an inky-black sky lit up with a billion dazzling stars.

Wrap up warm because it's bitterly cold.

It's a revelation, making you feel as if every time you've looked at the night sky before, you were wearing dark glasses. Now you've taken them off and are seeing the real thing. You can lie there for hours, drinking in the view, then fall asleep under the stars.

One word of warning though – the hotel is at an altitude of 1,280 metres and with more than 320 clear night skies per year, it can get very cold. In the winter months (July to September), you'll need to wear all your clothes in bed, and perhaps have a tot of pisco, the legendary South American firewater made in this very valley, on hand in case you need warming up.

There are telescopes in the domes too, but if you want to explore the stars, these are just the start. Unusually, many of the observatories in this

region allow public visits. The observatories at Cerro Tololo, La Silla (site of the European Southern Observatory's fourteen telescopes) and Las Campanas (run by the Carnegie Institute) all welcome visitors at certain times, but we chose to visit the Cerro Mamalluca, five miles from the town of Vicuña.

We left about 8 p.m. as night was falling for the drive of a couple of hours up to the observatory. As the van climbed up the hill we turned off the headlights, instead using only the hazard warning lights, in order not to cause any light pollution.

Up at the observatory, we spent some time looking through the reflecting telescopes, but the star of the show was the GPS-controlled main telescope. This isn't something you can get your hands on yourself, but the astronomer gave us a tour of the heavens using the GPS controls to seek out particular constellations. He showed how if you zoom in close enough, you can see that what looks like one star is actually a cluster of a dozen.

Enthusiasts would want to spend a few days here and make several visits to the observatories, but even in our three-hour visit, we saw stars and galaxies we never imagined existed, sights that would have been impossible to see back at home. Even if you're not interested in astronomy, I'd recommend this trip. It's a magical experience, and certainly the most distant bit of exploring you'll ever do.

Now do it . . .

For the star-gazing experience and accommodation, contact the Elqui Domos Hotel (www.elquidomos.cl). For more amazing adventures in Chile, visit Tourism Chile (www.turismochile.travel) and ProChile (www.prochile.co.uk).

'It's a magical experience, and certainly the most distant bit of exploring you'll ever do'

9   Deep sea fishing, Pacific style

Once in a Lifetime

Why	To catch your own dinner on a desert island
Where	Cook Islands **Duration**	Two days

As you approach Aitutaki in a small aircraft, you can't help but wonder if you're dreaming. For the previous forty-five minutes, since the plane had left Raratonga, the biggest of the Cook Islands, we'd seen nothing but the deep blue of the open Pacific. Then, suddenly, here was a vision of tropical perfection – a huge, white, coral reef, encircling a lagoon of turquoise water, at the centre of which was the deep green, palm-covered island of Aitutaki. It's a tiny place – we went round the whole island on a moped in about twenty minutes – and only two thousand people live here.

We'd come here not to lie on the beaches but to go fishing. Aitutaki is a great spot for all types of the sport, from fly fishing in the lagoon to deep-water game fishing for marlin, wahoo or yellow-fin tuna. There are several commercial sport fishing operators in Aitutaki, who you can book to take you out on a speedboat for the day, but we decided to go out with a local fisherman to learn how they catch fish. In Arutanga, the island's main village, we bumped into a Rasta fisherman called Junior who agreed to take us out with him.

Junior had a very simple boat, about 15 feet long and made of aluminium, and it took about two hours to get out beyond the reef to the spot in deep water where he knew there were often fish.

What followed wasn't like any fishing I'd ever seen before. Rather than trail a line behind the moving boat, Junior had a technique that didn't require the engine, and so wouldn't waste the fuel. He put a piece of fish on a hook as bait and placed it on a banana leaf. Then he surrounded the bait with a load of stinking fish guts and wrapped them up in the leaf. Next, he brought out a brick and attached it to the bottom of the leaf, tying the whole parcel together with twine.

The sea here was a mile deep, but Junior decided he wanted to fish at about 200 metres. He threw the whole parcel overboard and waited as the brick dragged it down to the right depth. Once it was there, he gave the line a sharp tug, releasing the special knots connecting brick and banana leaf. The brick dropped to the seabed and the banana leaf unfurled, releasing a cloud of fish guts to attract our prey, and there, floating in the middle of it, was the bait. It was a stroke of genius.

Except it didn't work. Not the first time, the second or third. After three attempts, we'd been at sea for three and a half hours. It was starting to get

'Then we saw it, a beautiful, bright greeny-blue Mahi Mahi, four feet long, its scales sparkling in the sunlight'

rough and we were about to give up and head to shore. Junior handed me the rod and started to get the boat ready to leave, when suddenly there was a tug on the line. I reeled it in slowly, and then we saw it, a beautiful, bright greeny-blue Mahi Mahi, four feet long, its scales sparkling in the sunlight as it jumped out of the water above the waves. It was an awesome sight.

As soon as it was close enough to the boat, Junior swung at the fish with a hook, spearing it through its back so he could haul it on board. Back went the bait and in the next half hour we reeled in two more, each of them worth $80 to Junior.

To be frank, seeing something so agile and graceful in the water meet such a violent death came as a bit of a shock. But it was raw, not sugar-coated for tourist consumption in any way, and I think it's important for people to see where their food actually comes from, rather than just finding it neatly packaged on the supermarket shelves.

That night we took one of the Mahi Mahi to Maina Island, an uninhabited speck of an island on the reef. We barbecued it simply, washed it down with some beers, then slept out under a tarpaulin on the beach, watching the sun set over Aitutaki. Fish has never tasted better.

Now do it . . .

Fishing tours with Junior Nicholls can be booked through the Aitutaki Tourism Office (www.aitutakitourism.com). To experience a real uninhabited island, we recommend you stay in Maina Lodge on Aitutaki (www.aitutaki.net/accommodation). For more information contact Cook Islands Tourism (www.cookislands.travel). Air Rarotonga (www.airraro.com) can arrange your flights.

Packing up the camp by the walking trees.

> We barbecued it simply, washed it down with some beers ... Fish has never tasted better

10

By Harley across America

Why	To have fun on the original motorcycling road trip
Where	USA	**Duration**	Two weeks +

Among British bikers, Harley Davidsons get mixed reactions. While the general public might think they say rebellion and rock 'n' roll, to bikers they conjure up images, not of Peter Fonda or Marlon Brando, but of a slightly overweight middle-manager having something of a mid-life crisis. Buy a Harley in the UK and you'd be worried that your biker mates would stop talking to you.

But in America, it's a totally different story. That is where the Harley was designed to be used, as a laid-back cruiser on long open roads. They are not about speed, they're not about ripping round corners, but they are perfect for chugging across great distances in comfort. So if you're going to ride across America, I wouldn't choose anything else.

The key thing is to decide which direction you are going to ride in – west from New York, or east from Los Angeles. Start in New York and you've got the treat of good weather and dramatic deserts to look forward to at the end; start in LA and you're straight into them.

The great thing is that, although this is an absolute classic adventure, it's so easy to arrange. I flew into Los Angeles, then went straight to the bike hire company, Eagle Rider. Twenty minutes later, I was rolling out on a huge Harley, with the whole of California in front of me.

First stop was Venice Beach, to dip my toes in the Pacific, then I headed for Route 66. Yes, I know it's a cliché, but who cares? Sitting astride a Harley on the open road, with 'Route 66' by the Rolling Stones on the iPod, who wouldn't have a grin on their face?

Officially Route 66 doesn't really exist any more. Opened in 1927, and running from Chicago to Los Angeles, it became ingrained in the American psyche as the route used by migrants heading west to seek their fortunes, particularly in the depression of the 1930s. All along the route, petrol stations, diners, motels and tourist attractions grew up to cater to the passing trade, so much so that the road became known as the 'Main Street of America' and the 'Mother Road'. But in the 1960s the new interstates started to bypass Route 66 and finally in 1985 it was removed from the US highway system. It's still very much worth seeking out though. With the real traffic and the

'Driving along the road today feels like driving through America's past' heavy trucks siphoned off on to the interstates, the towns along what was Route 66 feel quiet and marooned in the past, their brightly painted diners standing empty. Driving along the road today feels like driving through America's past.

In fact, everywhere you go on this trip you are running up against icons, clichés and legends – sights, sounds and places that are familiar from hundreds of films, songs and TV shows. I rode through the baking heat of the Mojave Desert, racing the huge freight trains on arrow-straight roads, then up to the edge of the Grand Canyon. I passed Lake Havasu, rode through majestic Monument Valley, then up to the ancient cliff dwellings of Mesa Verde, swinging round the windy mountain road, laughing like a maniac as sparks flew from the footpegs. Soon I was climbing up into the Rockies and suddenly huge snow banks appeared on either side of the road. It felt like the entire journey to Denver, where I arrived nine days later, was made up of one iconic American landscape after another.

Eagle Rider can pre-book your accommodation too, but I chose not to book anything and just see where I ended up each night. In Monument Valley, Goulding's Lodge – the only place to stay for miles around – was full but they gave us a trailer to stay in. It had a two-inch shag-pile carpet, and everything was made of brown formica. As bizarre as it sounds, I had a fleeting vision that I could live here, leading a simple life with the motorbike outside, a world away from the rat-race of London.

Another night, I pulled into a cheap motel where I had a shower, put the same T-shirt back on then went to the local bar to play pool and drink whiskey. There was a piano there and I played along with everyone clapping, then at 3 a.m. I staggered back to the room, fell on to the bed and slept in my clothes. There was no need to set an alarm – I'd wake up when I was ready, go outside and get back on the bike.

The whole thing sounds a bit like I was attempting to chase a cliché and live out a Hollywood fantasy. But the fun, and more importantly the sense of freedom, were very real indeed.

As a biking trip, this is an absolute 'must-do'.

Now do it . . .

To ride with the best, and to kick-start your cross-country adventure, contact Eagle Riders (www.eaglerider.com).

11

Riding the North Island of New Zealand

Why	For great views from great biking roads
Where	New Zealand	**Duration**	One week

Wherever you are in the world, just getting on a motorbike and heading out on the road is an adventure in itself. As soon as you drive out of your garage, there's a sense of freedom, whether you're in Surrey or Senegal. After a while, though, you want to get out there and explore the whole world on your bike, and that's why Ewan, Charley and I originally got together and cooked up various trips. The first thing is to decide if you're going to go off-road or stay on asphalt. If you choose to stay on asphalt, then I think that one of the world's best places to head for is the North Island of New Zealand.

You can easily rent motorbikes in Auckland – I hired a BMW 1200GS – but once you've done that, you should get out of the city as soon as possible. For some reason, it seems beset with traffic jams as bad as New York or London.

Almost as soon as you're beyond the city limits, the traffic seems to evaporate. I rode out to the Coromandel Peninsula, following the coastal road which is an endless ribbon of curves. It was heaven: sweeping bend after glorious sweeping bend, letting me lean the bike over and making me laugh like a maniac inside my helmet. The roads are like the best of Switzerland or Italy, but, crucially, without the cars coming the other way, so you can make full use of the width of the road.

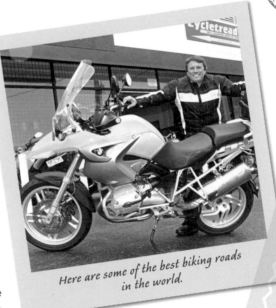

Here are some of the best biking roads in the world.

Next I looped back through Auckland and rode around the Northland, the northernmost strip of New Zealand, with the Tasman Sea on one side and the Pacific on the other. Again the roads were a dream, smooth asphalt and wonderfully twisty. Sometimes on a bike it's nice to let rip on a straight road, but for most riders the real pleasure is sweeping round corners like these.

The scenery is astounding too. On one side you have beaches and cliffs to rival the best of Cornwall or California, on the other you have semi-tropical

HAURAKI GULF

AUCKLAND
MANUKAU
PAPAKURA
COROMANDEL
MATARANGI
WHITIANGA
TAPU
TAIRU
KOPU
WHANGAMATA
NGATEA
PAEROA
WAIHI

It was heaven: sweeping bend after glorious sweeping bend

rainforest. You could spend a few days up here in the north, or a week or more and loop down to Wellington.

Finding a place to stay is a cinch. There are numerous great bed and breakfasts, many of which seem to be in whitewashed villas that look like they've been transported from the south coast of England.

Of course, this isn't a hardcore expedition to rival Paris–Dakar or the Road of Bones. But don't let the fact that it's safe, easy and comfortable put you off. This really is biking bliss.

Spectacular scenery is guaranteed in New Zealand.

Now do it . . .
The BMW 1200GS can be rented from New Zealand Motorcycles Rentals and Tours (www.nzbike.com). For other motorcycle adventures visit World of BMW at www.worldofbmw.com. Visit Tourism New Zealand (www.newzealand.com) for more information on travelling around the two islands.

12

Stilt village of Brunei

Why	To gain a cultural and economic insight
Where	Brunei	**Duration**	One day

Approaching from the water, you see what looks like a slum: a huge, dense cluster of buildings perched on wooden stilts. But get closer and you notice that the usual signs of a shanty town – the smell, the plastic sheeting, the corrugated-iron shacks – are noticeable only by their absence. This is actually a well-established community, it just happens to be balancing on stilts.

Kampong Ayer, or the Water Village, is actually more of a town than a village. More than 39,000 people live there, and they've been there, on the banks of the Brunei River, for a very long time – at least 1,300 years. In 1521 Italian scholar Antonio Pigafetta came here as part of an expedition that went on to become the first to circumnavigate the world. He described the Water Village as 'the Venice of the East', a title that has since been borrowed for everywhere from Bangkok to Srinagar, but which shows how well established it must have been as a fishing and trading hub.

Today Brunei is one of the wealthiest countries in Asia thanks to significant oil reserves, and its royal family are among the world's richest people. But Brunei's modern prosperity doesn't stop at the water's edge. The wooden houses of the Water Village may be small and closely packed but they have running water, air-conditioning, electricity, satellite TV and internet access. The village stretches for two miles along the riverbank, and is made up of over 4,000 main structures connected up by almost nineteen miles of wooden footbridges. There are schools, a health clinic, and fire and police stations.

It's a fascinating place to visit, just to stroll around on the walkways watching the village go about its life. Boats constantly buzz around beneath the stilts, either fishermen going out to tend their nets or water taxis for the local residents.

You can easily get out on the water yourself too. Boatmen in long canoes with outboard motors will take you upriver to fish and see the baboon colonies. The amazing thing is that within an hour you've gone from being in a major city to being surrounded by pristine jungle.

Kampong Ayer is a fascinating place to visit. If you find yourself changing planes in Brunei (as many people do en route from the UK to Australia), get out of the airport and come down to spend a couple of hours discovering a unique community.

Now do it . . .

To experience Kampong Ayer for yourself, contact Sumbiling Eco Village (www.borneoguide.com/ecovillage/).

Icebergs, igloos and dog sleds

Why	For an affinity with animals in a remote wilderness
Where	Greenland	**Duration**	Three days

Perched on the edge of the Ilulissat Icefjord, 120 miles north of the Arctic Circle on the west coast of Greenland, are five of the world's most amazing hotel rooms.

Perhaps 'rooms' is the wrong word – these are modern takes on the igloo, built not from snow and ice but sleek aluminium, and perched on wooden decks above the rocky banks of the fjord. They are run by the nearby Hotel Arctic, and inside each has a double bed, heating, a bathroom, TV, telephone and all the mod-cons you wouldn't expect an igloo to have.

But the things that make them really special are the windows. Pull back the curtains, or step outside and sit on the deck, and you will be treated to one of the greatest natural spectacles on earth.

The igloos, and the town of Ilulissat, sit at the end of a 25-mile-long fjord, a narrow, steep-sided inlet. But rather than being filled with seawater like most fjords, this one contains a glacier, the Sermeq Kujalleq (also known by its Danish name, Jakobshavn Isbræ). It starts as part of Greenland's vast central icecap, covering 80 per cent of the country's entire landmass, then flows down the fjord until it meets the sea, where great chunks of ice 'calve' off and float away as icebergs.

Like frozen rivers, most glaciers move forward very slowly. The Mer de Glace, a glacier above Chamonix in France, moves at about 90 metres per year, for example. The Sermeq Kujalleq, by contrast, flows at 20–35 metres *per day*, and is the most 'productive' glacier in the northern hemisphere. The result is that it dumps as many as 35 billion tonnes of icebergs into the sea every year.

And almost all of them float down past the igloos of the Hotel Arctic. They can be as high as tower blocks, or formed into arches, pyramids or jagged spires. Some are so huge they get stuck on the seabed, where they can stay for months. Watching these white giants float past in an infinite

variety of shapes and sizes is mesmerizing, and it can be hard to drag yourself away. (Apparently when Icelandic singer Björk came to visit, she ended up staying in an igloo for several weeks.)

But if you can rouse yourself from your igloo, Ilulissat has plenty more adventure to offer. You can go on helicopter tours over the ice, take boat trips through the icebergs or hike up neighbouring peaks to get views over the icecap.

The igloos are only open in summer, from May to October, but if you come instead between January and April, you can also explore by dog sled. You can arrange day trips by dog sled, but better to go for two or three nights. At this time of year the sea is frozen, and for much of the time the teams of dogs will pull the sleds along on the sea-ice, slaloming around the icebergs that are stuck solid until spring. You'll camp, or spend the night in basic cabins, and try to catch fish through holes cut in the ice. If you can stand the cold, you can arrange even longer trips, which last a week or more and take you up on to the icecap itself.

Be warned: up there, the igloos are not en suite.

"Watching these white giants float past in an infinite variety of shapes and sizes is mesmerizing"

Now do it . . .

Visit World of Greenland (www.worldofgreenland.com) for numerous dog-sledding adventure options. Greenland Air (www.airgreenland.com) operates flights to Greenland from Copenhagen.

14

In the footsteps of an outlaw

Why	To explore the crossroads where history meets adventure
Where	Bolivia	**Duration**	One week

In the middle of the table was a purple sheet, covering a large wooden box. 'What's that then, a coffin?' I joked. 'Si, señor,' the man said seriously, then pulled off the sheet, opened the glass cabinet and revealed a human skeleton. 'Esto es Butch . . . Butch Cassidy.'

I was speechless. I'd come to Bolivia on the trail of Butch Cassidy and the Sundance Kid, the celebrated American outlaws who led the Wild Bunch, robbing banks and trains across the Wild West while claiming to avoid violence wherever possible. As a child I'd loved the Robert Redford and Paul Newman film and I wanted to try to delve a bit deeper into the myth and legend surrounding the men and the mystery of their deaths in South America. But I'd certainly never expected to come face to face with Butch's body.

The adventure really started, like most South American journeys, at the bus station. South American bus stations seem to have a magical atmosphere, almost as if they are cathedrals honouring travel and human endeavour. They are usually big and airy with soaring roofs – La Paz's bus station was designed by Gustave Eiffel, creator of the Eiffel Tower, no less. Inside, rather than constant tannoy announcements, there are scores of women calling out the names of destinations as if they are ancient religious incantations.

We boarded an overnight bus to the city of Potosí, then changed on to one heading to the southern town of Tupiza, where Butch and Sundance lived for a couple of months near the end of their lives. The journey took seventeen hours and, to be honest, it was an ordeal. For much of it we were crammed into tiny seats bouncing along rough, dusty and pot-holed gravel roads over the vast, windswept Altiplano, the high, featureless plain that feels like the surface of the moon in places.

Already I was readjusting my view of Butch and Sundance. While the film portrayed their lives as happy and glamorous, the reality of life here must have been the complete opposite. Travelling by bus was hard enough, but crossing this barren, bitterly cold landscape by horse must have been miserable.

However, if the journey was tough, arriving in Tupiza was a delight. I'd been told that this pretty town was surrounded by beautiful red mountains, but I'd written that off as guidebook hype. It isn't – all the way around the horizon are fabulous peaks and ridges that glow a stunning red at sunrise and sunset.

> South American bus stations seem to have a magical atmosphere, almost as if they were cathedrals honouring travel and human endeavour

BRAZIL

PERU

LA PAZ

BOLIVIA

POTOSI

SAN VINCENTE

TUPIZA

CHILE

PARAGUAY

ARGENTINA

We spent a few days there, looking around, visiting the excellent museum and acclimatizing. Much of Bolivia is at extremely high altitudes – Tupiza is at 3,160 metres, Potosí is at 4,090 metres. Consider that the village of Val Thorens, Europe's highest ski resort, is at 2,400 metres and you start to see it in perspective. Even the airport at La Paz is at 4,061 metres, an altitude at which the air is so thin that planes must land and take off far faster than usual to avoid stalling and dropping like stones.

In the museum we learned about how Butch and Sundance had fled to Bolivia from the US, chased by the Pinkerton Detective Agency, and initially got jobs working as guards. Hearing stories about the great riches of the southern silver mines, in 1908 they travelled down to Tupiza

and checked into a hotel on the main square. Today, ironically, the legendary bank robbers' hotel has been turned into a bank, but otherwise the square looks unchanged from the photos of that time in the museum.

But better than anything the museum could offer was that we happened to bump into Dr Felix Chalar Miranda, a lawyer who lives in Tupiza and is one of the leading experts on Butch and Sundance. He took us into his home and described at length the various theories about how the pair had met their deaths. Then he showed us the memorabilia he had collected from the period – rifles, knives and files full of documents and eyewitness accounts relating to the outlaws.

Now it felt like the trail was getting warm. While in Tupiza, Butch and Sundance had learned of a mule train carrying a large amount of cash to a remote mine, as payment for the miners. They robbed the mule train (discovering that in fact it was only carrying the disappointing sum of 15,000 Bolivian pesos) in Huaca Huañusca – a place we visited on an epic journey through the mountains – then rode to San Vincente, a mining camp in the middle of nowhere, to hole up for the night. This was our next destination.

Driving that road to San Vincente would be worth it even if you had no interest at all in Butch's story. It passes the most awesome geological features I've seen: canyons, mountains, rock formations of a hundred different hues, and all the time there are massive views across the Altiplano and huge, epic skies up above.

Butch and Sundance must have thought they were home and dry when they got to San

But whether or not it was really him, the sense of discovery was amazing. We'd arrived from the other side of the world with only some hazy notions learned from a Hollywood film, and ended up following a trail that took us right to the heart of the story. It felt like we'd got inside the legend, and got under the skin of the country at the same time.

After a couple of hours, we left San Vincente. As we set off on the rough track to Chile that Butch and Sundance were hoping would be their path to freedom, it started to snow.

Vincente. Beyond here, there's nothing at all before the border with Chile, where they would be safe. But the owner of the house where they'd been put up for the night overheard them talking about the robbery and alerted the mayor. Four soldiers just happened to be staying in the town that night, and the mayor told them to arrest the bandits.

What happened next isn't clear. There was a gunfight, and Butch, Sundance and one of the soldiers were killed. Some say the outlaws were injured and ended up killing each other – one putting the other out of his misery, then committing suicide with his final bullet.

San Vincente is still an isolated, desolate place, and still a mining camp. It was freezing as we pulled up at the gate and asked the guard if we could go in to look around. We drove up to the small graveyard, surrounded by rough white walls to keep out the bitter wind. We couldn't find the man with the key to the cemetery gate, so I jumped over the wall. It was here that Butch and Sundance were buried, but as common criminals they weren't given headstones, so the trail seemed to have run cold.

Then, outside the cemetery, we bumped into a man who offered to show us the tiny, one-room museum, housed in a small stone building near by. He unlocked the door, showed me a few postcards and notices on the walls, and then we turned to the purple sheet and box on the table.

Was it really Butch? I'm not saying it definitely was. In 1991, two other bodies had been dug up from the graveyard, DNA-tested and found not to be them, but this body hasn't been tested yet.

Now do it . . .

Tupiza Tours (www.tupizatours.com) can assist with organizing not only your outlaw tour but also accommodation. We recommend Hotel Mitru in Tupiza.

On the route that the outlaws took on
their way to Chile.

IN THE FOOTSTEPS OF AN OUTLAW

15 Hong Kong kayaking

Why	To escape from the city and get into nature
Where	Hong Kong's islands	**Duration**	One day

Think of Hong Kong and you picture one of the world's great metropolises – teeming with people, lit up with neon, and with scores of skyscrapers jostling for position along the waterfront. But, bizarre as it might seem, it's also possible to combine a trip here with a wilderness adventure. The same day as you are shopping in the city or eating in one of its smart restaurants, you can also be kayaking through weird rock formations on uninhabited islands in the South China Sea.

For the only time in this book, for this adventure you can set off on the underground. You take the MTR out to Hang Hau station on the fringes of the city and from there it's a short bus ride to Sai Kung harbour, where you can catch a speedboat out into the islands.

Hong Kong has 263 islands, many of them inhabited. Our boat, the *Black Mamba*, sped past Bluff, and Wang Chau islands, arriving thirty-five minutes later at the village of Shar Kiu Tau on High Island. Here fishermen live in basic conditions in houses built on pontoons above the sea, working to supply live lobster, octopus, squid, and fish and crustaceans of every kind for the display tanks and tables of the city restaurants.

Here we picked up our kayaks and set out to explore the incredible rock formations of the surrounding islands. In places, there are hexagonal

'Most dramatic of all are the caves and tunnels through the rock ... you can paddle your kayak right through'

columns tumbling into the sea, like those of the Giant's Causeway in Northern Ireland – both the result of volcanic activity (though here the rock is not basalt like the Giant's Causeway but acidic silica-rich rhyolitic rock). Elsewhere the rock seems to be folded in thick layers, as if it were hundreds of sheets of soft marzipan, several feet thick. So unusual are the formations that the whole area has been declared the Hong Kong National Geopark, part of a network of 182 areas across China which have special conservation status because of their geological significance.

But most dramatic of all are the caves and tunnels through the rock – in some places you can paddle your kayak right through a narrow tunnel to the other side of the island, your paddle tips scraping the edges on either side as you squeeze

There are deserted beaches where you could camp, and numerous spots for a swim

through. There are deserted beaches where you could camp, and numerous spots for a swim. Unless you're an experienced sea-kayaker, you do need a guide, though, as it can get rough out there.

Later, we beached the kayaks and hiked up to a rocky ridge to get an aerial view of the islands and watch the coastguard ships patrol the channels between Hong Kong and the rest of China. We stayed to watch a stunning sunset over the surreal rocks and the deserted islands scattered about the sea all around us. It was amazing – but not quite as amazing as knowing that we were only fifteen miles from the centre of one of the world's most densely populated cities.

The perfect antidote to the business of Hong Kong.

Now do it . . .

Contact the adventure company Kayak and Hike (www.kayak-and-hike.com) to book your kayaking expedition. For luxury accommodation, we recommend the newly opened chic Harbour Plaza 8 Degrees hotel (www.harbour-plaza.com/hp8d), located near the former Kai Tak airport.

Diving SS *Coolidge*

Why	For an epic dive, suitable for all levels
Where	Vanuatu	**Duration**	One day

I love diving on coral reefs and in open water, but my real passion is wreck diving. And if you're at all interested in wreck diving, you have to make the long trip to the tiny island of Espiritu Santo, part of the Republic of Vanuatu.

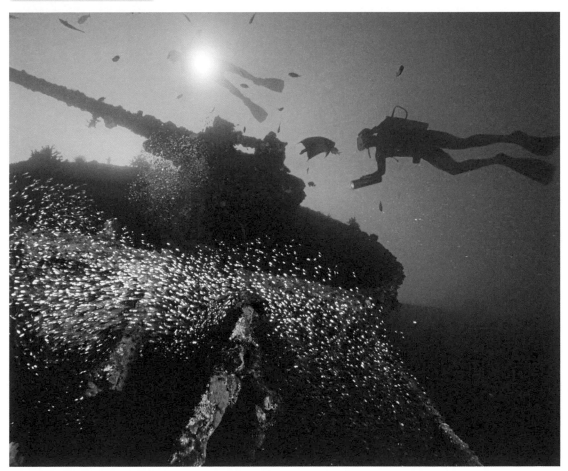

In many ways, Santo looks like any other South Pacific paradise island – white sand beaches fringed with coconut palms and clear, warm water. But what is unique is that lurking just below the surface of the water is the vast, rusting wreck of the SS *President Coolidge*, a 199-metre long troop-carrying ship that sank here during the Second World War.

The *Coolidge* was built in 1931 as a luxury cruise ship, taking wealthy Americans on tours of the Pacific and Far East. When war broke out, she was pressed into service as a troop carrier, and on 26 October 1942, she was approaching Santo with 5,000 troops on board, ready to be stationed throughout the region to fight the Japanese.

The captain, Henry Nelson, had not been given any information about landing but, fearing he would be a sitting duck for Japanese submarines if he sat at anchor offshore, he decided to enter the harbour by the obvious main channel. What he didn't know was that it had been heavily mined to protect the large US military base ashore.

A signaller on shore frantically flashed a warning in morse code, S – T – O – P, and the ship slammed its engines into full reverse. But stopping a huge ship takes time and at 9.30 a.m., still drifting forward, the ship struck a mine, then another thirty seconds later. Immediately the ship started listing and the captain ordered that it be rammed up on to the beach so the troops could get off.

Over the next ninety minutes, all but two of the 5,342 men on board got off safely, leaving behind all their belongings because they thought they would be returning to unload over the coming days. But the ship wasn't securely beached, only stuck on coral, and just before 11 a.m., it slid back down into the sea and sank.

Fast forward sixty-eight years and I'm wading into the sea from the beach in search of the wreck, which regularly appears in polls of the best dive sites in the world. As well as being one of the largest wreck dives, the *Coolidge* is also one of the most accessible – it lies just 45 metres off the beach.

Approaching it is an incredible experience. With most wreck dives, the depth and the murky water mean you can only make out the closest part of the ship at any one time. Here you see all of the ship at once, lying on its side and stretching away from you on the shelving seabed. The sheer scale is awe-inspiring.

The bow is closest to the beach, 25 metres below the surface, while the stern is 65 metres down. This means it's a great training ground for divers: the longer you stay, and the more training you have, the deeper you can go to explore the ship. The only requirement for the shallower dives is a PADI Open Water certificate (or BSAC equivalent), while the very deepest dives are reserved for those using nitrogen mixes.

We swam down to the deck of the ship, past the huge anti-aircraft guns and into the ship's hold, then through a hole cut into the internal corridors and cabins. It's hard to put into words quite how it feels to be down there – there's something fascinating about somewhere that used to be inhabited by humans but has now

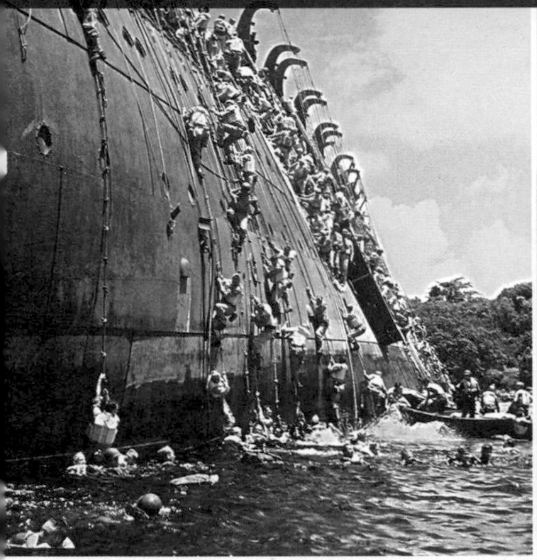

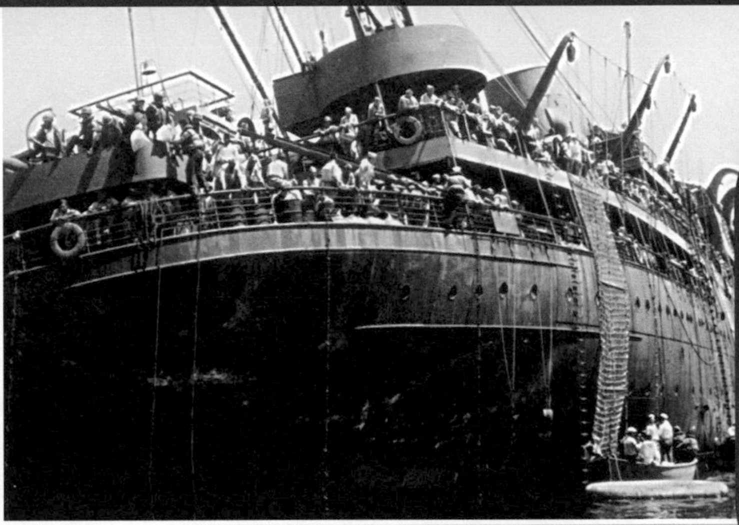

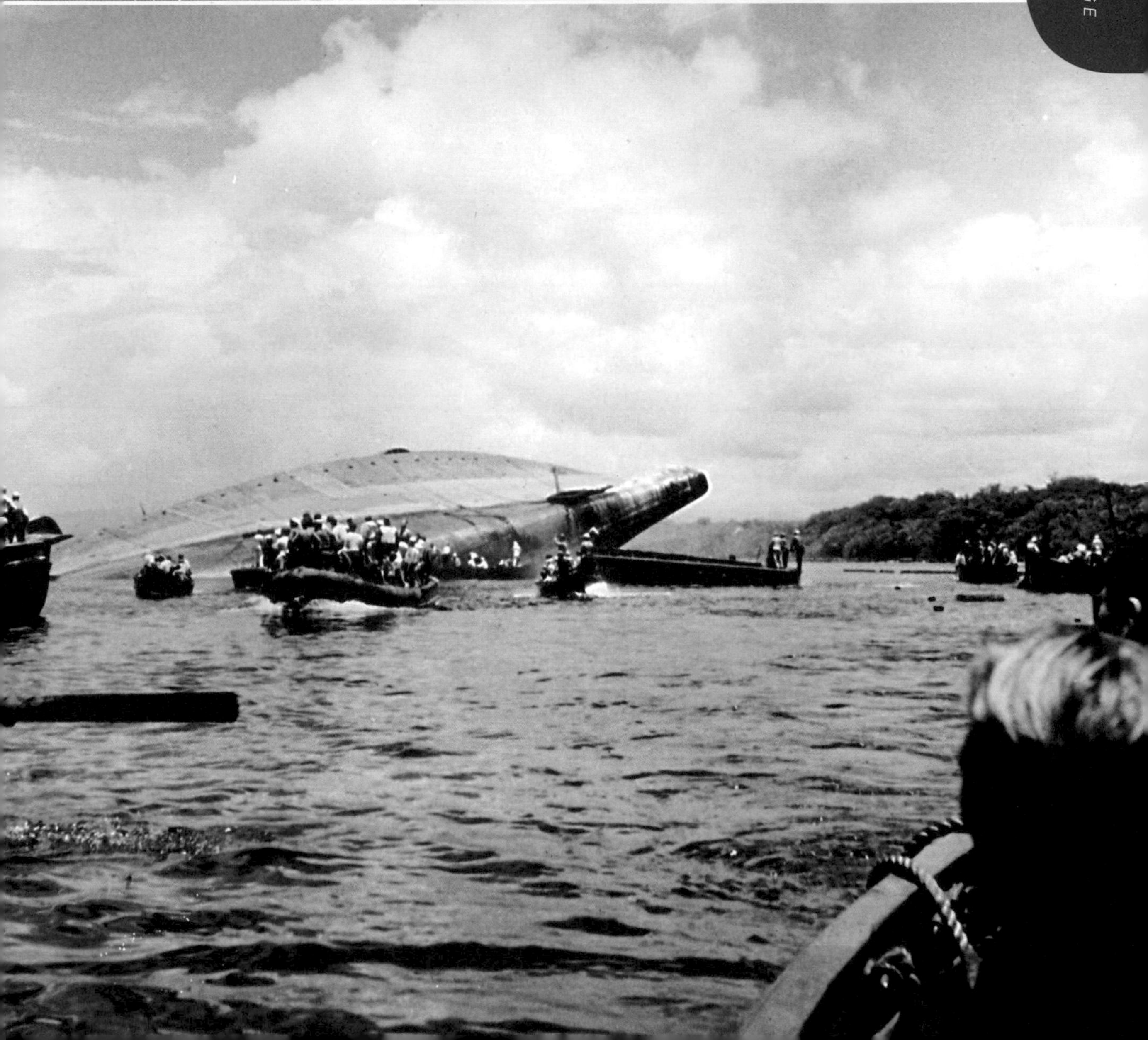

slipped into a totally alien environment. There are fish where men used to be.

Salvage teams have taken the valuable propellers, but otherwise it's pretty much as it was when the men abandoned ship – there are mustard and vinegar bottles in the canteen, medicine bottles in the pharmacy. At one point we found a GI's helmet that had been covered in coral sitting on the floor, then a rifle, also encrusted in coral, which I held up to my shoulder. It's phantasmagorical.

It's also pretty deadly. You must go with a guide who knows what they are doing because it's a labyrinth down there, and you could quickly get lost. Being unable to find your way out while you run out of air is the stuff of divers' nightmares.

We went down to about 35 metres, but you could spend days going deeper and pushing further into the ship, seeking out the captain's bathroom, where his hairbrush and talcum powder bottles are still there on a shelf, and 'the Lady', an ornate porcelain sculpture of a woman on a unicorn that once presided over the first-class smoking room.

After forty minutes we had to leave the sleeping giant and come back to the surface, stopping to decompress on the way. Walking back up the beach, into the bright sunlight, the whole experience seemed slightly unreal, as if we'd just stumbled on a time bubble where it will always be 1942.

Now do it . . .
Air Vanuatu (www.airvanuatu.com) operate flights from Auckland to Santo via Port Vila. Visit Aquamarine Santo (www.aquamarinesanto.com) to organize your dive. For all diving advice, visit PADI at www.padi.com

Why	For extreme speed, extreme thrill, extreme danger
Where	Switzerland	**Duration**	Two days

In the clubhouse, Lieutenant Colonel Digby Willoughby was giving us the 'death talk'. Behind him, the wall was covered in X-rays from club members who had crashed. Pieced together they made an entire human body – one full of broken bones and metal pins. 'These bits of metal,' he said, pointing to a set of pins, 'connect my head to my shoulders.' I was terrified.

The Cresta is a legend – one of the oldest adrenalin sports and still one of the most extreme. In the 1870s, before the arrival of skiing, bored British aristocrats who spent the winter in the Swiss resort of St Moritz had begun to race sleds through the streets. Then, to harness this enthusiasm, in 1885 the first Cresta run was built, a U-shaped track carved from the natural snow and ice, running from St Moritz downhill towards the neighbouring village of Celerina.

Perhaps the secret of its appeal is that today it doesn't feel as if much has changed. The track is still built from snow and ice each year (rather than having concrete foundations like most toboggan tracks), and still follows the same course, covering 1,212 metres, dropping 157 metres, and letting riders reach speeds of up to 80mph. A great way to get there is the ice train, which takes a scenic route through the Alps.

The equipment hasn't changed much either. You are given a helmet, hand, elbow and knee pads, and boots with sharpened teeth sticking from the toes – digging these so-called 'rakes' into the ice is the only means of slowing down.

In the early years, racers used the traditional 'luge' position, lying on their backs, feet first, but by 1890 everyone was riding head first in flimsy sleds known as skeletons. The danger isn't exaggerated – five have died on the course, and in 2008 Captain Bernie Bambury, a British soldier who had just returned from a tour of duty in Iraq, hit a marker post with his foot while travelling along at 80mph. He continued to the bottom and asked, 'Is my ankle broken?' Back came the reply: 'It's not broken. It's gone.'

So, heading out to 'the box', or the starting point, it's hard not to feel like a condemned man. Actually there are two start points, 'top' and 'junction', which is about a third of the way down and the point where beginners must start from. I lay down on the sled, trying not to think too much about what was to come, and gently pushed off.

Almost immediately, the feeling of speed was incredible. Your face is just inches from the ice as you fly into the sweeping corners. I scraped my spikes into the ice, trying to enter each turn

I've never been so nervous as at the start of my first Cresta run.

in control, but often sending the sled veering manically from one side to the other.

The most famous corner, and the thing you can't stop thinking about, is 'Shuttlecock'. According to the club literature, if you're out of control, you are 'certain to go out at Shuttlecock' – 'go out' being a euphemism for flying off the edge of the track at high speed. Although there is snow and straw on the ground beyond, injuries are common. On the upside, anyone who falls here is granted automatic membership of the Shuttlecock Club, and allowed to wear the Shuttlecock tie.

I dug my spikes in deeper – better a slow time than a flight out into the unknown. After that, everything became a blur of white ice and G-forces, and ninety seconds after starting, I swept across the finish line.

As I bent down to pick up my sled, blood pounding in my temples, there was only one thought in my brain – 'I have to do that again.'

It's amazing to ride on such a historic track ... try it.

Now do it . . .

The St Moritz Tobogganing Club is a private members' club, but you can get temporary membership in order to have a go (www.cresta-run.com).

Why	Last chance to see the faded charm of this bygone era
Where	Cuba	**Duration**	Two days

If you're going to go to Cuba, go soon. The island has been frozen in time since 1959, when the revolutionaries Fidel Castro and Che Guevara came to power. Apart from a few Stalinist statues and some nasty 1970s tourist hotels, the centre of Havana still consists of gloriously crumbling Spanish colonial buildings. The cigars are still rolled by hand, the men still wear moustaches and panama hats, and the terrace of the Hotel Nacional is still the place to people-watch while sipping a mojito.

Most excitingly of all, though, there are the cars – Havana's streets are still full of huge US cruisers from the 1950s. In 1960, the US imposed a partial trade embargo on its newly socialist neighbour, extending this to a total blockade in 1962. As well as devastating the economy, this meant no new cars could be brought into the country, and so the existing fleet were simply repaired and resprayed, coaxed along with home-made spare parts and lots of love and care. Some are as sprightly as the septuagenarian musicians of the Buena Vista Social Club, while others crawl round Havana coughing and belching blue smoke as if desperate for a long overdue retirement. It's estimated that

there are 50,000 such cars – Chevrolets, Buicks, Cadillacs, Pontiacs and Fords.

But recently things have begun to change. Even the most determined mechanic can only keep a car going for so long, and these cars are already well past their sell-by date. Soon the cost of repairs will be more than scrapping them and starting again. At the same time, more modern cars are arriving on Cuba – Toyotas, Kias and a host of cheap Far Eastern imports. And finally, there is mounting speculation that the US will relax its embargo some time soon, at which point the time bubble will burst for ever.

So go now, and spend a few days touring Havana and the rest of Cuba in a great whale of a car. Unfortunately foreigners are not allowed to drive these cars, but you can rent them with a driver, either officially from an agency, or usually far cheaper from your guesthouse.

The roads are good and there aren't many cars around at all – you can be driving along a dual carriageway and only spot a few other vehicles. Of course there are beaches, palm trees and jungle-covered hillsides, but for me the highlight of Cuba is cruising the streets in an old open-top Chevy, soaking up the unique atmosphere at sunset. And best of all, because you have to have a driver, there's nothing to stop you getting in the mood by stopping to sample a few mojitos and Cuba libres along the way. *Viva la Revolución*!

Now do it . . .
Intrepid Travel can organize a trip ideal for those wanting to experience Cuba via their classic cars (www.intrepidtravel.com/trips/QUSL).

19

Devizes to Westminster Canoe Marathon

Why	To take part in a hardcore race with great camaraderie
Where	England	**Duration**	One day +

LONG WEEKEND

There's something peculiarly British and a little bit eccentric about the Devizes to Westminster Canoe Marathon. It's not quite up there with cheese-rolling or bog-snorkelling in the silliness stakes, but there's something delightfully uncommercial and homespun about an event that grew out of a pub bet, was pioneered by the local Scout troop and now sees top international athletes and Special Forces soldiers compete alongside father-and-son teams and total amateurs (like me!) just along for a laugh.

The race traces its roots back to 1920 when a rail and bus strike was planned and locals in the Greyhound pub in Pewsey, a village just outside the Wiltshire town of Devizes, were discussing alternative methods of transport. The conversation ended with a bet on whether some of the men could canoe the seventy miles from Pewsey down the River Avon to the coast at Christchurch in under three days. They succeeded, and various teams went on to replicate their feat, achieving faster and faster times.

In 1947 one of the men who had done the Avon run was looking for a new challenge and came up with the idea of canoeing from Devizes to the Houses of Parliament at Westminster, and doing so in less than a hundred hours. The local Scouts took up the challenge, and achieved it at Easter 1948, their progress generating such interest that films at the Devizes cinema were stopped so the audience could be updated. In the following years the army got involved, using the event as a training exercise, and canoeists from around the world came to take part.

Today it's one of the toughest canoe races in the world. The 125-mile route starts on the Kennet and Avon canal before joining the Thames at Reading, and passes seventy-seven locks. Canoes aren't allowed in the locks, so at each one the competitors must haul their boats out of the water, carry them up and over the lock, then get

Getting our race number brings home the reality...

Planning our winning strategy.

MARLOW

NEWBURY

WESTMINSTER
BRIDGE

HUNGERFORD

READING

DEVIZES
WHARF

OLD
WINDSOR

ALDERMASTON

SHEPPERTON

*Heading for the start ... does anyone want
to take my place?*

back in on the far side. The élite competitors race non-stop all the way, paddling through the night and calculating their timings so they hit the final section of the Thames, which is tidal, in time to go with the direction of the water down to the Houses of Parliament. The record stands at fifteen hours and seventeen minutes. But there is also the so-called 'Endeavour' class of competitors, who take a more leisurely pace, stopping overnight at set campsites along the way and completing the distance over four days. You can do it in a single kayak, but most do it in double canoes or kayaks.

I'd read about the race and when Mungo, one of our cameramen, pulled up outside the office one day with a canoe on his roof rack, I asked him if he wanted to enter. Unfortunately the race was

> 'It's a team effort, a chance to bond as you chat and paddle along together'

the following weekend, so we didn't have a whole lot of time to train . . .

We went along anyway, just to get a taste of the atmosphere, and though we only completed the first day, it was abundantly clear that this was a very serious undertaking. At times it was miserable – hauling the boat up and down riverbanks; praying that we wouldn't capsize in the long, black canal tunnels; paddling on through wind and rain; battling to stay motivated when you turn the corner to see a mile-long, dead straight stretch of water before you. But at other times we were having such a good time that we sang as we paddled. Above all it's a team effort, a chance to bond as you chat and paddle along together hour after hour.

With only a week's training we never stood a chance of making Westminster, but I'd love to go back and do it properly. It must be an amazing experience to be paddling along the Thames then see Big Ben rise up in front of you, and know that you've completed an epic endurance test.

Now do it . . .
For more information on this race, visit www.dwrace.org.uk

Rwanda's mountain gorillas

Why	For a proximity to animals we normally fear
Where	Rwanda	**Duration**	One day

The guides had told us not to look into the gorillas' eyes, but we couldn't help ourselves. Just a metre from us, sitting in the undergrowth, was a mother feeding her two tiny babies, looking at us with their little eyes just like human children would. The mother stared at us too, her eyes big and baleful. It was the most moving wildlife encounter I've ever had.

We were high in the Virunga mountains of northern Rwanda, a string of volcanoes covered in bamboo and tropical rainforest. It was here that Dian Fossey carried out her pioneering research and conservation work with gorillas, a project that is credited with saving them from extinction and which was the inspiration for the film *Gorillas in the Mist*.

We'd started early that morning, driving an hour from our lodge then heading out on foot at an altitude of 1,800 metres. The gorillas live at around 3,000 metres, so we were soon gasping for breath in the thin air and drenched from pushing through the undergrowth. Thankfully, though, it's too cold for snakes up here, so there's no need to be on your guard. We climbed for a couple of hours, stopping at the occasional clearing to take in the view across to the other mist-shrouded mountains. And then, suddenly, we caught a glimpse of movement and there was our first gorilla family.

We'd been watching the mother and children for a few minutes when we heard a rustling

*Climbing up was an adventure
in itself.*

We climbed a bit higher. The disconcerting thing is that you hear the gorillas before you see them. We could hear the grass rustling alongside us, then saw a tree being shaken up ahead. You feel very much as if you're in their domain.

And then the gorillas were all around us, perhaps twenty in all. They were chewing on branches, eating leaves, playing with each other, and all the while the silverback sat on a mound keeping watch. The guides told us to keep quiet, and taught us to make a sort of grunting noise that conveyed we meant no harm.

And then, after what seemed like only a few minutes, our hour was up. Our privileged glimpse into the family life of the gorillas was over and we had to drag ourselves away. We set off back down the mountain, exhausted but elated.

behind us. We spun round and saw a huge silverback walking right up behind us, making use of the path we'd tramped down through the undergrowth. I was at the back of our line of people, so found myself looking right at him. He was huge – six foot high even when walking on all fours. I didn't know what to do, but one of the guides grabbed my arm and we quickly moved out of his way. He ambled past, little more than a metre away, staring at us imperiously.

Human visits to the gorillas are very controlled, to limit poaching and prevent visitors passing on coughs and colds. You're only allowed to stay with them for an hour, and a maximum of thirty-two people are permitted each day. This means you have to pre-arrange your slot, sometimes several months in advance. That might make it sound a bit touristy, but this couldn't be further from a zoo or safari park – these are wild animals.

*I took this photo as this silverback
walked past me.*

Now do it . . .

Visit Intrepid Travel (www.intrepidtravel.com/trips/YXOG) for a truly breathtaking, up-close-and-personal gorilla experience. You can find out more about Rwanda at the Rwanda Tourism Board (www.rwandatourism.com).

Why	To savour a slower approach to life
Where	Nepal	**Duration**	One day +

I'd always thought of elephants as big grey monsters, and sleeping out under canvas in Africa I'd often had anxious thoughts about being trampled by one in my sleep. Now here I was, tickling an elephant's tummy as I washed her in a Nepalese river.

We'd spent the night at Tharu Lodge on the edge of Chitwan National Park, and had arranged to spend the morning travelling through the countryside by elephant. Few people associate elephants with Nepal, but there are wild and domesticated populations here. Both have seen numbers decline sharply in recent decades – the domesticated ones as people have turned to machinery to do the heavy lifting, and the wild ones, which used to migrate here from northern India, because the growing human population has restricted their habitats.

As we washed the elephants, they playfully sprayed water from their trunks, and, as with a dog, you started to get a real sense that each one had its own personality. Then it was time to mount up. The idea is that you step on the back of the elephant's heel, and from there jump up on to its back. I was wearing cowboy boots, and after all those times fretting about being trampled by a marauding elephant, I suddenly found myself worrying about whether I was going to hurt one by treading on it.

Of course, it didn't feel a thing, and soon we were lolloping along through the countryside, holding up umbrellas against the tropical rain. It was far more comfortable than riding a horse and there was something supremely serene about the slow rolling motion. Best of all was the height. From the back of the elephant we could see the view above the bushes, and when we passed through villages, we could look over the

walls right into the beautiful houses – a little bit voyeuristic perhaps, but no one seemed to mind.

You can go into the heart of Chitwan Park by elephant, travelling through the jungle and, if you're lucky, spotting Bengal tigers, but our route took us through the Tharu villages at the edge of the park. The Tharu are a distinct ethnic group who have lived for centuries in the Teria, the lowland southern hills, and it's a side to Nepal that often gets overlooked in the excitement about Everest and the high mountains.

We'd only had a taster but I'd loved every minute of it, and certainly changed my mind about elephants.

Now do it . . .

Great Holidays Nepal (www.greatholidaysnepal. com) can arrange this adventure in one of their many package deals. You can contact them directly at nepalvacation@gmail.com

What an amazing beast!

Exploring the Atacama Desert

Why | To experience four perspectives in one great adventure

Where | Northern Chile | **Duration** | Two days

Covering 40,000 square miles, the Atacama is the world's driest desert and the very definition of the word 'barren'. It's windswept, cold and very high. Flying over it by plane, you see mile after mile of rocky nothingness. It's impossible to believe there's anything down there at all. And yet, look a little closer and you find there's more to the Atacama than meets the eye. The best starting point for exploring the area is San Pedro de Atacama, an oasis town at an altitude of 2,436 metres that sits at the meeting point of two rivers, the Rio Grande and the Rio San Pedro.

Our Atacama adventure began with a half-hour drive in a 4x4 heading southeast from San Pedro, after which we started out on foot into the flat, rocky desert. It was a bitterly cold day, and the wind was whipping across the plain. After a couple of hours' walking, we reached what looked like a low ridge of rock, a foot or so high, running across the horizon. As I got closer, then right on top of it, I could see it was actually the lip of a gorge. When we got to the edge and looked down, I couldn't believe my eyes.

In front of me was a beautifully lush valley, covered in all sorts of vivid green vegetation – giant ferns, fruit trees, long grasses and moss. In the middle was a crystal-clear river, which in several places turned into amazing cascading waterfalls as it travelled down the gorge. At the edge were giant cacti, some 20 metres high, which our guide told us were up to a thousand years old. We hopped along stepping stones at the side of the river, unable to believe the contrast between the wind-blasted desert and this Eden-like scene.

This isn't the only surprise the Atacama has in store. Eight miles west of San Pedro is the Valle de la Luna, the 'Valley of the Moon'. Here millions of years of erosion by water and wind have sculpted the rock into peculiar formations. It really is like the surface of another planet – so much so that NASA tested a prototype for the Mars Rover here.

As you walk along a winding path through the Valle de la Luna, the rock walls on either side grow higher and higher until they are towering 20 metres above you. It's like something from *Lord of the Rings*. At the end, the path goes into a tunnel, and with a torch you can press on beneath the desert, squeezing through narrow gaps in places and scratching your arms on the salty rocks. There are lots of these tunnels throughout the area – the result of erosion and the way the rocks have formed over millennia – though you'd never know from above.

The four dimensions: Valley of the Moon, Death Valley, the salt flats and the desert oasis.

> Approaching the salt flats is like driving towards a mirage ... you start to wonder if the altitude is playing tricks on you

Our next stop was the Valle de la Muerte, 'Death Valley', a few miles north, where there are huge dunes, some 200 metres high. Here you can go sand-boarding, climbing up to the summit, then sliding down on a wooden board, snowboard-style. We contented ourselves with running down the dunes, then moved on to our final stop, the Salar de Atacama, the great salt flats that start fifteen miles south of San Pedro and stretch for more than 1,000 square miles.

Approaching the salt flats is like driving towards a mirage. In the midst of the mountainous desert, with its myriad shades of red, yellow, black and grey rock, looms this perfectly flat, perfectly white ocean. As you get closer, it's odder still – in places there are pools of water, and standing in them are pink flamingos. You start to wonder if the altitude is playing tricks on you.

The salt flats are formed where ground water from the surrounding mountains collects into what would ordinarily be a lake, but here just evaporates, leaving its salt content lying on the surface. The flamingos are here to feed on algae in the pools of water, and it's this that gives them their pink colour.

Driving south from San Pedro, soon after the salt flats begin, you reach the Laguna Cejar, a sinkhole, perhaps 100 metres wide and some 40 metres deep, in which the water is five times more salty than the Dead Sea. On our trip I did what had to be done, stripped down to my shorts and dived in. I'm afraid I can't report too much about the flotation effect of the salt content – it was so cold (it would have been iced over if it wasn't so salty) I had to clamber out as quickly as I possibly could.

As I shivered in the back of the 4x4 on the way back to San Pedro, the desert slipped past the window – arid, empty, and yet full of surprises.

Now do it . . .

For eco-friendly accommodation, we recommend the Awasi Hotel (www.awasi.cl). For more information on eco luxury hotels, visit Eco Luxury Retreats (www.ecoluxury.com). For more amazing adventures in Chile, visit Tourism Chile (www.turismochile.travel) and ProChile (www.prochile.co.uk).

Once in a Lifetime

Why	To discover how spices affected history
Where	Indonesian Ocean	**Duration**	One week

Scattered in the middle of the Banda Sea, about 1,200 miles east of Java and 300 miles west of New Guinea, are ten tiny volcanic islands. Few people have ever heard of Indonesia's Banda Islands – in fact, they are not marked on some atlases – and even fewer have visited them. And yet, by a quirk of their turbulent history, they are forever linked with New York.

Until the mid-nineteenth century, these tiny specks in the ocean were the world's only source of nutmeg and mace. Their rarity made these spices so sought after that they were literally worth their weight in gold – and so control of trade with the Banda Islands was fiercely contested by the colonial European powers. First the Portuguese were dominant, then, by the seventeenth century, the Dutch, but the English kept a toehold in the area by controlling Run and Ai, the smallest and most remote Banda Islands.

Throughout the seventeenth century there were bitter battles between the Dutch and the English, including night-time raids during which hundreds were killed, and a month-long siege that allowed the Dutch to take Ai.

In 1667, the Treaty of Breda was signed. The English agreed to give up Run, allowing the Dutch to have a monopoly on nutmeg, and in return the Dutch would give up their claim to a small island on the other side of the world – Manhattan. The main settlement on Manhattan, New Amsterdam, was renamed after the future James II, the Duke of York, and New York was born.

This history makes the Banda Islands a fascinating place to visit. To this day the islands' lush palm and nutmeg forests are dotted with elaborate colonial Dutch houses, and there are

also crystal-clear waters, beautiful reefs for diving, a stunning backdrop of jungle-covered volcanoes and some delicious local food.

It's a long way from anywhere, but you can get there by air, flying on a small plane from Ambon (a much larger Indonesian island to the north), though flights are few and far between. We sailed there from East Timor, mooring up in the harbour of Banda Neira, the only real town in the region, on the island of the same name.

It's such a beautiful place that you might decide you want to stay there. To do so, you must pass the test to become an honorary citizen of Banda. And this is where the adventure comes in . . .

The challenge is to set off from Banda Neira, then cross by boat to the neighbouring island of Gunung Api, which is entirely taken up by a huge active volcano that rises 660 metres straight from the sea. You have to climb the volcano, return to shore, then swim back to Banda Neira. If you do all that, you can claim your citizenship.

We started climbing about 4 a.m. There is a route up the volcano, but it's not what you'd call a path. We were pulling on vegetation, hauling

ourselves up on tree trunks, struggling not to slip on the volcanic rock underfoot. It was pitch black, and though there was a group of eight of us, we didn't have a guide. All you could make out was the back of the person in front of you, and we were all scratching our arms on rocks or banging our heads into branches.

But when the first rays of sunlight broke the forest, things got even harder. Almost immediately, it became unbearably hot. People often had to stop to glug down water or bend over, hands on knees, panting for air. My heart was pounding.

Five hours after setting out, we reached the summit. In one direction was the vast crater, steaming with sulphurous gas. In the other was a sensational view of the emerald green Banda Islands, stretched out in front of us. The previous day in the Banda Neira museum we'd been looking at seventeenth-century paintings of the Bandas, and really it didn't seem as if much had changed. You could imagine the masts of a fleet of Dutch ships at harbour down below.

But we still had two-thirds of the challenge to complete. We slipped and slid back down the volcano, hanging off tree roots, tumbling through undergrowth and spending a lot of time on our backsides. By the time we reached the shore, I was saturated in sweat. What could be more delicious than to dive straight into the cool ocean?

This was a big mistake. The group leapt screaming and shouting into the clear blue water and swam off towards Banda Neira, 500 metres away on the other side of the channel. A few minutes in, an agonizing pain shot down my thigh. I put my hand down and felt my muscle completely rigid, then, before I knew what was happening, the searing pain moved down into my calf and I couldn't move my leg at all. It was cramp, but unlike anything I'd ever experienced before. All that exertion in the heat followed by plunging straight into the cold water must have brought it on. And then my other leg seized up.

I felt myself sinking; I was panicking, fighting to stay on top. I was a long way from land, the other swimmers were nowhere near me – there was no way out. I started shouting. 'Help! Help! Help!' What had started as a fun challenge had turned into one of the most dangerous situations I'd ever faced.

As I floundered, shouting and struggling to stay afloat, I heard an outboard. Someone from the yacht we'd arrived on, at anchor in the distant harbour, had heard my shouts and was coming to the rescue in a little dinghy. At first I didn't think I'd be able to stay up until he reached me, but as he neared, and I realized I would be OK, relief washed over me. 'Haul me in – I can't move my legs!' I shouted desperately, and my rescuer heaved me aboard, leaving me panting in the bottom of the boat.

Perhaps I should know when to give up, but that night, fully recovered, I went back and swam right across. And so the next day, the honorary president of the Banda Islands paid us a visit. He arrived dressed in long robes, sitting on an upright dining room chair in the centre of a small boat, shouting directions at his driver. Then he came aboard our yacht and presented us with our certificates of honorary citizenship.

Now, in theory, we can get married in the Banda Islands, buy a house and settle down there. And to be honest, I'm quite tempted.

Postscript: A couple of days later we had an even closer brush with Banda's history, in a peculiar way. We sailed to Run and camped out on the beach of Nailakka, a tiny neighbouring islet 400 metres long. It was here that the English soldiers had been forced to retreat when the Dutch were attacking in 1615 and many of them died here. In the bushes at the centre of Nailakka we found a very old grave, surrounded by candles which had only recently been placed there. That night we built a big fire on the beach and sat around it talking, singing, and taking the odd photo. When we looked at the photos the next day on the boat, we saw the most bizarre thing – a ghostly figure sitting within the fire.

> It's such a beautiful place that you might decide you want to stay there

Now do it . . .

Book your flight with Manado Safari Tours (www.manadosafaris.com) and they will arrange all the details for you, or Dive Happy (www.divehappy. com) can arrange a diving-tour around the islands.

For all diving advice, visit PADI at www.padi.com. You can contact the Indonesian Tourism Board for more information (www.indonesia-tourism.com).

Skiing the Haute Route

Why	For long-haul skiing with a sense of journey
Where	France and Switzerland	**Duration**	One week

TWO WEEKS OFF WORK

If you're looking for wilderness, for a chance to get out into the peaceful, majestic mountains, the last place you should go is a modern ski resort. With crowded pistes, overpriced self-service cafeterias, the constant hum of artificial snow cannons and the clanking of ever larger and more numerous lifts, today's ski resorts can feel like a kind of high-altitude suburbia.

Little wonder, then, that more and more people are choosing to take up ski touring, and so leave the resorts, queues and lifts behind altogether. Sticky skins attach to the bottom of your skis, allowing you to walk up to the top of the mountain where you take them off and stow them in your rucksack before skiing off down the other side.

Suddenly you are no longer tied to the network of mechanical lifts – it's as if, thanks to two sticky synthetic strips, you have discovered the freedom of the mountains. And the amazing thing is that even in the middle of Europe, even in the biggest and busiest resorts, you can climb up to the brow of the hill and discover utterly deserted, pristine valleys beyond.

A ski tour might last a few hours, a few days or even longer, with nights spent in high-altitude huts, or refuges, in the mountains. There are hundreds of possible itineraries throughout the Alps, and yet one is the undisputed king, the most celebrated ski tour of them all: the Haute Route.

It runs for eighty miles between two of the world's most famous ski resorts

> **The route was devised as a summer walking itinerary by the gentleman climbers of the British Alpine Club, then skied for the first time in 1911**

– Chamonix in France and Zermatt in Switzerland. Most people start in Chamonix, in the shadow of western Europe's highest peak, Mont Blanc, and finish in Zermatt beneath the Matterhorn, probably the world's most photographed mountain. It has been done in less than twenty-one hours (by a group of French soldiers), but most people take six days, staying in refuges along the way.

The route was devised as a summer walking itinerary by the gentleman climbers of the British Alpine Club, then skied for the first time in 1911. Today its fame means it attracts several thousand skiers each winter, but unlike most of the world's other celebrated and heavily marketed challenges – the trek to Everest base camp or the climb of Kilimanjaro, for example – the Haute Route remains genuinely tough and with a real level of danger. Less than half of those who attempt it manage to reach Zermatt.

In fact, many skiers don't get beyond the first day, arguably the hardest of all. You start by striking out across a glacier from Chamonix's Grand Montets ski area, then climb up to the Col du Chardonnet, a pass at 3,323 metres. After abseiling down the far side, you must climb again, up to the Trient Hut, perched on a rocky outcrop at 3,170 metres. It's a brutal introduction, and many people spend the night shivering in the hut's

dormitory, unable to sleep through a combination of the altitude and anxiety that they have bitten off more than they can chew. The morning brings comfort though – the hut's terrace has an epic view over a huge sea of snow without a single sign of human life to be seen.

The refuges along the way vary in standard. Some have showers and double rooms, others have no running water and long dormitory beds where up to eight people must sleep side by side (do not forget earplugs!). All provide decent and filling food, usually at a set time so everyone eats together, and you can buy beer and wine, though you might regret it the next day.

Apart from the abseil from the Col du Chardonnet, the Haute Route isn't technically difficult, but only the most experienced alpinists should attempt it without a guide because much of the route is on glaciers. These are covered in crevasses, which in winter are concealed by a layer of surface snow. With the weight of a person on top, the snow can give way like a trapdoor,

Off-piste skiing is amazing, but
beware of avalanches.

> " **The real secret of the Haute Route is that it doesn't matter if you make it or not** "

sending the unfortunate skier crashing down into the depths of the crevasse far below.

The draw of this trip is not thrilling powder skiing – there are some great descents, but perhaps 80 per cent of the time is spent climbing uphill, or traversing the high-altitude glaciers. The key is not to think of the downhill as the reward, but to relax into the meditative pace of the slow uphill trudge, taking the time to appreciate the awesome surroundings.

After a while you slow down into the rhythm of the trip: an early start, perhaps five hours' walking each day with a picnic lunch at a stunning viewpoint on the way, then finding the hut, drying equipment, reading a book and chilling out until supper.

If you make it to Zermatt you'll have the treat of skiing down beneath the iconic Matterhorn, aglow with the success of having bagged ski touring's biggest route. It's a moment you'll never forget, and yet the real secret of the Haute Route is that it doesn't matter if you make it or not. It may be a cliché to say that travel is about the journey not the destination, but it's never truer than with this trip. The prize isn't conquering the challenge, but having the chance to escape to a high-up and hidden mountain environment, beyond reach of ordinary skiers. It's a simple, ascetic existence up there but, above all, it's a complete break from normal life.

Now do it . . .
Wilderness Journeys offer inspiring adventure holidays to the world's wildest places, including the challenging Haute Route (www.wildernessjourneys.com).

Why	To conquer a personal achievement in swimming
Where	Turkey	**Duration**	One day

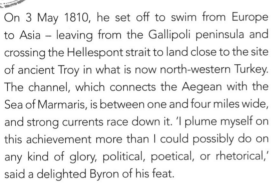

He is one of the most celebrated poets in English history, a leading figure in the Romantic movement, revered by the Greeks for fighting for their independence, and a legendary lover. And yet, Lord Byron himself was most proud of a swim.

On 3 May 1810, he set off to swim from Europe to Asia – leaving from the Gallipoli peninsula and crossing the Hellespont strait to land close to the site of ancient Troy in what is now north-western Turkey. The channel, which connects the Aegean with the Sea of Marmaris, is between one and four miles wide, and strong currents race down it. 'I plume myself on this achievement more than I could possibly do on any kind of glory, political, poetical, or rhetorical,' said a delighted Byron of his feat.

Numerous adventurers have copied Byron over the years. You could jump in to recreate the challenge at any time, but today the Hellespont, or Dardanelles as it's now more commonly known, is one of the world's busiest shipping lanes, considerably adding to the danger. Better to take part in the annual Hellespont swimming race organized by the local Rotary Club. It may have a less than catchy name, the Sahap Tarzi Swimming Contest, but there are support boats and, most crucially, the shipping lane is shut for two hours.

The race takes place in late August, and typically around 150 participants start the day taking the ferry from Çanakkale, on the Asian side, to Eceabat, where the swim starts. The actual distance directly back to Çanakkale, where a yellow balloon is set up to give the swimmers something to aim for, is less than two miles, but competitors have to plot a route that takes them 'upstream' for more than a mile. They then hit a current that brings them back down to Çanakkale, but means the total distance covered is three miles.

It can be cold and jellyfish are common so wear a wetsuit, but don't forget to smear your neck with suncream. The record stands at forty-eight minutes, but many of the participants are here for the challenge of taking part rather than to really race. If you take longer than two hours, you are disqualified (and, more worryingly, the shipping lane will reopen).

Do it in less than an hour and ten minutes, and you can toast the fact that though you may not be a celebrated poet, hell-raiser and lover, you are a faster swimmer than Lord Byron.

Now do it . . .

Swim Trek (www.swimtrek.com) offer great information about swimming the Bosporus, along with other great swimming adventures for you to tackle.

26

Hot-air ballooning over Guilin

Why | To view landscapes you only dream of from the sky

Where | China | **Duration** | One day

The scenery around the Chinese city of Guilin has to rank among the most dramatic anywhere in the world. Thousands of cone-shaped and tree-covered mountains reach up into the sky. Waterfalls crash down from their misty summits and the Li River snakes around their feet. It's an otherworldly scene.

So what better way to see it than from a hot-air balloon? There are several hot-air balloon operators in the town, and you can easily arrange for a sunrise, or sunset, flight. Don't expect the experience to be one of complete calm, though – if you haven't been in a hot-air balloon before, you are in for a surprise.

When our pilot fired the burner, there was an almighty roar and a blast of fierce heat. I felt like my head was burning and I had to crouch down to try to cool off. It was so hot and so noisy, it was impossible to think at all, let alone to have a spiritual moment looking at the view.

When we reached the top of our climb, turned

'There's something alien and unreal about the landscape, a little bit eerie but also very beautiful ' off the burner and just started to drift, the situation improved dramatically. The karst mountains, formed by millions of years of limestone erosion, rose above the morning mist and stretched away into the distance in every direction. There's something alien and unreal about the landscape, a little bit eerie but also very beautiful. It's quite simply a view you'll never forget.

Ballooning is an inexact science. There's no means of steering and no means of braking. So we just drifted along up a valley, gradually opening the vents on the balloon so the hot air escaped and we slowly descended. With a bit of luck, and by careful calculation of the wind direction and speed, the pilot should be able to bring you down gently in a field or other open space, but it doesn't always work out like that.

Bang! Bang! Bang! We bounced along the ground until, with a thwack, the bottom of the basket hit something solid and it tipped over, hurling everyone out in a jumble of arms and legs. The balloon itself fell across a road, blocking it and leaving the cars beeping their horns in frustration.

Thankfully no one was hurt, and as we drove back to the centre of Guilin, we laughed about what a strange experience it had been – incredible noise and heat and the chaos of the landing, mixed in with a few moments of tranquil perfection.

I guess it was two adventures in one, discovering one of the world's most bizarre landscapes, and one of the world's most bizarre means of transport.

Now do it . . .
To experience the magic of Guilin for yourself, visit China Fact Tours (www.chinafacttours.com).

27

Kaieteur Falls

| **Why** | For the most unblemished, awesome view |
| **Where** | Guyana | **Duration** | One to five days |

If there's one place that everyone reading this book should find their way to, this is it. I've been to Niagara, I've been to Victoria Falls, I've seen the Trümmelbach Falls in Switzerland and the Devil's Punchbowl in New Zealand – but without question this is the best waterfall in the world.

Kaieteur Falls is on the Potaro River in central Guyana and, with a clear drop of 226 metres, then a further drop that takes the total to 251 metres, is five times taller than Niagara Falls, and double the height of Victoria Falls. There are higher falls (Angel Falls in Venezuela is the world's tallest with a total drop of 979 metres) and there are bigger falls in terms of volume of water passing per second, but some argue that Kaieteur's combination of water volume and height earn it the distinction of being the 'largest single-drop waterfall in the world'. There's no official system for ranking waterfalls, and others complain this is a misleading title, but really such statistical hair-splitting completely misses the point – Kaieteur is the most beautiful waterfall in the world.

To get there from Georgetown, the capital of Guyana, you can either take an eight-hour bus trip to the town of Mahdia then trek for three or four days through the jungle, or you can fly to the tiny airstrip about two miles away.

Approaching the area by plane, you pass mile after mile of pristine tropical rainforest, then you see this immense brown river, the mist rising, then the breathtaking fall itself. Walking from the airstrip towards the fall only heightens the anticipation. The closer you get, the louder the thundering of the water until you can start to feel the energy through your feet. You can walk right up to the edge of it and out on a rocky promontory. From there you can look back straight into the falling water and down into the vast plunge pool, where a constant rainbow hangs amid the mist and spray.

In a way, the most surprising thing about Kaieteur is the total lack of any commercialization. There are no signs, no walkways, no guardrails – nothing. Just wilderness and, most importantly, no other people at all. Apart from the three of us, we didn't see another soul.

I was hot and dripping with sweat from the walk, and suddenly I felt compelled to get into the river. Jumping into a river just before it turns into one of the world's most powerful waterfalls is, in the cold hard light of day, a very stupid thing to do, but at the time it seemed like a terrific thrill. I just lay there, hanging on to a rock, watching the water cascade past and over the lip. Unforgettable.

'Statistical hair-splitting completely misses the point – Kaieteur is the most beautiful waterfall in the world'

> The closer you get, the louder the thundering of the water until you can start to feel the energy through your feet

Now do it . . .

Wilderness Explorers (www.wilderness-explorers.com) are the go-to company for adventures within Guyana, and they can organize your visit to Kaieteur Falls.

For more information on Guyana, contact the Guyana Tourism Authority (www.guyana-tourism.com).

28

Narrowboating in Wales

LONG WEEKEND

Why	For a peaceful journey with unexpected challenges
Where	Wales	**Duration**	Two days +

On the surface it seems so calm, serene and relaxing – hardly an adventure at all, in fact. But if you've ever been narrowboating, you'll know that the reality is very different.

You're chugging along happily, tending the tiller at the back of the boat, listening to the birdsong and keeping a careful watch on the bow, 60-odd feet in front of you. Your eyes flick down momentarily as you go to pick up your cup of tea, and then suddenly everything goes crazy. The bow swerves off course and straight towards the bank. You have to react fast, so you swing the tiller in the other direction, only to find you've over-compensated, and now you are zigzagging alarmingly across the canal, unable to regain control, with a boat coming the other way bearing down on you and its captain bellowing out with terror in his eyes . . .

Narrowboating is a relaxing way of life.

Don't let that put you off, though, because canal boating is brilliant fun. There are scores of canals across Britain and Europe where you can try it, but we chose one of the most scenic, the Llangollen canal in north Wales. We picked up a traditional 58-foot narrowboat at Chirk, travelled up to Llangollen and then south again towards Ellesmere.

It couldn't be easier – you have a thirty-minute briefing, then you're off, captain of your own ship. Almost immediately we entered the Chirk Tunnel, 459 yards long and built by Thomas Telford between 1794 and 1802. You have to turn on a lamp at the front of your boat, then peer down the tunnel, which is only the width of one boat, to check nothing's coming the other way. Only minutes after we arrived in our car on a sunny summer's day, we were right back in Victorian times, plunged into complete darkness, with the far end of the tunnel just a distant speck of light, banging off the damp walls in our boat.

For the next few days we motored through glorious countryside, stopping at country pubs along the way and mooring up for the night among the fields wherever we felt like it. There's a real sense of freedom.

I love the tranquillity but also the adventure.

The highlight, though, was crossing the Pontcysyllte Aqueduct on the way to Llangollen. Completed in 1805, it's the longest and highest aqueduct in Britain, 1,007 feet long and 126 feet high. It's an impressive sight, an iron trough supported on towering stone columns above the River Dee. A towpath runs over the aqueduct, beside a channel of water that is barely wider than a single narrowboat. The only guardrail is on the towpath side, so as you stand on the back of your boat, you look straight down over the edge into thin air.

After three days, I thought I'd really mastered narrowboating. Some friends had joined us for the final day and their three young daughters were sitting on the roof at the front of the boat as we pulled in to dock for the final time. I pointed the bow towards the bank, then moved the tiller to bring the stern in, but for some reason nothing happened. I had two options: to put the boat into reverse to slow us right down, or to open the throttle to full speed, making more water pass over the rudder so the steering would start responding again. I chose the latter. We surged forward, but the tiller still wouldn't work, so with a great 'crack!' we slammed into the concrete bank head first. The three little girls shot forward and disappeared from view. I thought I'd killed them.

Thankfully, though battered and bruised from their landing on the little front deck, the girls were OK. 'Don't worry,' said another boat's captain who had watched the whole thing. 'Canal boating is a contact sport!'

Now do it . . .
Black Prince Holidays (www.black-prince.com) can arrange your unique boating trip around the beautiful English countryside.

Why	For a slice of ancient history in the desert
Where	Libya	**Duration**	Three days

North Africa is not only a magical place to visit from a contemporary point of view, but historically it has much to offer. At Tobruk, visiting the graveyards of the fallen soldiers of Second World War battles between the English and the Germans is certainly an emotional experience. Walking among the gravestones, reading inscriptions of soldiers who lost their lives at 19, I strongly felt the importance of travelling to discover where significant historical moments had taken place.

The great irony about travel is that often we destroy the very things we've set out to see. We cross continents to reach the world's great sights – cathedrals, ruins, natural wonders – and then when we get there, all we can see are other tourists posing for photos. And with the tourists comes the whole food chain that feeds on them: the souvenir sellers, tour guides, ice-cream sellers and so on. At so many of the world's most celebrated sights, you end up feeling not wonder and awe, but merely a sense of mild irritation.

But Libya is different. For much of the last few decades, getting a visa has been tricky, and impossible for Americans. Now, though, the restrictions seem to be easing. You still need to travel with an officially recognized tour company,

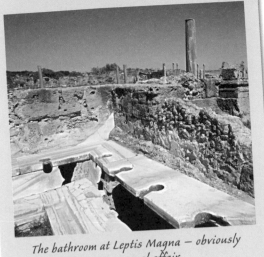

The bathroom at Leptis Magna – obviously a communal affair.

rather than on your own, but rules such as having to have all your hotels booked up in advance have been lifted.

You can feel the effects of the absence of tourists throughout Libya, from the souks of Tripoli where no one hassles you to the deserts of the south, where Tuareg children will stare at you shyly rather than scream for gifts. But nowhere is it more apparent than Leptis Magna, the ruined Roman city just outside Tripoli.

Founded as a Phoenician trading port in 1100 BC, Leptis Magna grew into one of the most important Roman cities of the Mediterranean. Its heyday began in AD 193, when Lucius Septimius Severus, a native of the city, became Roman emperor and proceeded to lavish the wealth of the empire on his home town.

Today it's one of the world's most impressive historical sights. Everywhere you turn there are incredible stone statues, mosaics, columns and carvings. There are temples, a marketplace and a huge amphitheatre. We had a laugh checking out the baths and their communal toilets – a long stone bench with holes cut into it and a channel of flowing water beneath. The men would sit there cheek by jowl, or rather, cheek by cheek . . .

There's a museum, but it doesn't feel like the ruins have been heavily restored and cleaned up for the tourists. Weeds grow up between the Roman cobblestones, and the place is all the more atmospheric for it. Best of all is that you have a good chance of having the place to yourself. You can wander around, clamber where you want to, and stop and chill out, totally undisturbed. It's such an unusual feeling that you almost feel as if you're trespassing. My advice is to go soon, before everyone else catches on.

There are few visitors, which is unique for such a historic site.

Now do it . . .

Since travelling as individuals in Libya is not yet accepted, you will need to go with a guide or tour group. To ensure you conduct your adventure with ease, we recommend travelling with Explore (www.explore.co.uk).

Mongolia by furgon truck

Why	For quirky travelling across the Mongolia steppe
Where	Mongolia	**Duration**	Two weeks

When travelling, it's always best to accept offers of food and drink to avoid offending your hosts. But when the old woman lifted the lid of a cauldron to reveal at least two hundred testicles of goats, sheep, horses and donkeys bubbling away, I had second thoughts.

We were in Mongolia and had been invited for tea by a nomadic family. Like all the country's nomads, they lived in a ger, a large tent made of felt wrapped around a wooden latticework frame (and known in other parts of central Asia as a yurt). The family were farmers, and moved their herds of animals over Mongolia's seemingly endless grassy plains, relocating their ger every few months. They told us that they castrated all the animals on one day each year. And by pure chance, today was that day.

Mongolia is a stunning, but not easy, country to travel through. There simply aren't many roads. The complete road network adds up to about 25,000 miles, but less than 2,000 miles of that are paved. And Mongolia is a big place – covering more than 600,000 square miles. Let's compare that to the UK, which covers 94,000 square miles, but has 250,000 miles of paved roads – Mongolia is six times bigger than the UK, but has less than one per cent of our network of asphalt roads.

And so, about an hour outside the capital Ulaanbaatar, the paved roads run out, and soon after that, the dirt roads too. For much of the time you are

> Mongolia is a stunning, but not easy, country to travel through. There simply aren't many roads

RUSSIAN FEDERATION

TSAGANNUUR

ULAANGOM   BARUUNTURUUN

ULAANBAATAR

MONGOLIA

CHINA

driving over grass. At one point we had stopped to ask for directions, and the man, on horseback, said: 'Keep going up this valley, then turn right after the third mountain.'

Clearly to travel in a country like this, you are going to need a special form of vehicle. Many people come to ride horses here, but it's hard to get far enough beyond Ulaanbaatar on horseback to really get into proper, wild Mongolia. No, the best way to get around is in a furgon, a small Russian-built van. Not only are they light, so don't sink into the mud and grass like heavier Western vehicles, but they have four-wheel drive and, most importantly, are widely used throughout Mongolia. If, or more like when, you break down, there will always be someone around with a spare part and who knows how to fix it.

It might be possible to hire one in Ulaanbaatar, but if not, you can buy a brand new one for $5,000. You can then spend two or three weeks exploring Mongolia, perhaps making a big loop out into the Gobi desert then back to Ulaanbaatar, and sell the furgon when you get back.

There is no guarantee of accommodation along the way, so you need to take camping gear, food and water. Petrol is widely available, from pumps which you have to hand-crank, but you should carry a few extra jerry cans of fuel on the roof, just in case. Be prepared for extremes of temperature – some nights I slept in the back of the furgon to try to keep warm.

I'd come to Mongolia as part of *Long Way Round*. We entered from the Russian border at Tsagaannuur in north-west Mongolia, driven across the country to Ulaanbaatar, then turned

north to re-enter Russia on the road to Ulan Ude, close to Lake Baikal. It took us two weeks to cover a little over a thousand miles, and was some of the hardest travelling of the whole expedition, with numerous breakdowns, mechanical failures and one serious crash. And yet Mongolia was one of the most magical, rewarding countries of all those we travelled through, where traditional ways of life seemed utterly unchanged by the modern world, and where the local nomads, clad in dells, their blue and red robes, would always be quick to offer us hospitality.

Which brings us back to the balls. I suggested that Charley and Ewan should try one, and they said they would only if we all did. And so the smiling lady dished up one testicle each, placed in a small white bowl on the table in front of us. Ewan went first, and somehow got his down. Charley put his in his mouth but quickly spat it out. I looked down at mine – white, with purple veins and with the sperm duct still attached. I looked back up and saw the eyes of everyone in the ger on me, waiting expectantly. I picked it up and put it in my mouth.

First I tried to swallow it whole, but this thing was as big as an egg and there was no way I was going to get it down. So I changed tactics and gingerly bit into it. Big mistake – it popped, and loads of fluid leaked out. A voice in my head screamed 'Noooo . . .' and I retched. The testicle flew out of my mouth, rolled across the floor and hit the leg of the father of the house. I thought I'd mortally offended him, and watched him anxiously, waiting for his reaction. We were camping just near by and it would not be good news to make enemies with the locals.

But slowly his face cracked into a broad smile, and then he, and everyone else, fell about laughing.

Now do it . . .

To arrange a furgon adventure, or any other adventures within Mongolia, contact Panoramic Journeys (www. panoramicjourneys.com).

Why	For danger, closeness to nature and total isolation
Where	Guyana	**Duration**	Two days +

Surama is a special place. A remote village in southern Guyana set in a small patch of open savannah, surrounded by the jungle-covered Pakaraima Mountains, it is home to fewer than three hundred people. The Makushi people lead a simple, basic life, based on farming as well as hunting and gathering from the forest. But since 1998, they've also run an award-winning community eco-tourism project.

At the edge of the village is the Surama Eco-Lodge, which, rather than being owned by a big foreign corporation, is owned, managed and operated by the local community. Today around 60 per cent of the village income is from tourism and more than seventy people are employed directly or indirectly by the lodge, which has become a role model for community-based tourism in this part of South America.

It has lots to offer the visitor too. The dozen rooms are quite basic – there's no electricity, for example – but the staff are welcoming and guests get a real insight into how the village works. There's plenty to do too, including birdwatching, mountain treks, canoe trips along the Burro Burro River to see giant otters and tapirs, and visits to the nearby Iwokrama Canopy Walkway, suspended 30 metres up in the tropical rainforest.

But we hadn't come for any of those delightful activities; we were here for a jungle survival training course. The lodge has a partnership with Bushmasters, a training company led by an ex-British Special Forces soldier, which runs jungle survival courses of up to two weeks – perhaps the most hardcore holidays in the world. Where other tour operator websites show beautiful sunsets and smiling clients, Bushmasters' site is full of photos of piranhas, edible maggots and other animals in the process of being gutted. 'Possibly the least relaxing holiday in history' says a quote from a previous satisfied client.

My girlfriend Vicks and I were going to do a far shorter course, just spending one day and one night in the jungle. Our guide Milner met us at breakfast time, and together we headed off on foot into the Iwokrama rainforest. This is virgin, or primary, rainforest, meaning it hasn't been cut down for timber or agriculture and then been re-grown, but is in its original, 100 per cent natural state. Almost as soon as we started walking through the vast, creeper-clad trees, Milner began to give us advice: always watch where you're putting your feet in case you stand on a snake, spider or something similarly nasty; never grab branches to steady yourself as you don't know what might be on them, and so on. My own tip is: always make someone else go in front; that way they will be first to walk into any spiders (which seem to have a nasty habit of spinning their webs right across the paths).

Soon we had our machetes out, cutting down trees to make our shelter for the night. I was hacking away when Milner shouted, 'Watch out!' and a big chunk of wood landed on the floor a foot from me. 'We're being attacked by spider monkeys,' he said.

I looked up and high in the canopy were two very agitated spider monkeys, one shaking with rage and baring his teeth, the other breaking off another branch ready to hurl at me. They are apparently very territorial and were trying to scare us off.

We persevered and managed to build a decent shelter with a roof of palm-tree branches to keep out the rain. Then Milner showed us how to make fishing rods and we headed down to a nearby river that seemed to be teeming with fish. After less than an hour we had ten catfish, though, ironically perhaps, the piranha wouldn't bite.

The next task was to build a fire. We collected a stock of wood, then tried rubbing sticks together to start the fire. After twenty minutes my hands were covered in blisters and we'd succeeded in making smoke but not fire, but luckily Milner had brought a lighter as insurance. We cooked and ate the fish, which were tasty but tiny, and then Milner announced he was off.

'Oh, OK then, see you later,' I said without really thinking. It was only as the light of his torch disappeared into the pitch-black forest that I began to think about the night ahead – it was 8 p.m., and it gets light at 5 a.m., so we had nine hours of darkness ahead of us. We got into our hammocks and started chatting. After a while I realized we were both babbling on about nothing in particular to block out the sounds of the jungle around us. It's simply alive – twigs constantly snapping, animals calling out, insects buzzing. Suddenly Vicks shouted out: 'Oh God! There's someone coming! I can see a torch!'

I realized I'd left the machete by the fire so I rushed to get it, toppling out of my hammock, getting tangled up in the mosquito net and crashing down on to the jungle floor. I got up, grabbed the machete and said, 'Where? Where is he?'

As she pointed out the direction, I turned and saw a firefly fluttering towards us – that was the torch. We laughed nervously, but by now we were really wound up and there was no chance of getting to sleep. Before he had left, Milner had

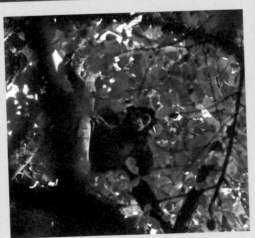

A spider monkey looks down on us, after trying to scare us away.

I picked up wood all night to keep the fire going. Luckily I didn't pick up a snake!

looking out at the glistening forest, the shafts of early morning sun catching the sparkling droplets of water as they fell from leaf to leaf, I realized how amazing this experience was. We were dry under our palm-leaf roof, in the middle of this pristine jungle, and, despite our terror, we'd survived the night.

Milner turned up about 6 a.m. and I asked how his evening had been. 'Well,' he said, 'actually I nearly died on the way home . . .' He proceeded to explain how, a short walk from the camp, he'd been stepping over a branch when he saw two red eyes staring back at him. He froze, shone his torch and saw a bushmaster. It's one of the largest and most venomous snakes in South America, and it was exactly where he'd been about to place his foot. As he was talking, all I could think of was fumbling around in the undergrowth in the middle of the night picking up logs by the light of my mobile phone. A shiver ran down my spine.

We packed up and headed back to Surama and the eco-lodge, whose basic rooms suddenly seemed very luxurious indeed. And the funny thing was that the further we got from the jungle, the more I started to appreciate it. Some adventures are an absolute joy in the moment, while others, like this one, seem nothing but an endurance test, and yet, when I got back to Britain, it was the first thing I wanted to tell everyone about. Sometimes you have to be pushed far beyond your comfort zone to really experience something new and challenging. And, as grim as it may seem at the time, those adventures are usually the most rewarding of all.

told us there was nothing around that was likely to harm us and that the fire would keep animals away, but in situations like that the real enemy is your imagination. With every branch that broke near by we had visions of a prowling jaguar.

And then the fire started to go out. As Vicks dozed off I hunted around the camp, using the light of my mobile phone to try to find new wood to put on the fire. Safely back in my hammock, I was just fumbling to put in some earplugs when the howler monkeys started. It was a horrendous sound, like the screech of a madman, and all the time they seemed to be getting closer. Howler monkeys are the loudest land animal and their call can be heard three miles away, even through dense forest. Lying there at 4 a.m., deep in the jungle, listening to the monkeys' blood-curdling screams, all I could think about was London and my own, comfortable, safe bed. What the hell was I doing here?

At 4.45 a.m. I finally got to sleep. At 5.15 a.m. it started raining and I woke up. But at that moment, a funny thing happened. Lying in my hammock,

Now do it . . .

Wilderness Explorers (www.wilderness-explorers.com) are the go-to company for adventures within Guyana, and they can organize your jungle survival experience. We recommend you stay at the Surama Eco-Lodge (www.suramaecolodge.com) during your stay there. For more information on Guyana, contact the Guyana Tourism Authority (www.guyana-tourism.com).

32

Night biking

Why	For a simple, cheap – but thrilling – adventure
Where	England	**Duration**	One night

In 1790, the French writer Xavier de Maistre published a travel book called *Journey Around My Bedroom*, in which he described spending six weeks exploring his bed, desk, armchair and so on. It might sound utterly bonkers, but in the introduction to a recent edition, the philosopher Alain de Botton argues there's a serious point: 'De Maistre's work springs from a profound and suggestive insight: that the pleasure we derive from journeys is perhaps dependent more on the mindset with which we travel than on the destination we travel to. If only we could apply a travelling mindset to our own locales, we might find these places becoming no less interesting than the high mountain passes and jungles of South America.'

Now I am not advocating you mount an expedition to your kitchen, or an exploratory hike round your back garden, but I do think it's true that we often ignore what's on our doorstep. The problem is that we become so familiar with what's near by – the sights and sounds of our home towns or cities, say – that they become invisible. What we need is to find different ways of exploring the areas closest to us, so those familiar sights come alive in a whole new way. And one of the best ways of doing this is simply to explore your home town in the middle of the night – on foot, by car, but probably best of all by bicycle.

We set off around 2.30 a.m., in the window of a few hours between the last revellers going home and the first early morning delivery lorries taking to the streets. The streetlamps of London were still on, but the roads and pavements were utterly deserted. No surprise in that, but what's shocking is how much it transforms the city.

It's eerie and dreamlike, but also liberating, as if you own the whole place. We rode over the Thames on the Millennium Bridge – cyclists aren't normally allowed, but at this time there are no rules. We wobbled through the narrow ancient lanes connecting the barristers' chambers around

spotting things you'd never noticed before.

It's not just about the absence of others – sometimes being out at an odd time lets you witness odd events. Coming down a spookily empty Mall, we saw that the Houses of Parliament were lit up by floodlights and surrounded by hundreds of armed police. The gates kept swinging open and closed as cars went in. It looked like a coup d'état. I stopped a policeman and asked what was going on – it turned out to be a rehearsal for the Queen's state opening of parliament, something you'd never otherwise know even happened.

Gray's Inn, then stopped to picnic in Lincoln's Inn Fields, the only time I've ever had a London park entirely to myself.

In Fleet Street, rather than the usual thunder of buses and taxis, there was complete silence, and I got off the bike and lay in the road, just because I could. And without having to constantly watch out for cars, you're free to stare up at the buildings,

The new bike hire schemes in London and Paris make this even easier to do, but of course you could do it in any city in the world.

We got home about 6 a.m. Climbing the stairs to go back to bed, I felt as if we'd just had VIP access to a strange city few get to see. We'd had a real adventure – and all before breakfast.

Now do it . . .
You don't need your own bike to experience this adventure. London is one of a handful of cities to have introduced its own bike hire scheme.

Visit Transport for London (www.tfl.gov.uk/ roadusers/cycling/14808.aspx) for more details.

33

Climb the Matterhorn

Why	To scale an iconic mountain and take in the world below
Where	Switzerland	**Duration**	One week +

TWO WEEKS OFF WORK

The Matterhorn is the world's most recognizable mountain, a jagged pyramid of rock that has graced a billion postcards and chocolate boxes. Look at the side of a Toblerone, and you'll see its picture; break off a chunk and you'll get a good idea of the mountain's shape.

Getting high!

And though it's an image you have seen all your life, when you finally come face to face with the mountain in reality, like the Taj Mahal or the *Mona Lisa* it doesn't disappoint.

The 4,478-metre-high peak towers above Zermatt, the famous Swiss resort, and dominates the view from every angle. When you step out of your hotel in the morning, it draws your gaze up to its sheer faces, with clouds circling around them. As you walk about the streets, you have to keep stepping aside to avoid people taking photos of it with their cameras or phones. And as you close your curtains at night, it's impossible to resist one last look at the moon shining off its icy flanks.

And yet, while everyone knows the Matterhorn, what many don't realize is that it's possible for ordinary people, as opposed to professional climbers, to reach the summit. From down in Zermatt, that idea seems ridiculous – the towering, near vertical faces look impregnable. But with a guide, anyone who is fit, doesn't suffer from vertigo and has some basic climbing experience can tackle it.

The peak was first climbed in 1865 by an English team led by Edward Whymper, but four of the seven climbers died in a fall on the descent. The story of heroism and tragedy was lapped up by the British newspapers, caused a sensation, and propelled Zermatt into the limelight as the destination of choice for adventurous tourists.

Today, most people follow the same route that Whymper took, and the climb takes one day, albeit a long one. You start at Hörnli Hut, a mountain inn and restaurant perched on the flank of the mountain at 3,260 metres. After a night there, you start out at 4 a.m. and scramble up the Hörnli Ridge to the summit. The climb normally takes four to five hours, but the descent often takes the same time or even longer, meaning many people are on the mountain for ten or twelve hours.

Whether you reach the top depends on weather conditions as much as your own skills and fitness. The route is usually possible from July to

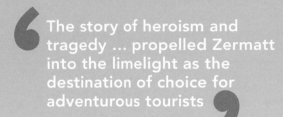

The story of heroism and tragedy ... propelled Zermatt into the limelight as the destination of choice for adventurous tourists

121

CLIMB THE MATTERHORN

mid-September, but storms can quickly blow in, making it inaccessible for days at a time. Often there's snow on the route, which means you need to climb in crampons, and you will be roped to the guide for most of the way.

So while it could be done in a weekend, most people allow a week or more, coming to Zermatt and acclimatizing while they wait for a good weather window. How hard is it? Of course, that's a bit subjective. It's graded as 'Assez Difficile', or quite difficult, but for most of the way it's a scramble rather than a technical rock climb. It is definitely 'exposed' though, at some points with drops of hundreds of metres on both sides, so those without a head for heights should certainly stay away.

Each guide will have different views on how much experience you need before they'll lead you, but you probably need to have done a couple of weeks' climbing in the UK or the Alps, and be familiar with harnesses, ropes and so on. At the guides' office in Zermatt, you can hire a guide just for the climb (for around 785 euros), but for the less experienced, a better option is to go on one of the week-long courses that are offered by several guiding companies in the Alps and the UK. You'll start by warming up with climbs of various easier peaks around Zermatt (the Pollux, Breithorn and Riffelhorn are ideal), so you are familiar with your guide and the equipment by the time you build up to an attempt on the Matterhorn at the end of the week.

But even if you don't fancy the climb to the top of the Matterhorn, coming to Zermatt to trek in the hills around its base would make a great adventure. There are mountain railways which give easy access to many of the routes and a network of high-altitude huts where you can have lunch or stay the night. For the real Matterhorn experience, you can walk up to the Hörnli Hut and spend the night with the climbers. Even if you've no intention of going any higher, you'll get to experience the atmosphere of the hut, and get up close with one of the world's iconic mountains.

Why don't we stay longer when we eventually get to the top?

Now do it . . .
Zermatt Matterhorn Group (www.matterhorn-group.ch) has all the details on the region, the mountain and the various climbs.

34

Fly a Tiger Moth

Why | To take off in a piece of history

Where | England | **Duration** | One day +

LONG WEEKEND

I was in Norfolk, lying on an empty beach with a few friends, when I heard the cough and splutter of an engine. I looked up and saw an old bi-plane fly out over the dunes and across the beach. It was very low, perhaps only 50 feet above the sand, and spotting us, the pilot turned the plane on its side and waved, his scarf flying in the air behind him. After circling round, he brought the plane down and landed on the beach, paused for a moment, then gunned the engine and took off again. We turned to each other dumbfounded – it was as if Biggles had just flown out of a timewarp straight from the Second World War.

The plane was a Tiger Moth, and after seeing one that close I knew I had to have a go. It may be small, but the Tiger Moth is a plane with an illustrious history. It was designed by Geoffrey de Havilland in 1931, only twenty-eight years after the Wright brothers made the first ever powered flight, but remained in service with the RAF until 1952 – and many are still in use today.

The two-seater, open-cockpit plane was used as a trainer for the fighter pilots who went on to fly Spitfires and Hurricanes in the Second World War. Such was demand that as well as being built by de Havilland in the UK, Tiger Moths were produced under licence in Australia, Canada, Norway, Portugal and New Zealand. The result is that today you can find Tiger Moths all over the world, in the hands of enthusiasts and flying clubs, and it's very easy to find someone to take you up in one. At least 9,000 were made in all, and experts believe more than 1,100 are still flying.

I had my first experience of flying in a Tiger Moth at Redhill Aerodrome in Surrey. Just getting into the cockpit evokes a bygone age – there's a smell of leather, oil and petrol. You have to wear big leather boots and a flying jacket to keep out the cold, and up close you can see that, rather than being metal, the wings and fuselage are made of wood and fabric. In front of you in the open cockpit, rather than the bank of controls and electronics you find in modern planes, there are just a few dials – speed, altimeter, engine temperature and fuel. This is flying at its simplest, and that's why it's so much fun.

With few pre-flight routines and checks possible on a plane this basic, we just roared off down the grass airstrip and, within a couple of hundred yards, were airborne. Because of its aerodynamics and because it's so light, the Tiger Moth can take off in 156 yards, little more than

the length of a football pitch – another reason it's used in many remote corners of the world.

Leaning out of that cockpit and seeing the ground fall away beneath you is a thrilling sensation, but my pilot had more in store. After a while he started looping the loop, and then performed a 'stall turn', flying directly upwards until the plane could go no further. It hung in the air for a second, then fell back down, twisting around until the speed of the fall gave it enough lift to start flying again. I just about hung on to my lunch . . .

As well as being capable of taking off and landing in a short distance, the Tiger Moth can fly very slowly and very low. After the war, many were used around the world as crop dusters, but this also makes them perfect for aerial sightseeing. As we flew back to the airfield, we hopped along over hedgerows, level with the taller trees and able to see everything in perfect detail. They say that in a Tiger Moth, you can not only wave at people on the ground, but recognize their faces.

Wherever you are in the world, it's worth seeing if there's a Tiger Moth pilot who will take you up. One operator I would definitely seek out is Tiger Moth Adventures based in Airlie Beach in Queensland, Australia. They will take you on flights from the mainland over the stunning rainforests and white-sand beaches of the Whitsunday Islands.

But an even more amazing adventure would be to take a longer journey by Tiger Moth. The planes typically have a range of about 300 miles before they need to refuel, so you would have to make a series of hops, just as Amy Johnson did when she spent nineteen days in 1930 flying from Croydon, England, to Australia in a Gypsy Moth, the Tiger's predecessor. If you wanted to fly from London to Paris, say, or on to the south of France, you could negotiate a price with one of the many flight schools with Tiger Moths in Britain. For something more serious, like a journey to Sydney or Cape Town, you'd probably need to buy your own. The good news is that they are cheap – starting from as little as £15,000.

Buying your own Tiger Moth and crossing continents in it would be an epic expedition, but even if you only go up in one for an hour, you'll be hooked.

Now do it . . .
For information on Tiger Moths and to organize your own flight adventure, visit Red Hill Aerodrome (www.redhillaerodrome.com).

35

Tbilisi to Baku by night train

| **Why** | For an unforgettable journey from capital to capital |
| **Where** | Georgia and Azerbaijan | **Duration** | One night |

There's something special about travelling by sleeper train. Perhaps it's because I grew up reading books like *Murder on the Orient Express*, and watching James Bond cross Europe by rail in *From Russia with Love*, but to me night trains always have an added excitement and romance.

There are fabulous, and famous, sleeper trains all over the world, of course, from the London-to-Fort-William Caledonian sleeper to South Africa's Blue Train, which travels in high luxury from Cape Town to Pretoria. But one sleeper

that few Western travellers have discovered is the train that runs three times a week from Tbilisi, the capital of Georgia, to Baku, the capital of Azerbaijan.

It's not so much that there's anything special about the train itself, rather that it lets you connect two fascinating cities to make an unforgettable trip. You can fly direct from London to Tbilisi, spend a few days there then catch the sleeper to Baku, from where you can return by direct flight to London. It's a corner of the world that is only just beginning to attract tourists from western Europe, but that is set to change.

Sitting where eastern Europe meets western Asia, Georgia has just 4.5 million people, but they are proudly independent and boast their own distinct language, culture and cuisine. Their capital is a stunning city, built on the banks of the Kura River, surrounded by snow-capped mountains and full of grand historic buildings, great restaurants and atmospheric narrow cobbled alleyways. You can shop in the smart boutiques, visit the opera house, cathedral and mosque (testament to the mix of East and West), then stop in one of the many cafés for some traditional dumplings filled with spicy meat.

Despite the short-lived war with Russia in 2008, the city seems to be confidently forging ahead, with numerous new hotels, several of them rising from the rubble of Stalinist-era blocks in the city centre. In 2009, the *New York Times* even said it was 'only a matter of time' before Tbilisi became a tourist draw on a par with St Petersburg or Moscow.

After the sophisticated delights of Tbilisi, hop on the train and prepare yourself for a surprise. Almost as soon as you leave the city, you find yourself crossing empty, barren steppes, which soon become desert. While Tbilisi feels distinctly European, you suddenly find yourself very much in central Asia.

The train leaves at 6.15 p.m. and arrives at 9 a.m. the next morning after covering 344 miles. There are usually cabins sleeping two or four, plus a restaurant car where you can get a good supper (though there may not be any choice) and local beer or wine to wash it down with.

I love that feeling of being cosy in your own cabin as the train races through the night, swaying left and right, clattering over points and whistling as it passes level-crossings. And from the tracks you have a whole new perspective on a country. Instead of looking at the front of shops, houses and offices, as you would from the road, you look right into their backyards. There's a sense of getting the real story rather than the official façade. The height helps too – after crossing the border into Azerbaijan we passed an enclosure the size of two football pitches, surrounded by a wall that would block the prying eyes of anyone passing by car or motorbike. From the train, we

On a long train journey, you meet local people ... and there's also the delicious sense of enforced idleness

were high enough to see that it was completely full of tanks, sixty or seventy of them.

On a long train journey, you also meet local people, as you never would when cocooned in your own car. And there's also the delicious sense of enforced idleness. Sitting in your cabin as the scenery rushes past, it's one of the few times in life where you can't really be doing anything else, so you can allow yourself time to digest what has happened on the trip so far or read a book or catch up on writing your diary.

At the border, the train stops and guards come through checking passports. It can be a nasty shock on an overnight, cross-border train, especially if the guards want you to get off the train while they search it. One minute you're in your pyjamas in a warm cabin, the next you're standing on a freezing platform being watched by a man with an AK47. Always check you have the right visas before getting on a cross-border train – if you haven't, the train will simply go on without you. Being left alone in a siding by the border in the middle of the night, with your luggage still on the train, is not a good situation to be in. Especially if you're only wearing pyjamas . . .

After hours of passing through arid, empty plains, you pull into Baku, on the banks of the Caspian sea. It's a crazy place, vibrant and booming. Oil revenues from the huge deposits beneath the Caspian sea, and from the pipeline that runs from here to Ceyhan, on Turkey's Mediterranean coast, are funding a spending spree, and the city is awash with fashionable new restaurants, bars and nightclubs.

Chefs, barmen and DJs are arriving here all the time from London, Moscow and St Tropez – while much of the world's economy is in the doldrums, Baku is really swinging. There are chic cocktail

The romance of boarding a night train is hard to beat.

bars like the Opera Lounge, live music venues like the Jazz Center, shops from every designer label you can imagine, and new hotels from the Four Seasons, Hilton and Marriott chains. Little wonder that 2010 saw the publication of a new guidebook to the city: *The Hedonist's Guide to Baku*.

If that all sounds a bit over the top, you can step away from the glitz into the eleventh-century mosque and the walled old city, where the fifteenth-century sandstone buildings have been restored, thanks to the new oil money. Later you can take a trip out of town to see mile after mile of nodding donkeys and the lakes of oil, or simply walk along the shoreline and watch the sun set over the Caspian.

Much as I love night trains, you often don't sleep that well on them. Stepping out of the station in Baku, blinking in the harsh sunlight and only half awake, we found ourselves confronted by Bentleys and Ferraris, skyscrapers of every colour imaginable and taxi drivers with gold teeth. It all felt fabulously surreal.

Now do it . . .

You can buy a ticket for the train either in Baku or Tbilisi train station. In summer buy your ticket a day in advance, as long waits in the queues should be expected. For more information visit Info Tbilisi (www.info-tbilisi.com/usefulinfos/railway/).

Horse riding in the Snowy Mountains

Why	For a chance to reflect on a different side of Australia
Where	Australia	**Duration**	Two days

With a flick of the reins and a click of the heels, Charley urged his horse on. I followed suit and soon we were galloping along the track side by side, splashing through mountain streams and rattling across wooden bridges. I was just thinking that we could be in Colorado or Arizona when the undergrowth parted and a kangaroo bounded out in front of us. My horse jolted to one side, throwing me forward so I had to grab it round the neck with both arms just to stay on. Perhaps I should stick to motorbikes . . .

I'm not a great horse-rider (I tend to prefer bikes on the grounds that they don't make your backside ache, and they go a lot faster) but if you do like horses, one of the best places to ride must be here, in the foothills of the Snowy Mountains of New South Wales. It's a surprise to come to Australia – which in most British minds is all about Bondi Beach, Sydney Opera House and Ayers Rock – and find yourself among snow-capped mountains. But the range here rises up to Mount Kosciuszko, Australia's highest peak at 2,228 metres, and gets snow from June to August.

Most noticeable are the beautiful pine forests. Look at a tree individually and it's green, but

merged together with a million others in forests that blanket the hillsides and they seem to take on a delicate blue tinge.

We set off from the small town of Khancoban and rode out with a guide called Peter and a stockman called Barry. Stockmen are the Australian equivalent of the cowboy, responsible for herding livestock across the huge expanse of Australian farms. As we rode across grassland dotted with gum trees, Barry told us about his life leading cattle through these mountains. We passed occasional log cabins, now used for overnight stops by hikers and cross-country skiers, but originally built by stockmen who would spend days at a time travelling through the hills.

We foreigners may think of Australia as largely about surf and sun, but for Australians this stockman's lifestyle, so similar in many ways to the Wild West, plays a powerful part in the national psyche. Andrew Barton Paterson, the Australian poet who wrote 'Waltzing Matilda', grew up in this area and dedicated much of his work to describing the lifestyle here. Paterson was better known as 'Banjo', a name he borrowed from his favourite horse, and one of his most famous poems is 'The Man from Snowy River', published in 1890. It's about a team of stockmen riding out to try to recapture a prize colt that has escaped from a farm and is living with a group of wild horses, or 'brumbies'. As we ride along it's not hard to imagine ourselves in the poem, riding 'through the stringybarks and saplings, on the rough and broken ground'.

Many people come here to ride precisely to experience the lifestyle Banjo celebrates. Though they may not have read his poems, they will probably have seen the Hollywood film of The Man from Snowy River starring Kirk Douglas, the 1990s TV series, or even the 2002 musical.

We stopped for a picnic lunch at Keeble's Hut, then rode on through the afternoon to Geehi, on the far side of the hills. Today there are fewer real stockmen riding these trails – farmers increasingly use small planes or helicopters to muster their herds – but the brumbies are still here, and you might also see possum, wombats, squirrel gliders and platypus in the streams.

At Geehi we got back into jeeps, but despite my feelings about horses I would love to have spent another few days riding here. I'd recommend plotting a route of three or four days, staying at the stockmen's huts or camping along the way. And for the real Aussie experience, when night falls you can build a campfire, cook your sausages, crack open some tinnies and serenade the kangaroos with a few verses of 'Waltzing Matilda'.

‘ For Australians this stockman's lifestyle, so similar in many ways to the Wild West, plays a powerful part in the national psyche ’

'Today there are fewer real stockmen riding these trails ... but the brumbies are still here'

Now do it . . .

Contact Peter Cochran at Cochran Horse Treks (www.cochranhorsetreks.com.au) for details on this trek and many others. For more information on the region contact Tourism Australia (www.australia.com/index.aspx) or The Snowy Mountains (www.snowymountains.com.au).

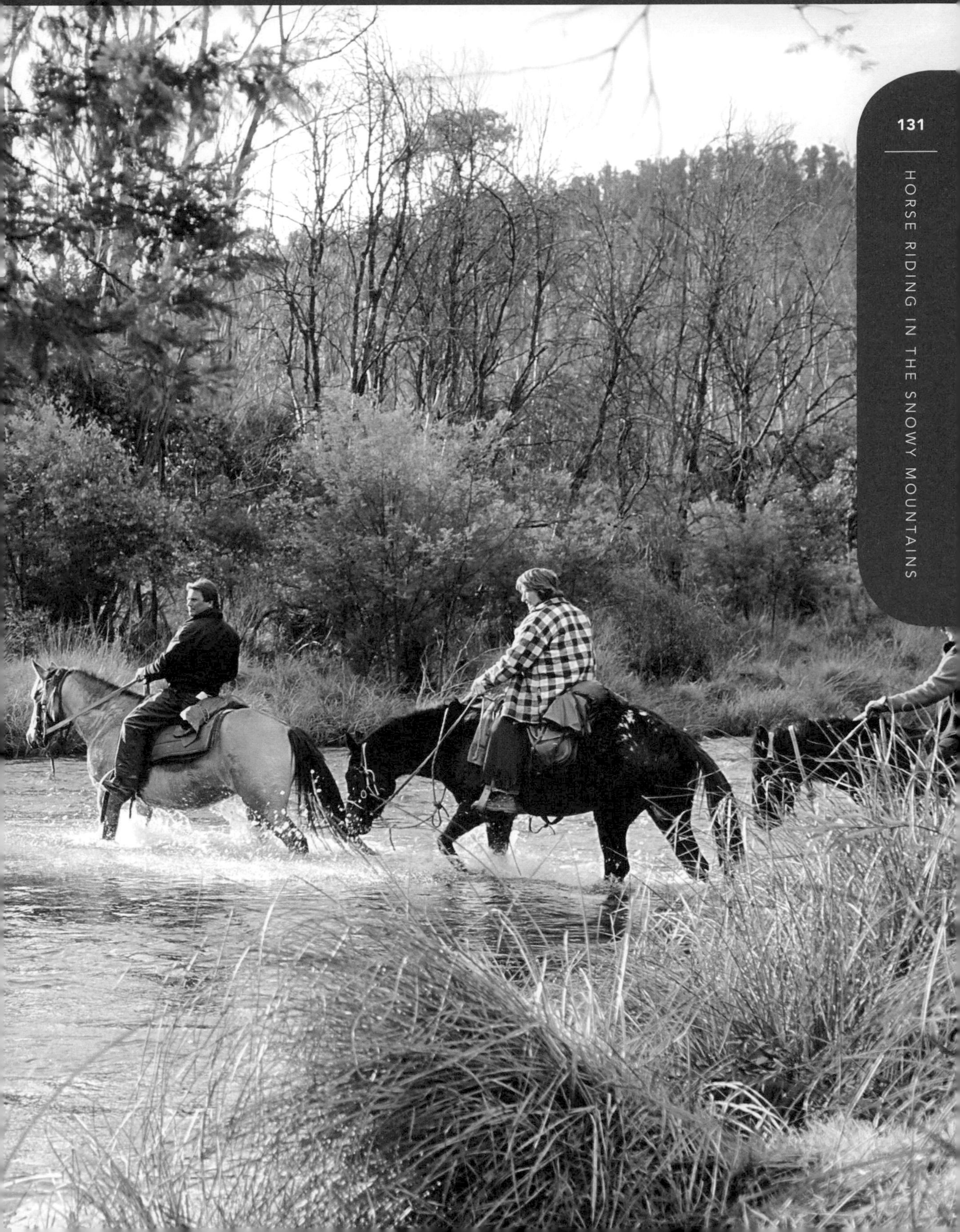

37

On Sherlock Holmes's trail on Dartmoor

Why	To hunt down the Hound of the Baskervilles
Where	England	**Duration**	Two days +

Some adventures, like the Paris–Dakar, are classic challenges, set-pieces against which you want to test yourself. But just as fulfilling, if not more so, are adventures you dream up yourself, tailored to your own interests or long-held ambitions.

The idea for this one was to have an adventure based on a book. I collect first editions of Sir Arthur Conan Doyle books, so I decided to set out on the trail of Sherlock Holmes, but you could take the same idea and apply it to any book, exploring Ian Rankin's Edinburgh, or Shakespeare's London, say.

Conan Doyle came to stay in Princetown, in Devon, in 1901, and decided to use it as the setting for *The Hound of the Baskervilles*. Even arriving there today, it's not hard to see why. Bang in the middle of the highest, bleakest part of Dartmoor, it feels cut off from the outside world. The town grew up with a grim purpose too, to service the prison that opened there in 1809.

Conan Doyle stayed at the Duchy Hotel, which now, conveniently enough, is a tourist information centre. We went to look at the prison itself, because the book's plot involves a convict escaping from it. Though today it houses mainly white-collar and non-violent criminals, it had a long-standing reputation for being an escape-proof jail where the hardest convicts would be sent. Even on a sunny day, there's something oppressive about its thick granite walls, stone arch and the heavy wooden doors through which the convicts pass.

Next we set out for the moor. Much of the plot of *The Hound of the Baskervilles* revolves around Grimpen Mire, a treacherous bog often covered in mist, in the centre of which the villain has an island hideaway, which eventually catches him out, sucking him down to a muddy death. Grimpen is based on the Fox Tor Mire, a bog covering close to a square mile just south of Princetown.

It's a strange place. In good weather it seems a perfectly pleasant area of moorland, with the paths through the bog easy to see and perhaps some wild Dartmoor ponies grazing on the long grass. But, as with much of Dartmoor, as soon as the fog rolls in, the atmosphere changes completely. With few landmarks and hardly any trees, navigation can be hard. You can imagine getting lost, wandering round in circles, and plunging into the bog. There are numerous local legends about people being sucked down into it, never

On the hunt for the Hound of the Baskervilles — a boyhood dream.

to be seen again. 'Rank reeds and lush, slimy water-plants sent an odour of decay and a heavy miasmatic vapour into our faces, while a false step plunged us more than thigh-deep into the dark, quivering mire, which shook for yards in soft undulations around our feet,' says Dr Watson. 'Its tenacious grip plucked at our heels as we walked, and when we sank into it, it was as if some malignant hand was tugging us down into those obscene depths, so grim and purposeful was the clutch in which it held us.'

We made it safely over the mire and continued across the moor, passing the remains of tin mines and Grimspound, the fallen stones of a series of Bronze Age dwellings, which were probably the inspiration for the stone hut in which Holmes takes shelter in the book.

The mist started to roll in so we pitched our tent beside a brook. I love the idea of wild camping. I think it's an adventure in itself wherever you are, a completely different experience to staying in an organized campsite with shower blocks and so on. Soon the wind got up and the tent was flapping around wildly. Even without the literary associations, we felt a bit vulnerable up there, a long way beyond the reach of mobile phones and protected from the elements only by canvas.

In the morning we cooked bacon and eggs and ate it surrounded by thick, eerie white mist. In some ways the Conan Doyle connection was just an excuse, a reason to bring us here, somewhere we'd never otherwise be, but it also gives a focus, a greater depth and sense of discovery to an adventure.

We washed up in the stream, then set off to try to navigate through the fog across the evil mire and back to Princetown. Was that the baying of a hound I could hear?

Now do it . . .

To plan your historic trip to Dartmoor visit www. dartmoor.co.uk, and for more information on Sherlock Holmes, visit The Sherlock Holmes Society of London (www.sherlock-holmes.org.uk).

"THE HOUND OF THE BASKERVILLES."
(See page 252.)

Dartmoor is wild, desolate, sometimes eerie – I'm definitely going back.

38

Boat trip down the Ganges

Why | For a spiritual journey and a cultural insight

Where | India | **Duration** | Two days +

TWO WEEKS OFF WORK

If I had to distil the whole of India into one experience, it would be this – rowing down the Ganges and arriving, as dusk falls, in Varanasi.

India is, to my mind, the most colourful and vibrant country in the world, and nowhere more so than Varanasi, the most sacred city in Hinduism. It feels as if there is a constant religious festival going on here, and more than a million pilgrims come each year to perform ceremonies at the temples and the ghats, the big stone steps that descend the banks of the Ganges.

Just walking down the street in an Indian city can be overwhelming – the traffic, the smells, the riot of activity. People rush up to talk to you, to see if you need any help or to ask if you want a cup of tea. Cows wander past. Rickshaws squeeze through the melee. The buildings may be crumbling, but in every corner of them someone is carrying on some kind of business, and every inch of space is covered with hand-painted signs advertising goods or services.

The spirituality, religion and history of Varanasi make it a 'must-do' stop on the Ganges.

It can be such an assault on the senses that it's hard to take it all in, but get out on the water and that problem disappears. Suddenly you have the space to think and quietly contemplate everything you are seeing as you float down the river.

And coming into Varanasi, there is certainly plenty to see. We'd set off in a small rowing boat from Ramnagar, three miles upstream, but to make this into a longer trip you could start from Mirzapur, nearly sixty miles upstream. Just speak to the boatmen at the ghats at either start point, and haggle for a good price. From Mirzapur, it will take two days to reach Varanasi, passing through countryside all the way, so you'll need to camp on the riverbank.

As we got closer we could see the ornate spires of the temples rising above the haze on the river. Children were leaping from the banks into the (heavily polluted) water, squealing with joy as they did so. Boats passed this way and that, ferrying people around. Soon we could hear the chanting from the religious ceremonies going on at the water's edge and smell the burning incense. Pilgrims clad in robes were bathing in the river, which is considered holy by Hindus and personified as the goddess Ganga. Others lit candles

'Suddenly you have the space to think and quietly contemplate everything you are seeing as you float down the river'

surrounded by flower garlands and sent these floating out on the water.

Closer still we could see the flames of funeral pyres. Hindus come from all over India to cremate their relatives here beside the holy Ganges. They hope that burning the bodies will break the cycle of reincarnation and allow the spirits to rise free. The corpses are not placed in coffins, but simply laid on fires of wood, with only the face wrapped in a cloth. When the bodies are fully burnt, the ashes are swept off the edge of the ghat, to float away in the Ganges.

It was a lot to take in. Strangely, it doesn't seem as gory as you might expect, and neither does it feel inappropriate to be carrying out what we would consider a private ceremony in full public view. As the flames licked up into the dark sky, you got a real sense of the cycle of life – the young children playing a few yards from where the funeral services were going on.

In a minute we would row into shore, back into the hustle and bustle of modern India, to seek out a hotel and a restaurant and transport for the next day. But for a moment we stayed there drifting, with the incense hanging on the water around our boat, and the candles floating past.

Now do it . . .

Visit Intrepid Travel (www.intrepidtravel.com/trips/HHSG) to experience this journey down the Ganges. For more information on India, contact the Indian Tourism Authority (www.incredibleindia.org/index.html).

39

Trawling in the Irish Sea

Why	To experience the tough working life at sea
Where	Irish Sea	**Duration**	Two days +

Sometimes the way to have an adventure is to step into someone else's shoes for a while. It could be staying with a tribe in Africa, or riding with cowboys in South America, but even closer to home you can leave behind your day-to-day life by trying out another job or lifestyle.

And so, at 4.30 a.m., I found myself shivering on the docks at Kilkeel in Northern Ireland. I'd arranged to hitch a lift across the Irish Sea to the Isle of Man on board a fishing boat called the *Q-Varl*. She was a scallop dredger, with a crew of six. I was lucky to be able to get a taster for just one day – usually these fishermen spend a week at a time at sea, filling three to four hundred large sacks of scallops before coming into port.

It took four hours to steam out to the fishing grounds, so I settled down in the narrow bunkroom and was lulled to sleep by the roll of the boat and the chugging engine. I was woken by alarms mounted on the bunks to alert the crew when there's work to be done. Two big booms swing out from either side of the boat and pull dredges, like great nets made of chainmail, along the seabed. Ninety minutes after the dredges are dropped, they are hauled up on winches, and emptied into two conveyor belts running down to the boat's lower deck.

This is where the hard work starts. As I stood and watched, the scallops came rolling down the conveyor belts, but so did everything else dredged from the seabed – starfish, lobsters, squid and lots of lumps of rock. Everything but scallops have to be picked out and thrown back by hand, as well as scallops that are smaller than the minimum legal size. In every job they do, the crew move quickly and smoothly, like an oiled machine. It was impressive to watch; these men have the kind of confidence only achieved through years of doing the job.

Once the dredges were dropped again, it was time for breakfast. On a two-burner stove in the tiny galley one of the crew had rustled up an absolute feast. He just cracked open a load of scallops, fresh from the seabed, fried them up and served them with black pudding, eggs and tomato. Order scallops in a smart London restaurant and you might be given three or four. Here there must have been about twenty on my plate. Squashed in around the tatty formica table, rolling from side to side in the swell as we ate, it was the best breakfast I've ever had.

> I was woken by alarms mounted on the bunks to alert the crew when there's work to be done

The engine room.

Why does every adventure start so early?

Watching the wild Irish Sea.

Now do it . . .

One of the great aspects of this adventure is the fact that you can't really plan it. Just head down to the docks, speak to the locals and haggle your way on board!

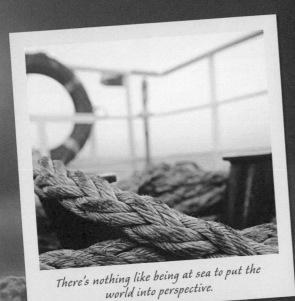

There's nothing like being at sea to put the world into perspective.

Snug in the wheelhouse.

The day wore on and it became clear that this is a very hard way to make a living. At the same time I was aware that environmentalists campaign vigorously against this kind of fishing, and you have to wonder at the damage caused by running the huge, clanking steel dredges along the seabed. But there was a great camaraderie on the boat, and you could imagine the crew all piling into port at the end of the week, painting the town red then coming back to their bunks to sleep it off.

As we approached the Isle of Man, I stood up on the deck, drinking a cup of tea. I was completely knackered, but at the same time it had been an invigorating glimpse of a totally different way of life. Staring out over the steely Irish sea, I felt utterly alive.

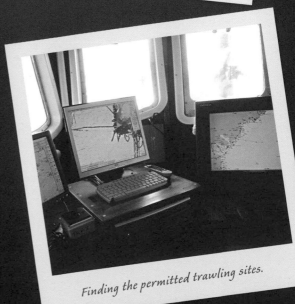

Finding the permitted trawling sites.

40

Ice climbing on Fox Glacier

Why	To understand glaciers by getting up close and personal
Where	New Zealand	**Duration**	One day

It was a place to fill you with foreboding: dark, cold, claustrophobic and resounding with groaning and cracking noises. I was 40 metres below the surface of New Zealand's Fox Glacier, dangling from a rope in a crack in the ice.

Glaciers are like huge frozen rivers, and where they pass over uneven ground, or drop sharply, the surface can crack, forming crevasses. The Fox Glacier, on the west coast of the South Island, is 13 kilometres long and drops 2,600 metres from top to bottom, starting in the high mountains and finishing among lush forest only 300 metres above sea level.

It's one of the easiest glaciers for people to get to, only a short walk from the village of Fox Glacier to its lowest end, and in summer as many as a thousand people a day come to look at it from official viewing points, separated from the ice by safety barriers.

We were getting a much closer look. With Fox's Glacier Guiding we'd flown by helicopter up on to the highest section. The flight was a thrill in itself. We got great views of Aoraki (Mount Cook), New Zealand's highest peak, then swooped low over the surface of the glacier, marvelling at the icefalls and crevasses. We landed, stepped out on to the ice and had to pinch ourselves to believe what we were seeing was real. In the space of a few minutes we'd gone from the pretty, bustling little village to an alien world of peculiar ice formations in a thousand shades of white and blue.

First we fixed crampons to our boots and learned to walk in them across the ice, adopting a slightly bandy-legged gait to make sure the metal spikes didn't catch and rip our trousers. Next we explored some caves that had formed in the ice. Bending down to walk inside them, we found ourselves surrounded by ice that was a rich blue. It was a magical, beautiful experience, but we had to remind ourselves that you can never relax too much on a glacier.

It may be only slowly, but glaciers are constantly flowing downhill. Their shape and the atmospheric conditions mean that the Fox and the nearby Franz Josef glaciers move about ten times faster than average glaciers elsewhere in the world; the ice here moves several metres per day. This may not sound that alarming, but it means crevasses can open up from one day to the next, and huge ice cliffs, or seracs, can collapse with no warning at all. In 2009, two Australian tourists were killed after crossing the safety barriers and walking up to take pictures of the bottom of the glacier. A hundred tons of ice fell and crushed them.

‘ It was a magical, beautiful experience, but we had to remind ourselves that you can never relax too much on a glacier ,

Our next challenge was to learn to climb up vertical sections of ice with a technique called front-pointing. Two spikes stick out from the front of the crampons, and in each hand you hold an ice axe. You swing the axe until it drives into the ice, giving you a solid hold, then kick your foot in so the spikes do the same. Gradually, moving only one limb at a time, you achieve what initially seemed impossible – climbing up a vertical, slippery wall of ice.

After practising on bits of open glacier, it was time for the main event. Each of us would take turns to be lowered into a crevasse, from where we'd have to front-point out.

It's exhausting work. Within minutes my calves and biceps were burning. Hanging on to the wall of ice with just a few inches of pointed steel, there's simply no way of having a rest. All you can do is switch your weight from your arms to your feet, giving one a momentary break but always at the expense of the other.

There was a strong incentive to get out of there fast. Down in the crevasse it was dark and lonely. At the bottom it narrowed so the opposite wall of ice was only a couple of feet behind me. Looking down, the crack continued into blackness. Worst of all was the noise, the groaning and cracking of the ever-shifting ice. I kicked my toe-spikes in and quickly carried on.

Emerging back into the warm sun, with the jaw-dropping view of the mountains all around, was an awesome moment. In front of me was the helicopter and soon we were inside again, heading back to the village for a well-deserved beer.

As we hovered over the valley, I nudged our guide and asked a question that had been on my mind all day: 'Is this where they got the idea for Fox's Glacier Mints?'

Disappointingly, it isn't. They come from somewhere altogether less dramatic – Leicester.

'Worst of all was the noise, the groaning and cracking of the ever-shifting ice'

Now do it . . .

Fox Glacier Guiding (www.foxguides.co.nz) can organize all your glacier adventures. We recommend staying at Te Weheka Inn (www.teweheka.co.nz), located right near to the Fox Glacier. Visit Tourism New Zealand (www.newzealand.com) for more information.

41

Riding or Driving the Nürburgring

| **Why** | For a scary, crazy bike and car adventure |
| **Where** | Germany | **Duration** | One day |

If it's true that Germans are a sensible and strait-laced people, then perhaps the Nürburgring is their pressure-release valve – a little bit of insanity in an over-sanitized modern world.

Since the late 1920s the Nürburgring had been the site of the German Grand Prix, but by the mid-1970s there was increasing pressure to move the race elsewhere because the track was too dangerous. There had been a string of accidents, and in 1976 Niki Lauda, the world champion, tried to get his fellow drivers to boycott the race on safety grounds. They refused, the race went ahead and, with horrible irony, Lauda himself crashed and was badly burned before other drivers pulled him from the wreckage. It was the last time the Grand Prix was ever staged there, and a new, safer and much shorter track was built near by.

So what did the authorities do with the track deemed too dangerous for the great Formula One drivers? Did they plough it up and turn it into fields? Turn it into a museum, perhaps? No, they decided to let the public race there instead.

Today absolutely anyone can race on the notorious Nürburgring. There's no speed limit and you don't need any special training, licence or insurance. You don't need a race-prepared car, a roll-bar or a helmet. You simply turn up, pay for a card (which works like an Oyster card) and wait in line. It's €22 per lap, with discounts if you buy several laps at once. When you reach the front of the queue, you swipe your card, the barrier goes up and you're off.

I spent the day at the ring and did five laps. My first experience was on a motorbike, my BMW, and the first lap was one of the most terrifying rides of my life. I then continued in a Jaguar XKR. The first time I went out, my heart was in my mouth. On the 14-mile-long track you see classic cars, super cars, hot hatches, ordinary family saloons, all kinds of motorbikes – when I was racing round there was even someone in a motorhome. There are teenagers, old people, nervous drivers and absolute maniacs. It's not a case of one type of driver being more dangerous than another, it's the combination of all of them that makes it so lethal.

You can be going along happily then check your rear-view mirror and see a Porsche flying up behind you doing 180mph. Then you look back through the windscreen and see a Ford Transit in

front of you doing 40mph. Add to that the fact that the track twists left and right, up and down, and you have no idea what's coming next. It really isn't for the faint-hearted.

Nearing the end of my first lap, I was cheered to see some spectators on one of the corners. It seemed touching that they were willing to come out to support mere amateur enthusiasts rather than the professional drivers. It was only later that another driver told me the spectators gathered on the corners where crashes were most likely. 'If you see someone watching you, watch out!' he said with a grin.

And crashes do happen. On the day I was there, there were five crashes serious enough for the track to be closed. By some strange quirk of German law, the track is classed as a public toll-road, so if you cause an accident through dangerous driving, you can be prosecuted as you

would be on any other road. And if you damage the track or the crash barriers, you'll be charged for it. The sad fact is that two or three people lose their lives here each year.

After a couple of laps you realize that the slower you go, the more dangerous it is, because cars are constantly coming up behind you to overtake. After the first lap, on which I was overtaken by a dozen cars, including a very prosaic Citroën Xsara, I wasn't sure I wanted to go out again. But by the fifth lap, I was sold. I was going fast enough to be rarely overtaken, and even doing some overtaking of my own. Without the panic of cars constantly passing, you can relish the swooping banked corners and the beauty of the pine forest that surrounds the track. It's incongruous that this piece of utter madness is in such a serene spot. It was probably one of the most dangerous experiences of my life, but I loved it.

Now do it . . .
For information on the Nürburgring and to book
your spot on the track, visit www.nurburgringuk.com.
For other motorcycle adventures visit World of BMW
(www.worldofbmw.com).

42

Guatemala's Mayan ruins

Why	To use local buses to explore extensive sites
Where	Guatemala	**Duration**	Three days +

'You see those hills covered in rainforest?' said my guide. 'Well, they aren't hills at all, those are the ancient ruins of a Mayan city – it's just no one has ever got round to excavating them.'

In Guatemala's Petén province, ruined cities are everywhere. Archaeological sites that elsewhere would be crawling with tourists and historians are simply left,

overgrown and unexplored. Even at Tikal, the most developed site of all and Guatemala's biggest tourist attraction, it's easy to find yourself alone beside an ancient temple, surrounded by nothing but jungle and with no sound except the calls of the birds and monkeys in the trees. For anyone with an interest in history or archaeology – or with Indiana Jones fantasies – coming to Petén is a must.

The Maya civilization was first established around 2000 BC, but only became the dominant power in the region during the so-called 'classic period' between AD 250 and 900. The first buildings at Tikal were erected during the fourth century BC, but in the classic period it grew into one of the most important cities of what is now Central America. At a site covering more than six square miles, archaeologists have discovered at least 3,000 separate buildings, including one temple 212 feet high, and pyramids, royal palaces and even seven courts for ball games. It's estimated that up to 90,000 people lived at Tikal, but in the late ninth century, some unknown catastrophe struck the city, and by 950 it was deserted, abandoned to the rainforest for the next thousand years.

Anyone coming to Guatemala has to see Tikal, even if only to watch the sunrise over the jungle from the top of Temple IV, the highest, and to spot the locations used by George Lucas in the first Star Wars film. But there are even greater treats in store.

From Tikal, we hopped on one of the brightly painted local buses, crammed with people taking their ducks, geese and sacks of corn to market, and with salsa music blaring on the stereo. After about 45 minutes, we reached Uaxactun, another complex of ruins only 12 miles north of Tikal, but which is overlooked by most visitors.

As we stood in Uaxactun's central plaza, surrounded by four ruined temples, we were

totally alone. We stood in silence and after a few moments saw a fox then a spider monkey dart between the ruins. Above us toucans glided between the huge mahogany trees.

Our guide explained that the pyramid-shaped temple before us also served as an astronomical observatory. When viewed from a particular spot below, the temple's three highest points line up with the sunrise on key dates of the calendar: one corresponds with the summer solstice, another with the winter solstice, and the third with the vernal and autumnal equinoxes.

Uaxactun was rediscovered in 1916 and excavated by American academics between 1926 and 1937, but today it still feels like you are exploring the ruins for yourself. And if that whets your appetite, your next adventure should be to visit El Mirador.

It is both older and larger than Tikal, but gets only a handful of visitors a year and remains completely undeveloped. The site, five miles south of the Mexican border, was found in 1926, but is so deep in the jungle and so hard to reach that it was then pretty much ignored until 1962, when it was mapped, and then 1978, when the first archaeological exploration began.

To get there today, unless you can afford to charter a helicopter, you start by taking a three-hour ride by jeep from Flores, capital of Petén, over rough roads north to the village of Carmelita. There you set out on foot for a five-day hiking and camping expedition – two days and 40 miles there, one day at El Mirador, and two days back.

It's definitely worth the effort. The site covers 10 square miles, there are several thousand structures and three colossal temples, including the 55-metre-high El Tigre, and La Danta which, at 70 metres, is the tallest of all the Mayan temples and one of the world's biggest pyramids.

Perhaps the most exciting thing, though, is that of the twenty-six known sites in the Mirador basin, only fourteen have so far been studied, and experts believe there are another thirty lost cities still to be found. So if you really fancy yourself as an Indiana Jones, your adventure awaits.

Now do it . . .

Guatemala Tourism Ministry (www.visitguatemala.com) can provide information about the country and the adventure. For detailed bus information, visit http://wikitravel.org/en/Flores_(Guatemala). Contact Journey Latin America (www.journeylatinamerica.co.uk) for tailor-made adventures or a private itinerary. For information on Central America visit www.visitcentroamerica.com

43

Building homes in the developing world

| **Why** | To change the world with a good deed or two |
| **Where** | Worldwide | **Duration** | Eight to fourteen days |

There can be few more satisfying experiences than coming back from a trip knowing you've done some good in the world. And there are few more tangible and visible ways of making a difference than building a home for someone who doesn't have one.

Various locations

This isn't something you could do by yourself, so you need to join up with a group of volunteers, led by an organization such as Habitat for Humanity. Its goal is to provide decent housing for the homeless or those living in slums, and in doing so to help them break out of the cycle of poverty. The charity runs house-building projects in developing countries around the world, and also in some of the poorest areas of the UK and US.

Currently there are projects going on in countries as diverse as Vietnam, Romania, Nepal and Honduras, and many African countries including Botswana, Malawi, South Africa and

Kenya. You sign up for between eight and fourteen days, and travel out with a group of volunteers. You don't need any special skills – you will be doing manual labour, perhaps digging foundations, laying concrete floors, building walls, plastering, mixing cement or decorating, all supervised by professional builders. Volunteers can be aged between eighteen and eighty.

To date the charity has built more than 350,000 homes, accommodating more than 1.75 million people. It was set up by the late Millard Fuller, an American who had become a millionaire by the time he was thirty but turned his back on commerce in order to devote himself to helping others. He moved to Zaire, now the Democratic Republic of Congo, for three years, returning to America in 1976 to set up Habitat for Humanity.

Of course, it has to be said that developing nations are not short of manual labour, and on the surface, there is something slightly odd about people who might be investment bankers or lawyers back at home flying in to haul bricks or dig foundations. But really the labouring is

draw in more long-term supporters. Habitat for Humanity has also had a fair bit of celebrity support – residents in one village in India found actor Brad Pitt, ex-Australian cricket captain Steve Waugh and former US president Jimmy Carter labouring away on a project.

And when you're on the ground, it's about more than just the building. Working side by side with local people, you'll learn about their culture and lives in a way you never could just by

just the start. To take part, volunteers must raise a minimum amount of money, typically between £1,800 and £2,400. Some of this covers flights, food and accommodation, but at least £400 will be a donation to the charity. Many volunteers raise more than this, and some donate as much as £1,235, the average cost of one of the charity's houses in the developing world.

But beyond the money, the sudden arrival of a group of Western volunteers in the middle of what are often remote, poor and neglected communities is a big boost. It can help generate publicity and encourage more donations, and

backpacking around. Plus there's time for some fun too – playing with the local kids, perhaps watching a traditional dance or celebration, or visiting a local school. You go home having given a lot to a community, but take away a great deal as well.

Now do it . . .
Visit the official Habitat for Humanity website (www. habitatforhumanity.org.uk) for more information on volunteering to help rebuild lives all over the world.

44

Climbing San Salvador

Why	To walk around the rim of this crater in its entirety
Where	El Salvador	**Duration**	One day

If you want to climb the volcano of San Salvador, first you need to find the right bus. The 1,893-metre-high volcano looms over the capital city of El Salvador, with which it shares its name. In fact, the volcano is so close that houses on the western fringes of the city actually rise up its slopes. Which must be a trifle unnerving because, although it hasn't erupted since 1917, this volcano is still considered active.

Being so near, it makes a great one-day adventure for anyone visiting the city. Take the bus to the village of El Boqueron on the flank of the volcano, from where it's only a half-hour's walk up to the rim.

Climbing up isn't the challenge here. Once you reach the top, you see the full extent of the vast crater – 1,500 metres across and 500 metres deep. The adventure is to follow the rim right the way around the crater, a hike that covers five miles, and which can take three hours because of the constant ups and downs.

There are fabulous views, both back to the city and across the plains to neighbouring volcanoes, and into the crater itself, at the bottom of which is a perfectly symmetrical, 50-metre-high cone, the result of the 1917 eruption. In some places the path narrows to a few feet and there are sheer drops down into the crater, while at others the gradient is gentle enough for local people to cultivate crops. Most of the volcano is blanketed in so-called 'cloud forest',

> Climbing up isn't the challenge here ... the adventure is to follow the rim right the way around the crater ”

Getting back to nature.

to go alone into the crater where it would be impossible to escape a mugger, but the situation seems to be improving.

It's amazing to be so close to a thriving capital city, yet walking amongst dense creeper-clad tropical vegetation on the rim of an active volcano. And best of all, you can have your adventure and be back in the centre of town for a few beers before sundown.

tropical forest that gets lots of moisture from the regular mist and cloud cover.

Incredibly, though the volcano is so close to the city, when we were there we didn't see another soul. El Salvador gets a fraction of the tourist visits that Costa Rica or Guatemala receive, thanks in part to a lingering image of danger. Throughout the 1980s it was riven by a bitter civil war that left 70,000 dead, but peace was achieved way back in 1992. A reputation for gang violence and robbery remains, but this seems to be played out between gang members rather than directed at tourists. Of course, you should check the security situation before you travel and take all the usual precautions, but don't be put off going by an out-of-date image.

We did have a guide and a guard when we walked the rim, and some travellers warn not

It's a full-day adventure to climb in and out of the crater and to walk around the rim.

Now do it . . .

Mayan Escapes (www.mayanescapes.com) can help you plan your own hiking adventure. For more information, contact El Salvador Tourism Board (www.elsalvador.travel), Journey Latin America (www.journeylatinamerica.co.uk) and www.visitcentroamerica.com

Swimming in a Guatemalan volcano

Why	To climb a volcano and swim across its crater
Where	Guatemala	**Duration**	One day

The small Central American country of Guatemala is dotted with at least thirty-five volcanoes, many of which make great objectives for treks. At 4,220 metres, Tajumulco is the highest, while the 3,557-metre-high Atitlan is considered by many to be the most beautiful, a perfect cone covered in forest, reflected in the huge lake at its foot.

Our destination was the far more obscure Ipala. This volcano is overlooked by most trekkers on account of its relatively modest height of 1,650 metres, but it does have a surprise in store.

The volcano is in the south-east of Guatemala and about 15 miles south of Chiquimula, the nearest town. We drove to Agua Blanca and started walking at about 10 a.m. Already it was hot and humid, but the path was wide and easy to follow, and occasionally we'd pass clouds of brightly coloured butterflies. Sometimes the dense foliage would clear to give us stunning views of the other volcanoes near by, their summits swathed in cloud.

After two and a half hours we reached the top, and before us was Ipala's secret – a huge lake entirely contained within the crater. We were here to swim across.

We scrambled down to the side of the lake, which is 150 metres lower than the rim. It was bigger than we'd expected – at least 400 metres across – and when I dipped my toe in the water, it was decidedly fresh. It was also clear that the rocks around the edge were too sharp to walk on in bare feet, so we'd have to swim across, then swim all the way back to pick up our clothes. We took some photos, and, when we could put it off no longer, jumped in.

We must have been about 100 metres across when thick black clouds rolled over the top of the crater. It was as if we were swimming across a giant saucepan and someone had put the lid on it. I started to feel a bit foolish, doing this crazy challenge without having done much research into the dangers. Then the lightning started, huge flashes of pink and purple, with thunder that echoed round the crater.

At this point I started to wonder whether you can get struck by lightning while swimming. The answer is yes, although if you're close to land, there will probably be objects higher than your head that are more likely to get struck first.

Thankfully the storm rolled over almost as suddenly as it had arrived, to be replaced by a mist so thick you couldn't see the other side of the lake. We ploughed on regardless, hit the other side and then started back.

By the time we reached dry land, the sun was out again and the storm might have been a bad dream. It had taken us fifty-two minutes to swim across and back – that's your time to beat.

Now do it . . .

Guatemala Tourism Ministry (www.visitguatemala.com) can provide information about the country and the adventure. Visit www.summitpost.org/volcan-ipala-guatemala/444835 if you want to climb Ipala. Contact Journey Latin America (www.journeylatinamerica. co.uk) for tailor-made adventures or a private itinerary. For information on Central America visit www.visitcentroamerica.com

Sailing on a Thames barge

| **Why** | For a taste of old-fashioned sailing, by wind alone |
| **Where** | England | **Duration** | Two days |

We had come less than 80 miles from London, but it felt as if we'd travelled a hundred years into the past. We were in the North Sea, just off Ipswich, aboard the *Hydrogen*, a huge wooden sailing boat whose oak timbers creaked and groaned as she ploughed through the waves. Salty spray crashed over the bows and we heaved on the ropes to trim the heavy flax sails.

Built in 1906, *Hydrogen* is the largest surviving Thames barge, a type of ship that at the turn of the century was a common sight up and down England's east coast. In their heyday, there were more than two thousand barges, typically 90 feet long and 20 feet wide, which could carry between 100 and 300 tons of freight. Without engines, they relied totally on their sails, which were a distinctive rusty red colour because of the coating used to waterproof them. Today, only a handful remain, kept afloat by a band of dedicated enthusiasts. You can occasionally see them sailing along the Thames estuary or around the coasts of Kent, Essex and East Anglia, and it's an evocative sight,

as if you're witnessing a ship sailing out of the pages of a history book. But even better to get on board.

A couple of barges are available to charter for the weekend (complete with a skipper) and it makes a unique adventure. *Hydrogen* is owned by a company called Top Sail, which is dedicated to preserving old Thames barges by keeping them working, either for weekend charters or as unusual venues for dinners and corporate events.

As we sailed past Felixstowe we could see the massive modern container ships lining up to dock. It was incredible to think how much the workhorses of the sea had changed in the space

of a hundred years. *Hydrogen* could carry 200 tons, powered by the wind; the modern boats we were sailing past could easily carry 100,000 tons, and had engines with up to 100,000 horsepower. Their size was impressive enough, but you can't really imagine people getting nostalgic about them in another hundred years' time, or devoting themselves to restoring and preserving them for future generations.

It was May, but when we moored up that afternoon beside four or five other Thames barges in Maldon, it was freezing cold. We went below deck and spent the evening huddled around the wood-burning stove, drinking wine and telling stories.

Even if you don't fancy sailing, you can come to get a taste of the Thames barges. When it's not chartered for sailing weekends, Top Sail rent out another of their barges, the *Reminder*, as a 'floating cottage' sleeping up to fourteen. You're not allowed to move it; instead you use it as you would a self-catering holiday cottage, albeit a highly unusual one.

In the morning I was up early and went on deck to watch the sunrise over the estuary. Mist hung over the water and about the rigging of the old barges, and the only sound was the occasional cry of a seagull. It was a scene that can't have changed much since *Hydrogen* first came here a century ago. They say the past is a foreign country – it certainly makes a great destination for a weekend away.

Now do it . . .

To arrange your own barging adventure, visit Topsail charters (www.topsailcharters.co.uk).

Why	For a beautiful walk laced with Roman history
Where	England	**Duration**	Two days +

LONG WEEKEND

'It's just a wall!' said my daughter Emily, fourteen. 'Why would anyone want to come and spend all weekend walking along next to a wall?'

It was raining and getting dark, we'd already walked 15 miles over the rough upland beside Hadrian's Wall and tempers were getting a little frayed. Up ahead the wall stretched away over hills and escarpments as far

as the eye could see. It was clear we'd bitten off more than we could chew for our first day, and yet, even though we were tired, cold and wet, it was incredibly atmospheric. It didn't require too much imagination to picture Roman centurions stationed all the way along the wall, huddled round fires to keep out the bitter chill.

A shiver went down my spine, breaking my reverie. Deciding it was too wet to camp, we struck out away from the wall, across a bog and to the nearest road. No one would stop so we walked two miles to a pub for the night.

Everyone knows the story of Hadrian's Wall, the great stone fortification built from coast to coast across England to mark the furthest border of the Roman Empire, and prevent attacks from what is now Scotland. But walking along it really brings the story to life. An 84-mile, signposted trail runs all the way from Bowness-on-Solway, on England's west coast, through to the ruins of the Roman fort of Segedenum in a suburb of Newcastle called Wallsend (because it's where the wall ends).

Originally built between AD 122 and 128, the wall was up to 3 metres wide and 6 metres high, with forts roughly every Roman mile along the route. Today some walkers take a week and complete the whole route, but many concentrate on the central third, between the town of Corbridge, Northumberland and the village of Gilsand in Cumbria. This is the best-preserved part of the wall, and also where it follows the Whin Sill escarpment, so you get stunning views of the rolling moorland scenery. Walking between Corbridge and Gilsand would take three days at a fairly leisurely pace, but you can tackle any section you like, even doing just a day trip.

I love this walk: with the history, terrain and views, it really has it all.

A special Hadrian's Wall bus runs along the roads closest to the wall, making it easy to reach the start and end points of any walk you pick. If you've driven, it means you can park, take the bus to the start, then walk back to your car, avoiding having to retrace your steps. (Always do it that way round – you don't want to be left waiting for ages at a bus stop when you're tired at the end of your hike.)

Our second morning dawned bright and sunny. Back on the wall, Emily was enjoying herself, and it was great for us two to be sharing an adventure. It's great to spend time with a member of your family. It gives you time to talk – something which is difficult in busy modern life. From the top of the hills we could see for miles across a patchwork of farmland and fields – you get a real sense of your home country. I particularly like the fact that the wall isn't covered with signs, guardrails and safety notices. There are lots of steep steps and dangerous drop-offs, but plastering it with warning notes would destroy the atmosphere.

In one sense, of course, it *is* just a wall, but it's also much more – a link with the past, with our national identity, and the focus for an adventure.

From the top of the hills we could see for miles across a patchwork of farmland and fields – you get a real sense of your home country

Now do it . . .

For all the information you need on the walk and the history of the wall, visit Hadrian's Wall Country (www.hadrians-wall.org).

48

Delhi to Agra by Enfield Bullet

Why	For a thrilling motorcycle ride with a mission
Where	India	**Duration**	One day

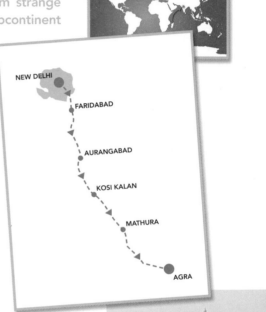

If you go riding across America, it has to be on a Harley. In India, it has to be a Royal Enfield. This might seem strange at first, because Enfields originate not in the subcontinent but somewhere rather less exotic: Redditch in Worcestershire. In the late nineteenth century, the Eadie Manufacturing Company of Redditch got a big order to supply gun parts to the Royal Small Arms Factory based in Enfield, Middlesex. At the same time, Eadie was experimenting with a new product – the bicycle – and to celebrate the parts order it decided to name its new bike 'the Enfield'. A new division, the Enfield Cycle Company, was set up, and soon it also borrowed the 'Royal' from its namesake. Keen to play on the connection for marketing benefit, it even introduced the slogan, 'Made like a gun, goes like a bullet'. Before long, bicycles were abandoned in favour of motorbikes, and in 1932 the firm produced its iconic model, the Bullet.

In 1949, Enfields were introduced to India. Initially Enfield would send Bullets in kit form to be assembled by Madras Motors, but soon the Indian engineers were making frames and parts themselves. Eventually Enfield sent over its jigs and tools so that Madras Motors could make the entire bike from scratch, and the design of the Bullet produced in India remained unchanged for thirty years.

While sales in Asia stormed ahead, buoyed by big contracts from the army and police, back at home Enfield ran into trouble. Production ceased in 1970, and the company was dissolved a year later. By the mid-1980s, Enfield India (as the firm was now known) was shipping coals to Newcastle – exporting entirely Indian-made Bullets back for sale in Britain. In 1995, Enfield India bought the rights to the name Royal Enfield, and the circle was complete.

All of which is worth mentioning only to explain why the Bullet is such an iconic motorbike, and how it is entwined with both British and Indian history. The look of the Bullets being made today have changed little (though recent models have far more modern engines), so if you're going for a biking trip across India, this really is the bike for you. Not only is there that sense of

A mad dash to Agra.

history, but wherever you break down, someone will be able to fix it.

Numerous companies will rent Bullets, and there's also a thriving market among travellers who want to ride for several months, then sell their bike on when they leave. Alternatively, you could join the Enduro India, an organized two-week charity ride that sees seventy or more Bullets tour the country together.

Of course, there are endless possible itineraries – through the deserts of Rajasthan, up into the Himalayas, or down through the rice paddies and beaches of tropical Goa and Kerala.

Charley Boorman and I decided to ride the iconic bike between two of India's most iconic cities – the capital Delhi, and Agra, home to the Taj Mahal. While I adore India and would encourage everyone to go there, I'd have to say that this isn't the place for novices on their first motorbike tour. The traffic is simply crazy.

We set off from Delhi at lunchtime, hoping to reach Agra, 125 miles away, by sunset. Immediately we were into some of the most chaotic riding of my life – weaving through cars, auto-rickshaws and horse-carts, past families of five teetering on a single motorbike, looking up to see lorries coming towards us, horns blaring, on the wrong side of the road, swerving to avoid the cows which wander, oblivious, across the tarmac, and all the while having to dodge the gaping potholes. For an experienced rider, it's testing but thrilling stuff; for anyone not completely confident, it would be hellish.

At the end of the journey, a treat lay in store. In Agra, a small boy directed me through a maze of narrow streets until I emerged on the banks of the Yamuna River. The final sliver of the sun was just dropping behind the horizon, turning the sky a flaming red, and there, on the far side of the river, was the beautiful white marble of the Taj Mahal. I turned off my classic Indian motorbike and sat astride it, taking in the most classic of all Indian views.

Now do it . . .
For all things Enfield, visit www.royalenfield.com

49

Hiking at Arthur's Pass

Why	For wilderness walking among stunning scenery
Where	New Zealand	**Duration**	Two days +

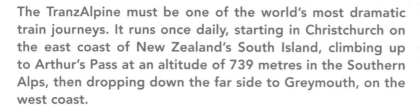

The TranzAlpine must be one of the world's most dramatic train journeys. It runs once daily, starting in Christchurch on the east coast of New Zealand's South Island, climbing up to Arthur's Pass at an altitude of 739 metres in the Southern Alps, then dropping down the far side to Greymouth, on the west coast.

The train leaves Christchurch at 8.15 a.m. and takes just over four hours to cover the 140 miles to Greymouth. It's a worthwhile trip on its own, but we'd planned to add an extra twist. We'd get off the train at Arthur's Pass, trek out into the mountains, camp out in a remote wooden cabin then come back in time to pick up the train the following morning and continue to Greymouth.

As soon as the train leaves the smart suburbs of Christchurch, you are struck by how few people there are on the South Island. In fact, only a million people live here, on an island that covers 58,000 square miles. England, by comparison, covers 51,000 square miles, but has a population of over 51 million.

The train pulled up to Arthur's Pass at 10.45 a.m. and we hopped out with our rucksacks. As soon as you get out, you are surrounded by mountains – we stopped and turned around in circles taking them all in.

We met up with our guide Karl and he led us off up the valley beside the Bealey River, across footbridges and through the beech forest. It was raining – something it does a lot here, so make sure you bring your waterproofs.

After only half an hour we reached a stunning waterfall, the 131-metre-high Devil's Punchbowl. You could hike up here, see the waterfall and have a picnic and return to Arthur's Pass to catch the 4 p.m. train as it makes its way back from Greymouth to Christchurch.

We'd decided to carry on, though, and hiked for several hours until we reached our destination, Fisherman's Cabin, a mint-green clapperboard hut beside a lake. We stripped off our waterproofs and piled inside to dry off socks by the fire.

It was basic but cosy, and most importantly dry. Watch out for the kea, though. These large, olive-green mountain parrots are known for their mischievous streak, and while we sat outside the cabin eating breakfast the next morning, they flew down and tried to steal snacks from out of our rucksacks. They're intelligent birds and can work out how to push and pull at things to get to the food inside. You could sit and watch them for hours, but we had to go – we had a train to catch.

GREYMOUTH · KOKIRI · MOANA · BRUNNER · JACKSONS · OTIRA · ARTHURS PASS Trek here · CASS · SPRINGFIELD · DARFIELD · CHRISTCHURCH

ARTHURS PASS NATIONAL PARK

ARTHURS PASS

HEIGHT ABOVE SEA LEVEL 737m

Now do it . . .

For more details visit TranzAlpine (www.tranzscenic. co.nz) and Arthur's Pass (www.arthurspass.com). Prior to your departure in Christchurch, we recommend you stay at the Crowne Plaza Hotel (www.crowneplaza.co.nz).

50

Staying with an African tribe

| **Why** | To experience a nomadic way of life first-hand |
| **Where** | Kenya | **Duration** | Two days + |

Africa has a huge amount to offer the visitor, from amazing desert, mountain and grassland scenery, to vibrant cities and incredible wildlife. But many visitors miss out on one of the most rewarding experiences of all – spending some time getting to know one of Africa's indigenous tribes.

Most safari companies will take their guests to visit a nearby village to buy jewellery and handicrafts. But while this can be interesting and worthwhile, often the visits are short and the tourists are whisked back to their luxury camp before they've had a chance to interact with the tribe. To get the most from the experience you need to stay a bit longer, ideally overnight in the village or near by.

The good news is that there is a growing number of community-tourism initiatives that allow visitors to do this. Crucially, they are organized by, or in partnership with, the local tribe, rather than exploiting them, which means visitors know they are helping their hosts and will be guaranteed a warm welcome.

In Ethiopia, for example, an organization called TESFA (Tourism in Ethiopia for Sustainable Future Alternatives) runs trekking holidays with a difference. Your guides are local villagers and they lead you between remote villages where you stay the night. In each village, the local community has constructed special cottages in the traditional style for the visiting tourists. The visitors' money goes to the communities they pass through, and there's ample time to sit and talk with the villagers about their way of life.

Meeting the leader of the tribe.

Elsewhere in Africa, the specialist travel company Expert Africa has a range of options, including staying with the Bushman people of Namibia at Nhoma Camp in the northern Kalahari. Visitors stay in tents (which have en-suite bathrooms and private verandas) on a hillside near the village and usually spend their mornings going out with the hunters, in search of everything from porcupine to wildebeest, which the Bushmen shoot with poisoned arrows. Along the way they point out the plants they gather for

food or use in medicines. As well as bringing money to the area, tourism has helped encourage the Bushmen to take pride in their traditional skills and knowledge, rather than viewing them as anachronistic. Afternoons are spent back in the village, processing the meat, berries or nuts collected by the hunters. Spend three or four days here and you will find yourself really getting to understand the community.

Alternatively, for something even more adventurous, an organization called Wandering Nomads arranges treks of six to eleven days through north-west Kenya's Turkana and Samburu districts, on which you are led by local guides and spend time in some remote villages along the way.

I got my own chance to stay with the Samburu tribe while we were filming Long Way Down. We had stopped close to the Losai National Reserve in central Kenya, where a group of nomadic Samburu had set up their camp on the grassland. We asked if we could camp alongside them and, after mulling it over, they agreed.

It was a fascinating scene. About three hundred people were living in wooden-framed tents covered in animal skins. All of them wore bright red robes and many had traditional beaded necklaces and giant earrings, which made large holes in their earlobes. Smiling kids were running around everywhere, helping to corral the cattle, donkeys and goats into an enclosure of thorn bushes where they would be safe from wild animals during the night. The tribe very rarely kill their animals, instead relying on them for milk and blood, taken while the animals are alive and drunk or used as an ingredient in other dishes.

When the villagers found out we had a doctor in our party, they became very interested. The doctor was taken from tent to tent and asked to examine a succession of ailments. It made us realize what little access these people had to healthcare and how serious a minor illness could become.

In the morning as we were packing up our camp, I became aware of an elderly man, walking slowly and gracefully among our tents and vehicles. He just stood for a while, taking it all in, unnoticed by the rest of our team. I walked across to introduce myself, and since some people were still eating breakfast, went over and got him a

> As well as bringing money to the area, tourism has helped encourage the Bushmen to take pride in their traditional skills and knowledge

sausage roll and a cup of tea. As he ate the roll and drank the tea, our translator came over to join us, and explained that this was the village chief. He seemed to enjoy his breakfast, so I fixed him up with the same again, and gave him a couple of our *Long Way Down* T-shirts and pens.

A few minutes later, I was back on the top of my car, ratcheting the cables over the roof rack, when the translator gave me a shout and asked me to come down. The chief was wearing one of the T-shirts and came over to give me a big hug, saying something in the Samburu language. 'He says thank you for your hospitality, and that you are welcome to return to stay with his tribe any time you wish,' said the translator. 'But there's more – he says, and by the way this is the biggest honour he could bestow, that if you come back, he'll kill a cow for you.'

I was really touched. The tribe had turned out to be warmer and more welcoming than we could possibly have imagined. If you are travelling through Africa and get a chance to spend some time with a tribe, leap at it.

Back in London, I still sometimes stop and think of the chief and his people, out there on the plains of Kenya. And it's nice to know I'm welcome back there.

Now do it . . .
Wandering Nomads (www.wanderingnomads.com) specialize in unique African tribal experiences.

51

The Road of Death

Why	For an exhilarating take on a former Bolivian trading route
Where	Bolivia	**Duration**	One day

The North Yungas road runs about forty-five miles from La Paz in Bolivia to Coroico, a town to the north-east. Built by Paraguayan prisoners of war during the Chaco war in the 1930s, it grew into a key route for lorries as one of the few ways to get between La Paz and the Amazonian region of north-east Bolivia. The more it was used, the more accidents occurred and the more its notoriety grew. In 1995 a study by the Inter-American Development Bank identified it as 'the world's most dangerous road', and in 2006 a BBC report estimated the annual death toll at between two hundred and three hundred. No wonder the locals call it El Camino de la Muerte – the Road of Death.

Why is it so dangerous? The road starts in La Paz, at an altitude of 3,660 metres, then climbs over the Andes, reaching a high pass at La Cumbre, 4,650 metres, before diving down towards the Amazon basin and Coroico, at just 1,200 metres. The road clings to hillsides or is carved into cliffs, with vast drop-offs down to the Coroico River in the gorge far below. Much of the road is only one lane wide, and most is gravel rather than tarmac. It can be dusty in summer, creating problems with visibility, and slippery in winter. Numerous lorries and cars have fallen off the edge, and in 1983 a bus careered over, tumbling into the canyon and killing a hundred people.

The situation is made worse by many of the drivers being in a fog of exhaustion. With few passing places, there can be horrendous hold-ups, but with nowhere to pull off the road to rest, the lorry drivers have to keep going.

In recent years, however, the very thing that makes the road so dangerous – the breathtaking mountain scenery – has been attracting growing numbers of travellers, while its notoriety draws thrill-seekers from around the world. Thankfully, the road is much safer than it was. At the end of 2006, a new route bypassing the most dangerous sections was opened. Now almost all the lorries go that way, removing at a stroke the main cause of accidents.

The Road of Death is certainly worth the trip. You can drive it, or better still mountain-bike it. Companies in La Paz will drive bikers up to La Cumbre, where you can saddle up for a five- or six-hour ride to Coroico – downhill all the way. It's a stunning trip. You start in the arid, cold, high-altitude desert, gasping for breath in the thin air, then finish in humid, tropical jungle, toasting your efforts with a cold beer.

> You start in the arid, cold, high-altitude desert ... then finish in humid, tropical jungle

Now do it . . .

Visit Crillon Tours (www.titicaca.com) to book your adventure and accommodation. Round the World Experts (www.roundtheworldexperts.co.uk) can arrange your flights from London to Bolivia.

52

Wildlife-spotting in the Okavango Delta

Why	For a close-up of a remote habitat and its animals
Where	Botswana	**Duration**	Two days +

The lone bull elephant was about 10 metres from Ewan when it started to charge. Ewan had been filming him from behind some bushes, edging closer and closer for a better shot. He looked up from the viewfinder and realized that perhaps he was pushing his luck, and at exactly that same moment the elephant stopped grazing and decided he'd had enough.

Ewan scuttled behind a tree, and the elephant, a big, fully grown bull, gave out an almighty trumpet and started to pound the earth with his feet. That was enough for Ewan. Unsure what else he should do, natural instinct took over and he legged it as fast as he could back to the safety of the lodge.

We'd come to Botswana's Okavango Delta to see the wildlife, but we had no idea we'd get this close, or that it would be quite so wild. Okavango is one of the best places in the world to see animals. Lion, elephant, buffalo, hippo, crocodile, giraffe, leopard – all the African animals you've seen in school textbooks and on wildlife documentaries are here in the flesh, drawn by the delta's water and abundant food.

Okavango is the world's largest inland delta. The Okavango River flows down from the Angolan highlands but never makes it to the sea, instead breaking up into thousands of smaller and smaller channels that spread out over 6,000 square miles of north-western Botswana. It's highly seasonal. In

'It was a good reminder that this is real, untamed Africa, where the animals are in charge'

> **'Okavango is one of the best places in the world to see animals'**

The Okavango Delta is alive with wildlife.

January and February the heavy rains fall in the highlands, and then the water takes four months to spread out through the delta. Between June and August the entire delta is flooded, and animals come from miles around to drink and feed.

All this water makes driving in the area very difficult, so we flew in on a light aircraft that picked us up at the Ngwasha Fence near Odiakwe and took us to our base for the next few days, the Mapula Lodge. This is a great place to visit and a perfect spot for a few days' rest and recuperation if you're on a difficult overland trip. You can lie in bed in your cabin at the end of the day, watching the sky turn a vivid red and listening to the hippos moaning and the birds calling.

And while Africa is full of safari parks, this is something totally different. The animals are wild and there are no fences. On our second day there, a few of us borrowed a Land Rover and drove off to go animal spotting. After a couple of hours we caught sight of a pack of hyena and stopped to watch them devouring their kill. And then the Land Rover wouldn't start.

For a nervous hour, we became the ones being watched, first by the hyena, and then by a whole load of baboons, presumably alerted to our plight via the animal grapevine. We were twenty miles from the lodge, and with lions, leopards, crocodiles and numerous other dangerous animals around, that seemed like a very long walk.

Eventually we managed to bump-start the Land Rover – an adventure in itself – but it was a good reminder that this is real, untamed Africa, where the animals are in charge. I wouldn't have it any other way.

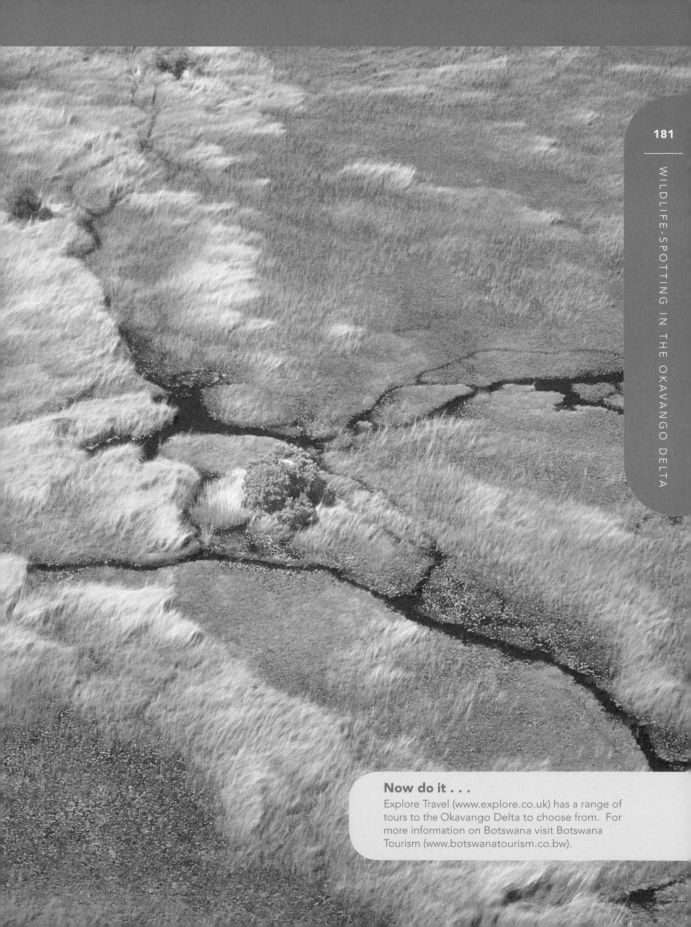

Now do it . . .

Explore Travel (www.explore.co.uk) has a range of
tours to the Okavango Delta to choose from. For
more information on Botswana visit Botswana
Tourism (www.botswanatourism.co.bw).

PANAMA CANAL RAILWAY

53

Panama Canal

Why	To understand colossal engineering, ships and trade
Where	Panama	**Duration**	Two days

TWO WEEKS OFF WORK

I don't think I've ever felt smaller. We were bobbing around in a small open boat, perhaps a couple of metres long, in the harbour of Panama City. In front of us were some of the world's biggest ships, their sides rising vertically from the water, forcing us to crane our necks just to see their decks. The sheer scale was awe-inspiring. Even the tugs, manoeuvring the giant freighters around as they waited for their turn to enter the Panama Canal, were bigger than any I'd seen before.

I'd always wanted to see the great ships sail down the Panama Canal. Lots of people travel to see the engineering achievements of ancient times – from Machu Picchu to the Pyramids and Stonehenge – but few dream of visiting those that are still in use. To me, though, it was a chance to see one of the most important man-made constructions of all, and witness the spectacle of these monsters of the sea squeezing their way down a narrow channel in the middle of a tropical rainforest.

We started in Panama City, simply by wandering down to the docks, finding a boatman and offering him $40 to take us out for a couple of hours touring around the big ships. Later we went a little way out of town to look at the colossal locks that lift the ships from the sea into the canal.

The canal runs for 48 miles from Panama City on the Pacific, southern coast, to Colón on the Atlantic, and offers a shortcut that saves the ships a journey of as much as 8,000 miles around South America. It comes at a price, though – the tolls can cost more than $200,000 for the biggest ships.

The idea of such an impressive shortcut had been obvious for centuries. In 1534 Charles V, the Holy Roman Emperor, ordered a survey to examine its feasibility, but it wasn't until 1880 that the French embarked on the first attempt at building a canal. Their efforts were badly planned and abandoned as a failure within a decade, but not before 22,000 workers had died, mostly of malaria. In the end it was the Americans who built the canal, from 1904 to 1914.

In fact, Panama's existence as a country is closely entwined with the canal. Between 1821 and 1903, Panama

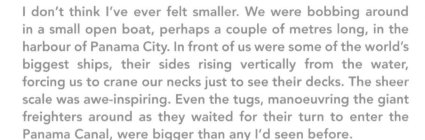

The Panama Canal – an adventure in so many ways.

Now I know why it's called rainforest!

was part of Colombia, but the US backed its struggle for independence in return for rights to the strip of land where the canal would be built, and the right to run it 'in perpetuity'. This was renegotiated in the late 1970s, but it wasn't until 2000 that control of the canal fully passed back to Panama.

Having seen the ships up close, we wanted to see more of the canal. A train line runs alongside it, mainly to transport freight between ships that stop at either end rather than travel the canal themselves. However, once a day, at 7.15 a.m., a passenger train makes the journey, returning from Colón at 5.15 p.m. And while the ships take between eight and ten hours to complete the route, the train only takes an hour.

Each carriage has an open section at the end, so you can stand outside with the wind in your hair. As you travel on the train, you realize that the canal, for much of its length, is not so much a canal as a series of lakes. The train runs over bridges and causeways and you see great expanses of water on both sides.

We spent a few hours in Colón then travelled back to Panama City in a local bus, hand-painted in crazy colours, with flashing lights and air horns on the front, and crammed with people and hens. We trundled along through the jungle, music on the radio, fat tropical raindrops beating on the roof. And every so often, through a gap in the glistening wet trees, we'd catch a glimpse of a great wall of painted steel – a ship literally sailing through the jungle.

Now do it . . .

Contact Miraflores Visitor Center (www.pancanal.com/eng/anuncios/cvm/index/html) for details on how to traverse the Panama Canal. For more information visit Panama Tourism Board (www.visitpanama.com), Journey Latin America (www.journeylatinamerica.co.uk) and www.visitcentroamerica.com

54

Animal-spotting in the Pantanal

Why	For an eye-opening experience of wildlife in their habitat
Where	Brazil	**Duration**	Two days +

Say Brazil, and people immediately think of Rio or the Amazon, of samba dancers or dense rainforest. Few have even heard of the Pantanal, let alone visited it, and yet it's a region as big as England and Wales combined.

The Pantanal is the world's largest freshwater wetland. Each winter, between November and March, the rains swell the rivers that crisscross the region and up to 80 per cent of the land is covered in water. When it eventually recedes, the land is left super-fertile and the ponds full of fish that failed to make it back to the rivers as the water level dropped. As a result, the region can support an astonishing diversity of plants and animals.

The Amazon may be similarly rich in biodiversity, but there, in the deep, dark rainforest, it's actually quite hard to see animals – though you can hear life in the forest all around you, the animals are just too good at hiding in the trees. By contrast the Pantanal is far more open, a mix of savannah, woodland and fields. All of which makes this one of the world's best places to watch wildlife.

We flew from Rio to Campo Grande, capital of Mato Grosso do Sol, the western Brazilian state that borders Paraguay and Bolivia and contains most of the Pantanal. There, we picked up a 4x4 and spent the next three days driving through the area, stopping for the night at eco-lodges along the way.

The incredible thing is that the wildlife is just there, all around you – you hardly even need to seek it out. We saw armadillos, a giant anteater and the world's biggest rodent, the capybara, which looked more like a pig as it snuffled through the undergrowth. Lying by the side of the roads were caiman, members of the alligator family, some alive, others dead, their tails, seen as a local delicacy, cut off by poachers. Up in the trees we spotted a group of brilliantly plumed red macaws, then two toucans with black feathers and giant orange and green beaks, and later a huge vulture, just sitting on the fencepost by the side of the road. The animals just kept coming, one after another.

Top of most visitors' wildlife wish-list for the Pantanal is the jaguar, the world's third biggest cat after the lion and tiger.

We didn't manage to spot a jaguar, nor the other famous Pantanal inhabitant, the anaconda. These snakes, which crush their prey, can grow up to 5 metres long and weigh close to 100 kilos. The locals take great pleasure in telling stories about anacondas carrying off small cows and unsuspecting fishermen. Just tall tales, I think, though that's one animal-spotting opportunity I'm not too bothered we missed out on.

Now do it . . .

Pantanal tours can be organized through Pure Brasil (www.purebrasil.net), and a great place to stay during your trip is the Fazenda San Francisco (www.fazendasanfrancisco.tur.br).

Why	For a motoring challenge with an historic twist
Where	Western Europe	**Duration**	Two days

Dudley Noble had a cunning plan. A former motorbike racer, he worked for Rover and was building a name for himself as one of the motor industry's first, and most influential, PR men. He had been responsible for one of the earliest promotional films, which ended with a sequence of him falling off his Rover motorbike, then in January 1930 he came up with his best wheeze yet.

At that time a famous luxury train ran from Calais overnight all the way across France to the Riviera resorts of St Raphaël, Cannes, Nice and Monaco. The Calais–Méditerranée Express, nicknamed 'the Blue Train' after the colour of its carriages, was entirely first class, and in the dining car five-course dinners were served to the likes of Winston Churchill, Evelyn Waugh and Coco Chanel.

Noble decided he would set off from Calais to race the train to its destination, and thereby just happen to demonstrate the speed and reliability of the Rover Light Six. It was a brilliant stunt – while the train had the image of great glamour and speed, Noble knew that, taking into account all the various stops, it only averaged about 40mph. He beat the train by twenty minutes and was splashed all over the *Daily Express*.

Many more races against the train followed. In March that same year, Woolf Barnato, the chairman of Bentley and a former winner of Le

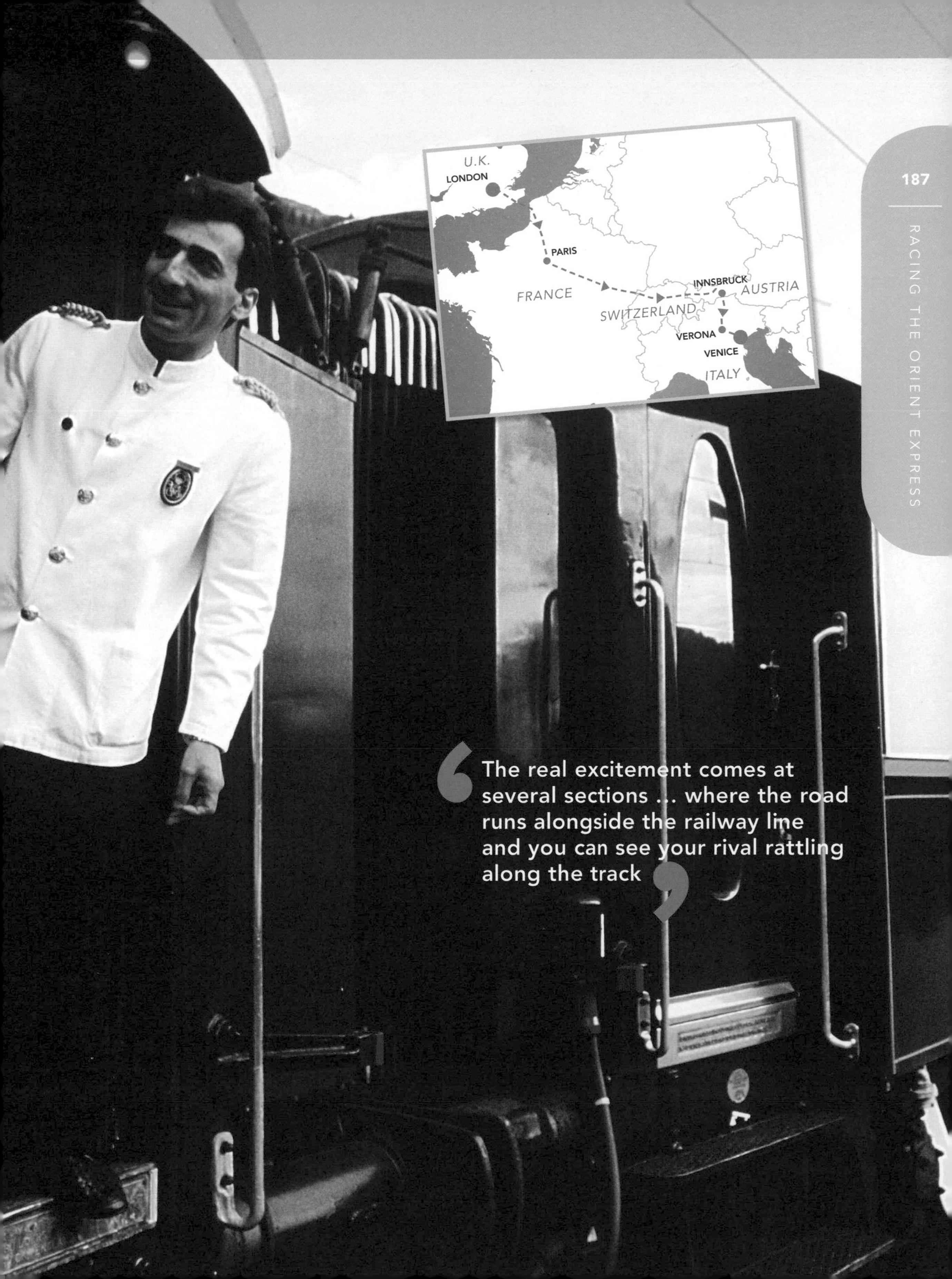

U.K.
LONDON

PARIS

FRANCE

SWITZERLAND

INNSBRUCK

AUSTRIA

VERONA

VENICE

ITALY

'The real excitement comes at several sections ... where the road runs alongside the railway line and you can see your rival rattling along the track'

Mans, was having dinner at the Carlton hotel in Cannes. When his friends started talking about Noble's achievement, he said he wasn't impressed, and bet £100 that the following day he could leave Cannes in his Bentley Speed Six at the same time as the train, and be at his London club before the train reached Calais. He made it – by four minutes – and was later fined by the French police for racing on public roads.

Today the Blue Train has long since been consigned to history, but it is still possible to recreate a little of the glamour and excitement of those days. With the Blue Train gone, the next best thing is the Orient Express from London to Venice.

It leaves London Victoria mid-morning then guests cross the channel by ferry at Dover. Once in France, they board another Orient Express train, and finally arrive in Venice the following afternoon. Which doesn't sound particularly fast, but to beat it you basically need to drive non-stop through the night. A co-driver is absolutely essential, and even then, with breakdowns, map-reading mistakes and everything else that can go wrong, only about half of those who try manage to beat the train.

As with all silly challenges, it's better in a group, and we did it in a convoy of classic cars that we'd begged, borrowed and hired for the occasion. Of course there's some fabulous scenery as you cross Europe and the Alps, but the real excitement comes at several sections, mainly in Italy, where the road runs alongside the railway line and you can see your rival rattling along the track.

Best of all is the arrival in Venice. We drove across the causeway, parked at the bus station, ran across the bridge to the train station, then down the steps, two at a time, to the platform – just as the Orient Express was starting to pull in. Victory!

The nice thing about the whole experience is that once the adventure – the race – is complete, you have to drive back. Only this time, you can go as sedately as you like, taking a week or two to relish the drive and soak up the scenery. Just remember to stop and raise a toast to Dudley Noble.

Now do it . . .

For the various routes and train times so you can plan your trip, visit the Orient Express website (www.orient-express.com/collection/trains/venice_simplon_orient_express.jsp).

Rocket boat down the Mekong

Why	For a wind-in-the-hair rush, Cambodian-style
Where	Cambodia	**Duration**	One day

We were in Voen Kham, a small town on the border between Laos and Cambodia, following our guide through a down-at-heel market, along narrow alleys between houses and across plank walkways to the banks of the Mekong. We emerged through some scrub, and then, bobbing beside the jetty, we saw it – probably the most bonkers form of transport ever invented.

Picture a drag racer. Now picture it floating on water, and you have a pretty good idea of what a Mekong rocket boat is like. They operate as fast taxis all along the Mekong in Cambodia, and are basically light, narrow, open wooden boats, a bit like canoes with high curved prows. Mounted on the back, completely incongruously, is an engine from a car, attached by a shaft a metre or more long to a big propeller. The two we would be taking had 1600cc, 16-valve Toyota engines, and would, we were told, easily top 40mph. To be honest, the boats looked a little flimsy and we'd heard there were rapids up ahead.

'Don't worry,' said the guide. 'The only thing

that's rapid round here are these boats.'

He wasn't wrong. The drivers fired them up and we were off, accelerating across the glassy, flat Mekong as the sun started to set, turning the sky a vivid orange. It was petrol-head heaven. With the engine roaring, we flew across the water at an incredible speed, jumping over the wake of the other boat, darting between the mangrove trees that poked out of the water, and all the while we were laughing, shouting and taking pictures.

But just as a drag racer wouldn't be the most practical choice for a long journey, the longer we travelled in the boats, the more we began to notice their downsides. When a short rain

shower blew in, we were going so fast that the rain stung our faces like a thousand needles and, as the boats are completely open, everything got soaking wet. It began to get dark and choppy, and soon the boats were banging off the waves, setting up a relentless bone-jarring rhythm. It was so exciting, though, that none of this seemed to matter . . .

After a couple of hours we reached our destination, Stung Treng, and the drivers rammed the boats up the bank and cut the engines. Suddenly there was silence. We slowly unfolded ourselves from the bottom of the boats and gingerly stepped out, ears ringing, nerves jangling from the vibration, faces raw from the wind and rain, our hair swept back like startled cartoon characters.

Next morning we were back on the river, this time on a large, slow boat. We sat in wicker chairs, sheltered under a roof, drinking cups of tea and watching the scenery drift slowly past. It felt like something from colonial days, peaceful, relaxing and refined. But give me the rocket boat any day.

Now do it . . .

You can book a flight at www.cambodia-airports.com and contact Nick Ray to organize the Mekong adventure. For more information on Cambodia, contact the Cambodia Tourism Authority (www.tourismcambodia.com).

57

The Skeleton Coast

TWO WEEKS OFF WORK

| **Why** | For the chance to value complete isolation |
| **Where** | Namibia | **Duration** | Three days + |

If you want to get away from it all, there are few better places than Namibia. The stats speak for themselves – it is four times the size of Britain, but has a population of just 1.8 million. There are fewer than seven people per square mile in Namibia, compared to 1,023 in England. Most of Namibia's people live in a central strip between the Namib and Kalahari deserts, or in the fertile far north, so in much of the rest of the country you can drive a hundred miles without seeing a soul.

The coast is lonelier still. Along 980 miles of coast, there are just three seaside towns. Everywhere you go in Namibia you feel like a tiny insignificant speck in a vast landscape, but perhaps that feeling is most acute on the Skeleton Coast, which runs north from the town of Swakopmund to the Angolan border. Travel along it and you find yourself sandwiched between the baking heat of the world's oldest desert on one side and the freezing breakers of the Atlantic on the other. The only sign of man's 250,000 years of toil and effort on this planet is the occasional rusting wreck of a ship, half buried in the sand.

The Bushmen of the Namibian interior called the Skeleton Coast 'the land God made in anger', while Portuguese sailors christened it 'the gates of hell'. The cold Benguela current means there's very often dense fog hanging along the shore, and ensures big waves constantly pound the beach. Blinded by the fog, ships would run into the rocks just offshore. If they made it to the beach, the waves would stop them getting off again, and climbing the steep dunes and making it through the desert to civilization would be practically impossible. The sailors marooned here were in trouble.

It sounds bleak, and it is, but the Skeleton Coast is also deeply impressive, utterly unearthly. And the odd thing is that all this glorious isolation is very easy to reach, and very safe to travel through (provided you don't drive on the beach!). You can fly straight from Europe into Windhoek, the capital, hire a car at the airport, then off you go. The roads are mostly gravel but

You can completely lose yourself in Namibia.

Now do it . . .

Visit Intrepid Travel (www.intrepidtravel.com/trips/ UBKC) for a fantastic 8-day trip to Namibia and the infamous Skeleton Coast. You can learn more about Namibia through the Namibia Tourist Board (www.namibiatourism.com.na).

Map labels: ANGOLA, ZAMBIA, GTOOTFRONTEIN, TSUMKEW, OTJIWARONGA, SWAKOPMUND, WALVIS BAY, BOTSWANA, NAMIBIA, SOUTH AFRICA, ATLANTIC OCEAN

are well maintained. And though you may have to drive for hours to reach a human habitation, when you get there you are more than likely to find it's an upmarket lodge, a stylish tented camp or a friendly guest farm. Food is fabulous, as is the top-quality red wine from South Africa.

Driving south down the Skeleton Coast, we eventually reached Swakopmund, and coming into town it's hard to believe your eyes. After days of travelling through sun-blasted African desert, you find yourself in a town that looks like it's been transported from Bavaria. There's a Becks brewery and street-corner cafés selling 'Kaffee und Kuchen'. There are Lutheran churches, whitewashed and half-timbered hotels, wood-panelled bars with roaring fires and framed maps of Germany, and neatly tended public gardens.

It's not a mirage. Namibia was a German colony from 1884 to 1915 and large numbers of settlers arrived from the fatherland. A third of white Namibians still speak German and restaurants across the country offer sauerkraut and bratwurst.

It's a fun place to hang out for a few days. Swakopmund also happens to be Namibia's adrenalin sports capital and you can try quad-biking in the dunes, sandsurfing, skydiving and many more before coming back to the numerous bars and the only nightlife scene in the country that extends beyond 10 p.m.

And when you've had your fill of that, it's time to head out into the grand emptiness once more.

58

Skiing the Himalayas

Why	For remote skiing with epic vistas
Where	India	**Duration**	Two days +

'If there is paradise anywhere on earth, it is here, it is here, it is here . . .' So said the Mughal Emperor Jahangir when he visited Kashmir in the early seventeenth century. It's easy to see what he meant – a fertile valley filled with crystal-clear streams, lakes, orchards and ornamental gardens, and surrounded by the snowy peaks of the Himalayas. Except today there is trouble in paradise.

When skiing, always expect the unexpected and go prepared.

Kashmir's borders are disputed by China, Pakistan and India, and for much of the last fifty years it has effectively been off-limits to travellers. Thousands of soldiers have died here on what are the world's highest battlefields, and there have been numerous bombings and riots in Kashmir's towns as pro-independence or pro-Pakistan campaigners clash with the Indian police and army.

Yet bizarrely, over the last few years, Kashmir has been building a reputation as the ultimate ski destination. An hour and a half's flight from

Delhi brings you to Srinagar, capital of Kashmir, and from there, a two-hour drive up into the hills brings you to the village of Gulmarg. While tensions rumble on in Srinagar, in Gulmarg, on a plateau at 2,600 metres, you feel a long way from the political strife.

Gulmarg grew up as a colonial hill station in the nineteenth century. British army officers and civil servants would come up to escape the heat, to hunt and play golf. By the start of the twentieth century there were three golf courses – one for women only – and a small Anglican church in the middle of the fairways.

Today St Mary's church is still there, but tourists come not for the golf but the snow. Indian tourists travel up from the southern states to get their first ever sighting of the white stuff, while international visitors are here for the ski lifts. Well, actually, the ski lift.

Gulmarg has four lifts, three of which are ancient, tiny, drag lifts suitable only for beginners. But the fourth is the world's highest ski lift, extending from the village to an altitude of 3,979 metres, just below the summit of Mount Apharwat. (In fact, there are two higher cable cars in the world, both in China, but they are designed for sightseeing tourists, not skiers, and there's no official ski area at the top. Venezuela and Bolivia used to have higher lifts too, but both have now closed down.)

Gulmarg's gondola may be record-breaking but it is a rickety old thing, out of date by the time it opened in 2005. Construction had started back in 1989, but the project had been mothballed due to an escalation in violence. Breakdowns are common, opening hours fluid and modern skis are too fat to fit in the racks, so you have to wedge the gondola door open and carry them half in, half out.

But as you rise up Mount Apharwat, above the haze in the valley, the Himalayan panorama opens up around you and all gripes about the lift are forgotten. From the top, you can ski off in any direction, and the snow is usually deep, deep powder.

Don't expect the trappings of a normal resort, however – this is for experts only. None of the mountain is groomed into pistes, and only one small section is monitored for avalanche risk. Everywhere else, you are completely on your own. But for those with the right experience, equipment and a guide, the skiing here is among the best in the world. There are steep sections, glades of paperbark trees (a type of beautiful pink-tinged birch) and huge forests of gigantic Himalayan pines. You ski past monkeys in the trees, spot the tracks of snow leopard, eat curry for lunch, then ski right down to remote villages in the valley where children will run out and ask to ride along on the back of your skis.

The snow conditions are usually great, with deep powder all over the mountain, and there are usually very few people to share it with. Typically around 250 people might use the lift per day, and once they have spread out across the mountain, you won't see anyone else.

In all the fun, it's very easy to forget the Kashmir conflict altogether and simply enjoy your holiday. But the reminders are there, if you want to look. At the very top of Apharwat, ski down for a little way in the opposite direction from Gulmarg and you will be able to see a lone, unbroken line stretching its way across the distant peaks. At first you might think it's a ridge in the snow, or the fences of a farm, but in fact these are the barricades and barbed wire of the demilitarized zone between Pakistan and India, somewhere which Bill Clinton identified in 2000 as 'the most dangerous place in the world'.

> **You ski past monkeys in the trees, spot the tracks of snow leopard, eat curry for lunch, then ski right down to remote villages in the valley**

Now do it . . .
Visit Mountain Tracks (www.mountaintracks.co.uk) to organize your own skiing adventure.

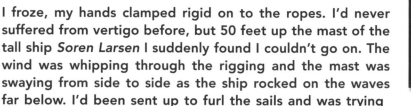

59

Sailing *Soren Larsen*

Why	For a fantastic voyage, sailing the traditional way
Where	South Pacific **Duration** Five days +

I froze, my hands clamped rigid on to the ropes. I'd never suffered from vertigo before, but 50 feet up the mast of the tall ship *Soren Larsen* I suddenly found I couldn't go on. The wind was whipping through the rigging and the mast was swaying from side to side as the ship rocked on the waves far below. I'd been sent up to furl the sails and was trying to clamber up on to the top galley, a platform halfway up the mast. But to get on to it, I had to climb out and over the base of the platform – all without being tied on. And this was only day one.

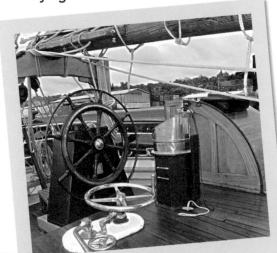

We had joined the ship in Port Vila, the capital of Vanuatu, for a five-day voyage through the South Pacific. Built in 1949 in Denmark, the *Soren Larsen* is a 145-foot brigantine, built entirely of oak. Until the 1970s she carried timber and grain between European ports, and then, having been saved from destruction and restored by enthusiasts, she starred in the BBC drama *The Onedin Line* as well as appearing in *The French Lieutenant's Woman*, *The Count of Monte Cristo* and *Shackleton*. Today, she travels around the Pacific as a cruise ship with a difference – the guests sail her themselves.

Soon after boarding, we were allocated our watches, either from twelve o'clock to four o'clock, four to eight or eight to twelve, and so on around the clock. As long as the ship was sailing, we would do two four-hour shifts a day, ringing the ship's bell once for every half hour that passed. Ringing eight bells means you've reached the end of your shift (the reason why so many pubs are called the Eight Bells).

And though the ship has all the modern navigational aids and technology, the crew don't like to use them, so the tasks are much as they would have been on the high seas two hundred years ago. You might be assigned to watch

Sailing, the traditional way.

> **We spent the next few days sailing between beautiful uninhabited islands**

Sailing on the Pacific was one of the most amazing adventures I've had.

because it was a little bit like living in the days of Nelson, or maybe just that it was one of those moments when you catch yourself realizing this is something you'll probably never do again in your life.

But don't think it's all about hardship, either. We spent the next few days sailing between beautiful uninhabited islands – we'd moor up offshore then land in a small dinghy for a few hours of the most idyllic sunbathing. On one day, the sea was like a millpond, so the crew rigged a knotted rope from the yardarm so we could swing on it and leap 20 feet down into the water. On other days we'd snorkel among the reefs, or fish off the side of the boat watching the amazing South Sea sunsets.

From May to November the ship cruises the South Pacific, setting off from its home base in Auckland, New Zealand, and making a loop, usually including the Cook Islands, Samoa,

duty, up in the bow with the waves breaking over you, or to man the wheel, learning how to hold it just off centre to allow for the effect of wind on the hull. Or, like me, you might be asked to climb the rope ladders, or ratlins, up the mast to furl the sails.

Safely back on the deck after my aborted attempt, the crew reassured me and told me not to worry. The *Soren Larsen* isn't about gruff naval officers beasting the new recruits.

Later that night, we hit a force seven gale, and soon we were rolling up and down the waves, feeling seasick, with water splashing over the midships and the sails flapping furiously above. But as I stood there in the dark, soaking wet and tied to a safety line to stop being swept overboard, I realized I was grinning. Perhaps

Stopping off at small islands.

Climbing up the ratlines — not for the faint-hearted!

Travelling with my daughter Emily made the adventure even more special.

Fiji, Vanuatu, New Caledonia and Australia. You can join for a few days or a few months.

Don't expect cruise ship comforts, though. The cabins are absolutely tiny, with two bunks next to a narrow space where you can just about stand and get dressed. But the food is delicious, the atmosphere great fun, and the crew, led by the charismatic bearded Captain Jim, were delightful. There's space for up to twenty-two passengers, or 'voyage crew' as they are known, and thirteen crew, enough that if you ever decide you want to skip your watch, you can.

But my experience up in the rigging was nagging at me, so, on the final day, I gave it another go. Trying not to make too much of a big deal about it in my mind, I rushed up the ratlins, clambered up on to the top galley, then, before I stopped to think, I was out along the yardarm, hands holding the wooden beam, feet inching along a rope strung below. As I stretched forward to start tying up the sails in the special way we'd been taught, feet wobbling on the rope below, I couldn't help thinking what madness this was, and how much I was loving it.

What made this adventure even more special for me was that I was accompanied by my fifteen-year-old daughter Emily and my girlfriend Victoria. It is sometimes difficult to have adventures with your family, particularly teenagers, but I would highly recommend this. Emily really connected with the crew and embraced the watch system – in fact she called the 4 a.m. watch, and at 5 a.m. when I came on deck to find her she was helming the ship in rough seas and had also spent an hour with the cook, baking bread for breakfast for the rest of the crew. I knew that she was safe and well looked-after, and she really embraced life on the seas, having the time of her life.

There's always a place where you can be alone.

Now do it . . .

Escape around the South Pacific with Tallship *Soren Larsen* ships (www.sorenlarsen.co.nz). For accommodation in Port Vila, we recommend staying at Fatumaru Lodge (www.fatumaru.com), an idyllic waterfront beach hotel. Air Vanuatu (www.airvanuatu.com) operates flights from Port Vila to Santo.

Why	To live out a dream via fire, steel, steam and water
Where	Australia	**Duration**	One day

LONG WEEKEND

I've always loved travelling by train. After long journeys by motorbike, switching to a train gives you the chance to look up from the road, relax, watch the scenery unfolding outside your window and talk to local people. I've had some glorious train trips everywhere from Azerbaijan to Argentina, but I'd always hankered after going one better: following the line of the Ghan railway, riding on the footplate of a steam train.

The Pichi Richi Railway Preservation Society is a heritage railway in the Australian outback where enthusiasts run regular services between Port Augusta and Quorn in South Australia, using elderly steam trains on a 25-mile section of track that used to be part of the Central Australia Railway. This was the route of the famous Ghan train which ran from Adelaide through the heart of the outback to Alice Springs, and was named, depending on who you believe, either after an Afghan passenger who got out to pray to Mecca, or the Afghans who ran camel trains to take goods through the outback before the train track was built.

The few hours I spent on the footplate were the absolute fulfilment of a boyhood dream. I didn't get to drive the train, but I was the fireman – and that was plenty hard enough.

The volunteers who ran the train explained that you can't just shovel loads of coal in then have a break, you have to make sure it goes in at an even rate, and that it is spread around all the corners of the firebox. You need to keep the fire burning evenly to make sure the steam pressure stays between 180 and 220psi – below that, the engine loses power; above it, the safety valve blows to stop the whole engine exploding.

I soon understood what a hard job this was. On a non-stop run, the fireman couldn't get out and swap with anyone else, so he was stuck on the footplate. And on a long trip, he could end up shovelling 25 tons of coal.

It's hard to put the thrill of a steam train into words – it's as if the machinery comes alive, with the squeaking wheels, the roaring flames and the whoosh of steam. Soon I was exhausted, sweating from the heat of the outback and of the furnace in front of me, not to mention the effort of shovelling. My face was black with coal dust and grime, but I couldn't stop smiling.

Now do it . . .
The Pichi Richi Railway Preservation Society (www.prr. org.au) operates regular heritage-train journeys in South Australia, and can provide all the details you need for your own steam adventure.

Three peaks by tuk tuk

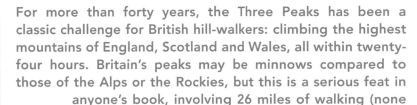

61

LONG WEEKEND

| **Why** | To undertake an established challenge, your way |
| **Where** | Great Britain | **Duration** | Three days |

For more than forty years, the Three Peaks has been a classic challenge for British hill-walkers: climbing the highest mountains of England, Scotland and Wales, all within twenty-four hours. Britain's peaks may be minnows compared to those of the Alps or the Rockies, but this is a serious feat in anyone's book, involving 26 miles of walking (none of it on the flat), a vertical ascent and descent of over 3,000 metres and around 475 miles of driving.

The clock starts when you head off from the car park at the foot of the first peak, and ends when you get back down from the final one. There are no breaks for sleeping, eating or driving between the mountains – that all has to be done in the twenty-four hours.

Most people start with Ben Nevis in Scotland, at 1,344 metres the highest mountain and, for many people, the most remote. You can do it at any time of the year, but if you do it in midsummer you should be able to avoid walking in the dark. The normal itinerary is to start about 5 p.m., reach the summit of Ben Nevis by 8 p.m. and be back down by 10 p.m., ready to jump in the car for the six- to seven-hour drive to Scafell Pike, in the English Lake District.

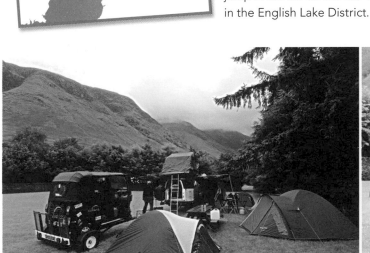

Often success depends on having a support crew, who can have a meal waiting for you to eat in the car, and a designated driver so you can sleep during the journey. You need to keep your fingers crossed that you don't run into any traffic jams too.

Once you reach Scafell Pike, at 4.30 or 5 a.m., you start straight up it, reaching the 978-metre summit by 7 or 8 a.m. and getting back down ninety minutes later. None of the mountains are technically difficult to climb, but gearing yourself up to start hillclimbing so early in the morning, and after just a few snatched hours' sleep, is a significant mental challenge.

The drive to Snowdon should take two to three hours, meaning you can start up from the Pen y Pass car park by lunchtime and reach the 1,085-metre summit at 3 p.m., leaving two hours to dash back down before the 24 hours is up.

It's a great event, proof that you don't have to go to the other side of the globe to have an epic adventure, and the sense of achievement for anyone who completes it is immense. But at the same time, it's also worth remembering that, with celebrated set-piece challenges like this, there's nothing to say you have to do them 'by the book'. Often it's more fun to adapt them to create your own, individual adventure, and once you get over the notion that you're somehow 'cheating' by straying from the accepted norm, a whole world of possibilities opens up.

I decided to do the three peaks in three days. I wanted to enjoy the experience, to have fun with friends and have time to take in the surroundings. Plus, just to throw something silly into the mix, instead of using a minibus like everyone else, I'd drive between the peaks on an Indian tuk tuk, or auto-rickshaw. People have asked me why, and of course there's no sensible explanation, other than that for me adventures are all about leaving ordinary life behind, and there are few things less ordinary than buzzing through the Scottish Highlands on an Indian tuk tuk.

Plus, I just love tuk tuks. They may only go at 40mph, but they do 150 miles to the gallon and only cost £4,000 to buy new. They are exempt from the London congestion charge, you don't have to wear a helmet and you can park in a motorcycle bay. I fell in love with them while in Varanasi in India, bought one and had it shipped home.

The only downside is that they can only really carry three, and when they heard about the trip, loads of people I knew said they wanted to come. In the end there were eight of us, so we took a couple of cars and towed the tuk tuk from London up to the start point at the foot of Ben Nevis. We set up our tents, had a good Scottish supper of haggis, neeps and tatties washed down with whisky, and looked up at the looming mountain we'd have to climb first thing the next morning.

The next three days passed in a blur of trudging feet and the buzzing of tuk tuk engine. Ben Nevis was a long haul, but worth it for the porridge we made on the summit and the snowball fight in August.

Our top speed was 40mph.

I love the freedom of a tuk tuk - like that of a motorbike.

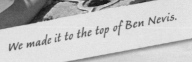

We made it to the top of Ben Nevis.

Unfortunately, the tuk tuk ran on LPG, and there aren't too many LPG-equipped petrol stations in the Highlands, so I ran out on the way to Scafell Pike and had to wait for the car to rescue me. We camped en-route, got to the bottom of the English peak at 5 p.m. the next day and immediately set off up it. We were at the top by 8 p.m. but I wished we'd brought the tents up with us. Wild camping on the summit would be an awesome experience, and you would wake up to England's best view.

The next morning at the crack of dawn we set off for Snowdon. In between the climbs I was driving cross-country and passers-by couldn't help waving and smiling when they saw an Indian tuk tuk in the lanes of north Wales. We started climbing about 5 p.m. and got to the top about 9 p.m., just as the sun was going down and a cold mist was rolling in. We were getting tired by now, and we trudged down in a sober mood.

It was nearly 3 a.m. by the time we got back to the car park at the bottom of Snowdon, but suddenly the atmosphere came alive. As each person came over the line, we cheered and clapped, and they punched the air. We were standing in the drizzle in a remote Welsh car park in the middle of the night, but everyone was full of energy, beaming and saying it was the best thing they'd ever done. If we could have done, we would have had a party right there.

Now do it . . .

To buy your very own tuk tuk, visit TukTuk UK (www.tuktuk-uk.com) who specialize in the importing of authentic Indian rickshaws. For information on the Three Peaks Challenge, visit www.thethreepeakschallenge.co.uk. For additional information on the region contact Visit Scotland (www.visitscotland.com).

Vietcong tunnels of Vietnam

| **Why** | To understand the effects of the Vietnamese war |
| **Where** | Vietnam | **Duration** | One day |

Vietnam is a delightful country to travel through, and Hanoi is one of my favourite cities. Where Bangkok has sections that are very traditional and sections that are very westernized and modern, in Hanoi the old and new, east and west, seem to be integrated. There's a buzz of activity and optimism in the air, and a thousand scooters careering around every corner, laden with goods and people. It's a place where you can live well.

And yet the war is indelibly imprinted on Vietnam. From the wreckage of the downed B52 bomber that pokes up out of Huu Tiep lake in the centre of Hanoi, to the old American uniforms, helmets and even medals on sale from stalls at Khe Sanh, site of a long and bloody battle, it's impossible to forget what happened here.

But the fascinating thing is that, having seen numerous films about the war, all made from a US perspective, by coming here you can get a sense of what it was like for the Vietnamese. Vinh Moc, just south of what was once the demilitarized zone separating North and South Vietnam, is a great place to visit to learn more. When war broke out it was

a village. Suspecting the residents of helping pass supplies between North Vietnam and the Vietcong soldiers in the South, the Americans set about bombing the area so the residents would leave.

Instead, the villagers simply moved underground, creating a network of tunnels in which they could survive the bombardments while continuing to supply the Vietcong. The tunnels were dug between 1965 and 1967 and used until 1972. The Americans never found them so they are still there today.

As you approach, there's no sign of what lies beneath the ground, but then you enter a ditch that becomes a trench and at the end is a door. Inside, you go down steps, dropping deeper and

deeper until you find not just a shelter, but an entire underground village. There are classrooms for the children, a hospital, alcoves set back where individual families would sleep, a well, kitchens, eating and storage areas and a meeting room with space for 150. There are ventilation shafts, and concealed chimneys for the stoves. The clay soil was perfect for tunnelling – soft enough to be easily dug out, but structurally sound without the need for extensive wooden supports. There are three levels, the lowest of which is 30 metres below ground, beyond reach of even the biggest American bombs, but the deeper you go, the narrower and tighter the passages become.

The tunnels stretch for three miles all the way to the coast, where supplies of arms and food would be transferred from boats under cover of darkness.

At first you are struck by the ingenuity of it all. Then you start to consider what the conditions must have been like. Three hundred people lived here for more than five years while their farms and village above ground were carpet-bombed into a wasteland. Incredibly, seventeen babies were born underground. And though today it looks reasonably clean and pleasant, with the body heat of three hundred people and poor ventilation, it must have been hot, humid and claustrophobic.

It's an enthralling place to visit purely for historical reasons, but there's more than that. Seeing what lengths the villagers were prepared to go to, and what hardships they endured to protect their community, gives you a real insight into why modern Vietnam is such an industrious, determined and positive place to be.

Now do it . . .
Visit Intrepid Travel (www.intrepidtravel.com/trips/ TVAM) to experience the eye-opening history of Vietnam. For more information on Vietnam visit (www.vietnam.com).

WORK · TWO WEEKS OFF

Why	To learn how to become a real cowboy
Where	Guyana	Duration	Three days

Just getting to the ranch is an adventure. We flew to Boa Vista in northern Brazil, then took a bus for an hour and a half to the border with Guyana, where we crossed the bridge into the town of Lethem. There, we were picked up by a 4x4 and set off up a dirt road towards the Dadanawa Ranch, the largest and most isolated cattle ranch in the whole of Guyana.

It had been raining and the dirt road had become a morass of deep red-coloured mud, rivulets and giant puddles, some of them 20 feet across. We travelled in a convoy of three 4x4s, so if one got stuck – and they all did, over and over again – the others could help pull it out. In good weather, the journey from Lethem can take as little as three hours. It took us almost six to cover the 60 miles.

By the time we arrived, it was 1.30 a.m. and pitch black outside. It was pretty dark inside too – the ranch doesn't have electricity. Dadanawa isn't a place for tourists in search of luxury. It's a working ranch, covering 2,000 square miles, with around 28,000 head of cattle. I'd come to ride out with the cowboys who herd and corral them, and get a taste of their tough lifestyle. Here, the cowboys go by their Spanish name, vaqueros (from which we get another word for cowboy – the buckeroo). They don't wear cowboy boots, preferring to ride barefoot. Their saddles are handmade, and they ride small horses that look a little like polo ponies.

Early the next morning, I was introduced to my steed. His name didn't exactly conjure up the Wild West, nor the golden age of South American exploration. He was called Trevor.

Soon Trevor and I were making ourselves useful. With six vaqueros we were tasked with moving a herd of several hundred cattle from their fenced enclosure down to the river where they could drink, and then taking them back again. The rough wooden gate slid back and the cattle surged

Rounding up the herd.

forward, frantically mooing and snorting, hooves clattering on the ground, some clambering on top of each other. Suddenly the vaqueros were shouting and whooping, darting into position to control the cows. A tingle of excitement went down my spine.

What Trevor lacked in the macho name department, he more than made up for in his ability to control the cattle and to make me feel at home on his back. He turned left or right with the barest movement of the reins, and soon we were chasing wayward cattle out of the scrub and herding them across the savannah to the river. I've enjoyed riding holidays before but this was something else, something genuinely thrilling. This wasn't riding for fun, but horses doing real work.

Later, we separated the cattle into calves, steers, bulls and heifers, sending them into separate enclosures and branding some of them with the ranch's mark, an 'H'. Next we had to lasso two bulls that needed to be castrated. The vaqueros offered to let me have a go.

It's not easy. As they swing the rope above their heads, experts can twist their wrists with a fluid motion so the lasso stays open in the air before being pulled taut around the animal's head. Novices tend to jerk it so the metal ring that acts as a slipknot slides straight to the end, closing the lasso before you've even thrown it.

And so I found myself standing there, concentrating so hard on trying to swing the lasso that I'd completely forgotten I was in a field with

It was amazing to see cowboys at work on a real ranch.

Now do it . . .

Wilderness Explorers (www.wilderness-explorers. com) are the go-to company for adventures within Guyana, and they can organize your Dadanawa Ranch visit. For more information on Guyana, contact the Guyana Tourism Authority (www.guyana-tourism.com). Round the World Experts (www. roundtheworldexperts.co.uk) can arrange round-the-world flights from the UK via Guyana.

two bulls. When the bull I was trying to catch stopped and turned to stare at me, breathing heavily, all I could think was, 'Oh good, now he'll be an easier target.' It was only as he charged towards me that the reality hit me of who was the target, and by then it was too late. He butted straight into my chest, knocking me backwards. Within seconds, the other bull came and battered into me from behind. Thankfully both were small, young animals without horns, so they only managed to wind me – and prompt howls of laughter from the vaqueros, sitting on the fence watching the comic attempts of the greenhorn.

It was a glorious day. The vaqueros are great fun, and riding alongside them is a thrill. Even more than that, staying at the ranch gives you a real sense of a different, slower pace of life.

That night we sat out on the porch, swinging in hammocks, drinking fine 15-year-old Guyanan rum and watching the sun set behind the distant mountains. With no electricity, and no towns for miles around, the modern world seemed a long way off. It was hard to reach Dadanawa, but it was harder to leave.

Trevor and I.

This is the hole that we had just ridden across.

We stayed near a piranha- and
caiman-infested river.

| **Why** | For feeling alive, close to both nature and history |
| **Where** | Italy | **Duration** | Two days |

We had arrived at the mountain refuge in darkness, exhausted after a gruelling climb, so when I pulled back the curtains in the morning, the view came as a complete shock. We were looking out over a misty ocean, from whose depths the spires of great limestone cathedrals emerged and reached for the sky. It was like a mystical scene from *Lord of the Rings.*

In truth, of course, the ocean was a sea of clouds below us in the valleys, and the cathedrals were the peaks of the Dolomites poking up through them, but I'd never seen anything like it. Surely this must be the most beautiful battlefield in the world?

For although today the Dolomites in northern Italy are a playground for skiers, hikers and climbers, not to mention food lovers who come to feast at the numerous Michelin-starred restaurants, in the First World War they were the scene of horrendous human suffering. In 1915, Italy joined the war on the Allied side, tempted by the prospect of winning great chunks of Austro-Hungarian territory. In the end, at Versailles in 1919, Italy got the land it wanted, but, with 689,000 of its men dead, it was a hollow victory.

For much of the war, the frontline went right through the Dolomites, with thousands of Italian and Austrian troops dug into the high mountains. Some carved machine and artillery positions into the rock faces and opened fire whenever they saw movement, while others dug mines through the rock to attempt to blow up the enemy positions from below.

It must have been a miserable existence, baking hot and without running water in summer, freezing cold in winter. The elements were known as the 'third army', and this was the most deadly of all – it's estimated that the snow and the cold killed more soldiers in the Dolomites than bullets or bombs. On one day, 13 December 1916, 10,000 men were killed by avalanches. It became known as White Friday.

All of which isn't to dwell on past sorrows for the sake of it, but because the soldiers and the modern-day climbers are tied together by a very tangible link. So the troops could move around safely and quickly, a network of 'via ferrata', or iron roads, was installed. These were metal cables bolted to the rock, in places augmented with iron rungs, short sections of ladder and the occasional hanging bridge.

They are still there, nowadays an extensive range of modern stainless steel cables firmly attached to the rock face by embedded steel pins. It is these via ferrata that allow today's visitors to tackle routes that would normally be the preserve of serious rock climbers. You need a harness, to which you attach a Y-shaped piece of rope, sometimes called the 'bull's horns', ending in two carabiners. You clip one carabiner to the metal cable, then climb up to the point where the cable is bolted to the rock. Here you attach your second carabiner above the bolt before removing the first one from the cable below it, thus ensuring you are secure at all times. Good walking boots, lots of water and plenty of sunscreen are equally important.

There are via ferrata throughout the Dolomites, some rusty, others repaired and modernized, and many allow you to access the high-altitude mountain huts used by skiers in winter. We'd chosen to climb to the Rifugio Lagazuoi, on a mountain that was the scene of some of the fiercest fighting.

The via ferrata vary greatly in difficulty too. The easiest are scarcely steeper or more precipitous than ordinary mountain paths, and the cable is there for peace of mind more than anything else. The hardest are close to vertical, and it's advisable to use an additional safety rope unless you're very confident.

We were in at the deep end. Our route up from the Passo Falzarego began with some hardcore rock climbing, before the gradient eased off. It took us three hours of climbing then another four hours of walking to reach the refuge. We stumbled in at 9 p.m., for a hearty dinner of pork chops and gnocchi.

Next morning we got an even closer insight into the lives of the troops up there. The tunnels and gun emplacements have been preserved as a sort of high-altitude museum. For an hour and a half, we descended the mountain inside a tunnel, stopping occasionally to peer from the shooting points. In their tunnels and lofty camps, the terrified Italian soldiers were often so close to their Austrian enemies they could hear them talking.

How bizarre that half an hour before, we'd been eating a leisurely breakfast on the terrace of the refuge, soaking up the sun and drinking in that glorious view.

Now do it . . .

Mountain Tracks (www.mountaintracks.co.uk) can organize your adventure at the Via Ferrata. The Rifugio Lagazuoi (www.rifugiolagazuoi.com) is a great place to stay and offers spectacular views.

Why	To test your physical endurance in a traditional way
Where	Cook Islands **Duration** Two days

For hundreds if not thousands of years, the people of the Pacific islands have sailed in vakas – canoes stabilized with one or more outriggers. In their heyday, they ranged from large ships with multiple sails that could take people and freight over the vast distances between islands, to one-person vessels that were paddled offshore to fish. Far more than just a means of transport, they were central to communities' livelihoods, culture and even social lives, and they are still used today. So if you come to this part of the world, you have really got to get out in one.

I tried two, very different, types of vaka. The first was a 45-foot-long catamaran, one of seven traditional vakas that had been rebuilt by enthusiasts concerned that boats of that style would die out. The seven have been dispersed throughout the region, and one, the *Marumaru Atua*, is stationed on Rarotonga, the largest of the Cook Islands, and takes paying passengers out on voyages.

This is sailing at its most basic. On longer trips you sleep in bunks in the hull, with your belongings in a net. There is a toilet, but you have to flush it with a bucket.

Up on deck is a small cabin with a couple of gas burners for cooking and a sink. There are four crew members, and space for about six passengers. There are two sails, and a huge oar hanging down in the middle of the two hulls which acts as the rudder. The clever thing is that the boat has a very shallow draught – you can sail in two foot of water or less – so that if a storm blew up, the boat could come into the nearest island and find shelter in even the shallowest of bays.

We set off from Rarotonga in an eight-foot Pacific swell. I was holding the rudder, trying to steer a straight course, but it was a beast – I was wrestling with it. There's no compass; you have to try to steer a course by the sun. How the early Pacific sailors ever navigated between islands, which, after all, are tiny specks in hundreds of miles of open sea, is beyond me. They must have been so brave, and so skilled.

My favourite spot on the boat was the little seat at the back of each of the hulls. Sitting there as the boat rocked up and down the waves was like riding a rollercoaster – you couldn't help but smile. Don't think of trying it if you get seasick, though . . .

Completely different was my experience of racing a V6 canoe (V stands for vaka, six is the number of paddlers on board). Think *Hawaii 5-0* and you have the picture. Racing these canoes isn't something laid on for tourists, but a central part of the island's social life – teams practise in the evenings after work then compete on special occasions. One of the local paddlers told me that racing the canoes is a welcome way of getting off a tiny island that can feel claustrophobic at times. Being out on the vaka gives them a sense of escape.

To get a chance to go on board, you have to talk to the Cook Islands Voyaging Society in Avarua, capital of Rarotonga, to see if they have a spare place in a boat. It's well worth making the effort, because it's a thrilling experience.

Be prepared to work hard, though. Three people paddle to the left, three to the right, with a leader controlling the rhythm. When you're starting to tire, the leader shouts 'whoa', and you do one more stroke, then switch to the opposite side. Working well – i.e. without me on board – it should be a fluid, rhythmic motion. And it's fast – we had a motorboat sail alongside trying to take pictures, and it was struggling to keep up.

The leader also has to work with the waves. By upping the paddling tempo at just the right time, he can make the boat surf along on the top of the waves, giving a burst of speed and a brief respite for the paddlers.

But as well as the adrenalin and the sense of teamwork, perhaps the best thing is looking back at Rarotonga. Of course, when you're on the island, you don't really take it in, but looking back I could see the big waves rolling in and crashing on the reef, the volcano shrouded in mist and a huge double rainbow above. Stunning.

Rowing as part of the team.

Now do it . . .

For the chance to experience a vaka, contact the Cook Islands' Voyaging Society (www.voyaging.co.ck). While in Rarotonga we recommend you stay at the award-winning Little Polynesian Resort (www.littlepolynesian.com). For more information, contact The Dive Centre (www.thedivecentre-rarotonga.com) and Cook Islands Tourism (www.cookislands.travel). Air Rarotonga (www.airraro.com) can fly you from New Zealand to the Cook Islands.

Why	To see spectacular reef wildlife, guaranteed
Where	Belize	**Duration**	One day

If you want to dive amid beautiful coral and see a spectacular range of fish, Belize is hard to beat. The 186-mile-long Belize Barrier Reef is part of a chain of coral that stretches from Mexico to Honduras, making it the second largest reef in the world after Australia's Great Barrier.

But where the Great Barrier is a long way offshore and takes at least 90 minutes to reach by boat, in Belize the reef is, in places, a stone's throw from the beach. So while lots of divers on the Great Barrier end up committing to stay for days at a time on a 'live-aboard' dive boat out at sea, in Belize you can dip in and out whenever you want. It's easy, relaxed and cheap – perfect for the inexperienced.

We stayed on Ambergris Caye, Belize's largest island, a strip of sand and palm trees 25 miles long and one mile wide. From here we could have struck out for the Great Blue Hole, an almost perfectly round sinkhole 300 metres wide and 124 metres deep. From the air it looks dramatic, like an ominous dark-blue eye, or a gaping mouth, surrounded by beautiful turquoise water. It's a famous dive-site and can get busy, but we were advised to give it a miss – once in the water, there is apparently little to see.

Instead we headed ten minutes by boat to the reef, and we weren't disappointed. I've dived a

lot around the world but here it was as if every fish I'd ever seen had been brought together in one place. There were manta rays, turtles, conga eels, vast tuna and shoals of tiny sardines like shimmering silver clouds. There were sharks too – seven of them, at least 2 metres long. Thankfully these were nurse sharks, partial to crustaceans and fish rather than humans.

The coral is in fabulous condition and everywhere you look there are vibrant colours. When you're diving, the deeper you go, the more the colour fades, until about 15 metres down everything becomes monochrome. On the Belize Barrier, you are rarely more than a couple of metres down, so there's abundant sunlight and vivid shades of every hue imaginable.

There are numerous outfits on Ambergris and nearby Caye Caulker that will teach you to dive and help you pass your PADI course, but my advice is to do it before you go. PADI and the British Sub Aqua Club (BSAC) run evening courses at swimming pools around Britain, so you can get your qualification and not waste any time while you're away.

This isn't diving at its most adventurous or hardcore, but it just might be diving at its most enjoyable.

Now do it . . .

Contact Chaa Creek Belize Resort (www.chaacreek.com) or www.thebelizecollection.com to book your diving adventure. For all diving advice visit PADI at www.padi.com. For more information, contact Journey Latin America (www.journeylatinamerica.co.uk) or visit www.visitcentroamerica.com

Why	For an uninterrupted aerial view of tropical rainforest
Where	Belize	**Duration**	One day

We'd flown over miles of pristine rainforest, over ancient temples lost in the jungle and the thatched roofs of remote villages, when Mick spotted a small landing strip far below. With a flick of the controls, he tipped the microlight on its side and began a rapid corkscrew to lose altitude. I was strapped to a flimsy seat behind him, and with the aircraft tilted right over, was looking straight down at hundreds of metres of thin air.

The microlight before take-off.

This is not something to try if you suffer from vertigo, but I loved it. To me, microlights are the motorbikes of the sky and training to fly one is definitely on my 'to do' list. Microlights bring the thrill of flight into the reach of those without the time or money to buy a plane and get their pilot's licence. Second-hand ones can cost as little as £3,000, and even new they might only cost £13,000, less than the average price of a new car. In the UK, you can get a licence with as little as 25 hours' experience, though 40 hours is more normal. Even if you don't learn to fly yourself, getting up in one as a passenger is a fabulous adventure.

My pilot was Robert Combs, an Englishman who since the late 1970s has run Chaa Creek, a lodge in the Belizean rainforest, close to the border with Guatemala. He'd agreed to let me go up for the day to show me the area and give me a taste of microlighting, but it's something you can try all over the world.

One of the best places to go microlighting is on safari in Africa. The beauty of the microlight is not its speed, but how slow you can fly. As they weigh so little (less than 450 kilos for a two-seater, 300 kilos for a single-seater), they can fly as slow as 40mph without stalling. This means you can take in your surroundings – a different experience to zipping past in a small plane. And though there is noise from the engine, it's a world away from the roar of a helicopter's rotors.

All of which makes them brilliant for spotting game. You can cover far more ground than in a Land Rover, and get further off the beaten track to see many more animals than you would in a conventional game drive.

Now do it . . .
Contact Chaa Creek Belize Resort (www.chaacreek.com) or www.thebelizecollection.com to book your microlighting adventure. For more information, contact Journey Latin America (www.journeylatinamerica.co.uk) or go to www.visitcentroamerica.com

Microlights aren't available everywhere, but a growing number of lodges, such as Tafika in South Luangwa National Park in Zambia, and Tanda Tula Safari Camp and Kwa Madwala Private Game Reserve in South Africa, are offering them as an alternative to driving or walking safaris.

Another fabulous experience is to microlight over Victoria Falls, the famous waterfalls on the Zambezi, between Zambia and Zimbabwe. You can swoop low over crocodiles sunning themselves on the riverbank, pass a few metres above the heads of the hippos swimming in the water, and see elephants and giraffes drinking. After that comes the main event, flying over the 1,708-metre-wide falls and watching the water thundering down more than 100 metres.

Great microlight adventures are on offer beyond Africa too. There are pilots who will take passengers up everywhere, from the wild coast of Northumbria, to Wadi Rum, the famous desert valley in Jordan, and the vineyards and beaches of the Hunter Valley in New South Wales, Australia.

My own trip had started at a landing strip close to Chaa Creek, then after about an hour's flight we landed at a remote airstrip in the jungle. This, it turned out, belonged to Blancaneaux Lodge, a jungle retreat owned by film director Francis Ford Coppola. We had a drink in the lodge's Jaguar bar (where Coppola has installed the ceiling fan used in the disturbing opening scenes of *Apocalypse Now*) and dreamt up possible microlight expeditions. There are few limits to where you can get to with them – enthusiastic microlighters have travelled from London to Sydney, and, more impressive still, from Tierra del Fuego to Cape Town, in a series of hops through the Americas, the Arctic, Europe then Africa.

Afterwards we wandered back to the airstrip, strapped ourselves in, fired up the little four-stroke engine and taxied to the end of the mud runway. Robert gunned the engine and within only 40 metres we were airborne, soaring steeply upwards over the jungle canopy. What a way to travel!

Make sure you have a good pilot.

There are truly amazing views from your seat in the sky.

A different geographical perspective.

The Simien Mountains and Lalibela

Why | For a high-altitude journey back in time

Where | Ethiopia | **Duration** | Five days

Ethiopia is years behind the rest of the world. Eight years to be precise. Through a quirk of history, based on variations in how branches of the church calculate the date of Jesus' birth, the date in Ethiopia is always eight years behind us. And yet, as you travel through the country, it can feel far more than that.

Ethiopia came as a shock to me, not because of poverty or famine, but because of how friendly and welcoming it was. Everywhere we travelled, we'd be greeted by smiling people and invited into houses. Sitting in one of them, with three generations of the same family, I couldn't help thinking that they had something we'd lost in the West a long time ago. We travel constantly, leading busy lives in cities miles from family and friends. Here the families were all together, leading a very simple existence, but with smiles from ear to ear. I'd travelled through lots of countries where there are traditional lifestyles, but never been quite so struck by how much pleasure and comfort people were gaining from having their extended family all around them.

Although there certainly is poverty in some places, in others I was struck by how fertile the land is, and how delicious the espresso. Coffee was first cultivated in Ethiopia, and strong historic links with Italy have only encouraged the appreciation of the black gold here. I'd given up coffee thirteen years before arriving here, but it smelled so good as they ground the beans and roasted them before our eyes that I had to try it again.

Travelling anywhere in Ethiopia is a worthwhile adventure, but the best itineraries have to include the Simien mountains of the north, where you find the churches of Lalibela. We'd ridden on motorbikes from Sudan, and after hundreds of miles of dry, arid desert, to be suddenly up in the mountains, riding above the clouds or through the rain, was another shock. The range rises up to 4,543 metres, and the peaks are often covered by snow in winter. There are dramatic gorges, waterfalls, green vegetation everywhere and roads that cling to the edge of cliffs.

And most impressive of all must be Lalibela, one of Ethiopia's holiest cities, where thirteen churches are hewn directly from the rock. Guidebooks sometimes refer to them as 'Africa's Petra', and when Francisco Alvares, the sixteenth-century Portuguese writer, visited, he finished his breathless account: 'I weary of writing more about these buildings, because it seems to me that I shall not be believed if I write more.'

KHARTOUM

SUDAN

ERITREA

GEDAREF

ADIGRAT

AXUM

MKELE

METEMA

MAYCHEW

GONDER

ETHIOPIA

LALIBELA

The churches are thought to have been built in the twelfth and thirteenth centuries, and are still used by the local people who are almost entirely Orthodox Christians. Approaching the Church of Saint George, perhaps the most impressive of all the churches, you walk along a rough, rocky hillside, then look down to see a big hole, where the rock has been carved away and formed into a building in the shape of a perfect cross. Some 30 metres high, it has windows, staircases and ornate columns. It's breathtaking.

Visitors can go inside most of the churches. You don't need to book or pre-arrange tours – you just have to buy a ticket (about £4) which allows you to wander into the churches as you please. Standing inside those rock rooms, listening to the incantations of a white-robed priest and breathing in the incense, it certainly feels like you've stepped back in time, and by a lot more than eight years.

Now do it . . .

Visit Intrepid Travel (www.intrepidtravel.com/trips/YDOG) for your own Ethiopian adventure. You can learn more about Ethiopia through the Ethiopian Tourist Board (www.tourismethiopia.org).

We had only just stepped from our tiny seaplane on to the beach at Kodiak Island when our guide motioned urgently for us to stop. We looked up and saw a huge bear prowling along the beach, less than 20 metres from where we were standing.

Any bear up close can seem pretty big, but this one was a monster.

The bears that live on Alaska's Kodiak Island and its surrounding archipelago are a subspecies of the brown (or 'grizzly') bear and grow far bigger than their relatives on the mainland. An adult male can stand 10 feet high on his hind legs, or 5 feet when on all fours, and can weigh more than 600 kilos. In fact, apart from polar bears, which are roughly the same size, Kodiak's are the biggest of all the world's bears.

Coming to see them up close is one of the planet's best wildlife experiences – though it can be distinctly scary. Once the bear on the beach had moved off, we walked inland through patches of woodland, constantly aware that bears might wander on to the path at any point. Only one person has been killed by a bear on Kodiak in the last seventy-five years, but someone is injured every other year on average. Not the most comforting statistic, especially for the person at the back of the line.

Kodiak is the second largest island in the US, about 100 miles long and between 10 and 60 miles wide, sitting about 40 miles off the southern coast of Alaska. Its biggest town is Kodiak, on the north-east of the island, home to some 6,600 people. The best place to see bears is the Kodiak National Wildlife Refuge, set up by the US government in 1941 to protect the bears' natural habitat. Today some 2,300 bears (not to mention 600 pairs of bald eagles) live on the refuge's 1.9 million acres of land, covering the south-western two-thirds of Kodiak Island, plus land on the neighbouring islands of Uganik, Afognak and Ban. To get there, you can travel by small plane (with floats to land on the sea) from either the town of Kodiak or Anchorage on the mainland. Several operators offer bear-watching packages, and they will drop you by plane close to where bears have been recently sighted, and provide a guide to make sure things stay safe.

We might have been a little bit jumpy on our walk from the beach, but it was worth it. After about half an hour, we came to a spot where a river dropped 6 or 7 feet over a small waterfall.

There, standing in the shallow water in front of us, were sixteen bears, some of them colossal adults, others quite young cubs.

Every summer, salmon run up the rivers of Alaska to spawn, and as we watched, the big silver fish leapt from the water, flew gracefully through the air and, if they were lucky, landed in the river above the waterfall to continue their journey upstream. Those that were unlucky would land in the jaws of the bears, who casually – nonchalantly, even – swung their heads to catch the fish in mid-air.

It was an amazing natural spectacle, the power of the fish matched by the skill of the bears. You could sit and watch it for hours, and the bears seemed completely untroubled by our presence on the sidelines. Only once did we get a hint of how ferocious these giants can be. A lone bear walked across the river, coming between a big mother bear and her cubs. The relaxed mood changed instantly. The mother reared up on to her hind legs, bared her huge teeth and then swung at the other bear, pushing and shoving it with her claws and eventually chasing it off downriver. In the space of about ten seconds, we'd all gone from thinking how cuddly the fishing bears were, to realizing they could tear us apart in moments.

After a couple of hours on the island, we headed back to the plane for the one-hour flight back to Anchorage. The whole experience had only taken half a day, but we'd got up close with one of the world's largest land predators and seen it hunting in its pristine natural habitat. Back on the busy city streets, none of us could quite believe our luck.

Now do it . . .

If you want to search for the Kodiak bear for yourself, visit Kodiak Treks (www.kodiaktreks.com) for more information.

Why	For a tour through unbelievable geographical features
Where	India **Duration** Three days

The ancient kingdom of Zanskar, high up in the Indian Himalayas, is hard to reach at the best of times. In summer you can get there by driving over high passes on rough tracks. But for six months of the year, snow blocks the passes and no cars or trucks can get in or out. For the area's 14,000 people, the deep snow makes it hard even to visit the neighbouring villages.

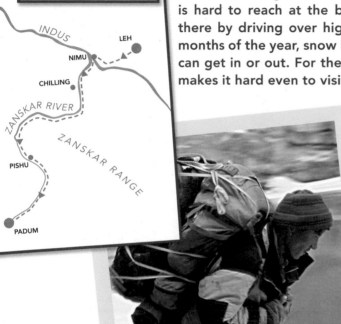

Remember to pack light!

In winter, the only ways of getting to Zanskar are by helicopter or by making the so-called Chadar (meaning 'white blanket') trek. Rather than battle through snow-covered roads or footpaths, the Chadar follows the Zanskar river itself — you walk on the frozen water. It really is a trek like no other.

The route starts at the village of Chilling, where trekkers strap crampons to their boots and head south, upriver, into the heart of Zanskar. This isn't something invented for tourists — in fact, few tourists have ever done it. For hundreds of years farmers and tradesmen would slip and slide along the river ice to transport supplies to the isolated communities upstream.

The scenery is stunning. The river flows through a deep gorge, with cliffs of hundreds of metres on either side, and above them mountains rising to more than 7,000 metres. Deep in the gorge, the river ice is in the shade for much of the day and temperatures can drop to −30° C. There's no option but to camp, so you must have the warmest sleeping bag money can buy. Some guides suggest it is warmer to sleep beside a fire in one of the caves at the edge of the river, as the local traders do, rather than using tents. You should still take tents, though, in case you need emergency shelter, as well as good supplies of food.

Walking on ice is exhausting.

Listen out for cracking ice!

Now do it . . .
To take on the Chadar Trek, contact Peak Adventure (www.peakadventuretour.com) who can help arrange your trip.

Conditions vary, but typically it might take a week to reach Padum, the capital of Zanskar, and a week to get back. Along the way you pass the villages of Lingshed, Pishu, Pidmo, Stongde and Zangla, places that get a handful of trekkers passing through in summer, but in winter will see few visitors, let alone Western ones. You'll be welcomed with open arms, asked in to share warming cups of tea and feted by over-excited children as soon as word spreads that you're approaching the village.

This isn't a technically difficult trek – you don't need to know any climbing techniques – but a guide is essential and you need to be pretty tough to take on a fortnight or more of walking in such cold conditions. But if you are looking for a taste of splendid isolation, and want to meet people leading a totally different way of life, there's nothing like it.

'For hundreds of years farmers and tradesmen would slip and slide along the river ice to transport supplies to the isolated communities upstream'

Riding Mont Ventoux

Why	For leg-burning, heart-pumping, full-on pursuit
Where	France	**Duration**	One day

LONG WEEKEND

As he neared the end of the thirteenth stage of the Tour de France, Tom Simpson, Britain's top rider, started zigzagging wildly across the road. He was cycling up the flank of Mont Ventoux, one of the most notorious climbs of the race, in temperatures of over 40° C. Simpson had always been a popular rider, impressing colleagues and fans with his ability to push on through the pain barrier. But that day he was pushing himself too far.

Near the top of the mountain there are no trees or bushes, just white rocky scree that reflects the sun's rays and makes the road even hotter. Suddenly Simpson fell to the ground. The legend has it that, though chronically dehydrated and fighting for breath, he whispered, 'Put me back on my

Do plenty of training before you go.

bike.' Fans and team staff did what he asked and, with a push, set him on his way again. Only 500 yards further on, he veered to the side of the road, fell again and died. The official cause of death was heart failure, caused by dehydration and exhaustion, and exacerbated by the amphetamines he'd been taking to block out the pain.

That was 1967, but today the roadside shrine to Tom Simpson is still covered in water bottles and spare inner tubes, left every day by cyclists as tributes to the fallen hero. Yet even if it hadn't claimed the life of one of the sport's top personalities, Ventoux would still be a place of pilgrimage for cyclists. For many, it represents the spiritual home of the sport.

At 1,912 metres, Ventoux isn't the Tour de France's highest point. Rather, its reputation comes from the steepness of the road up it, and the fact that, instead of being part of a chain of mountains, Ventoux stands alone above the lavender-covered plains of Provence. You can see it for miles around, a vast bulk looming on the horizon, and cyclists talk about it taunting them as they ride towards it.

For any cyclist, climbing Ventoux is a rite of passage. For a real adventure, rather than simply starting at the foot of the mountain, many cyclists follow the route taken by the Tour de France on one of the many times it has passed through here. (The race's route around France changes each year, but Ventoux is a frequent fixture.) An obvious section to choose is the 104-mile stage of the 2009 race, which started in Montélimar, to the north, and ended at the top of the mountain. Montélimar is on the direct TGV route from Paris, as is Orange (two hours' cycle to the west of Ventoux), so you can take your bike on the train, stay one night in Montélimar and another close to Ventoux, and squeeze the adventure into a long weekend.

From Montélimar, the route winds through beautiful countryside, sleepy stone villages like Taulignan and Rousset-les-Vignes, and the bustling rural markets at St Jalle and Buis-les-Baronnies. But it's hard to really enjoy the scenery when you know what's coming.

The real test begins at the village of Bédoin, to the south of the mountain. From here, it's 14 miles of constant climbing, and an altitude gain of 1,617 metres to the summit. The road starts in the forest, and is soon climbing far steeper than most of the other famous Tour de France climbs. Where other classic routes have hairpins every few hundred metres, which at least allow a momentary respite, here the road rises constantly and relentlessly. When you do finally reach a bend, your spirits sink as the next long stretch of tarmac is revealed, even steeper than the last.

Four miles from the top, you break out from the trees into the open, blinking in the direct sunlight. The gradient eases but the heat increases. It can be windy too – 'ventoux' means windy, and speeds of up to 200mph have been recorded.

As you pass Simpson's memorial, you can't help but be touched by the tragedy of it. With little more than half a mile to go, he was within touching distance of the summit, and safety.

By this stage, you will be so tired you can barely think, so it may come as a surprise when, after perhaps 90 minutes of constant climbing, you turn the corner to find yourself at the summit observatory. You are at the top. You can call yourself a real cyclist. And from now on, it's downhill all the way.

Now do it . . .
Rail Europe (www.raileurope.co.uk; 08448 484 064) can arrange train tickets from London to Montélimar and back from Orange. In Montélimar, we recommend Hôtel Kyriad (www.kyriad.com); in Bédoin, we recommend Hôtel des Pins (hotel-des-pins.fr). To book an organized ride or for information on hiring bikes, contact Saddle Skedaddle (www.skedaddle.co.uk).

| **Why** | To conquer a lung-bursting climbing goal |
| **Where** | Argentina | **Duration** | Five days + |

Once in a Lifetime

At 6,962 metres, Aconcagua is the highest peak in the world outside the Himalayas. The summit of the Argentinean giant is covered in snow all year round and temperatures regularly drop below –20° C. It's so high that you can clearly see the curvature of the earth from the top, where the air pressure is only 40 per cent of that at sea level. And yet, amazingly, this is a mountain anyone can climb.

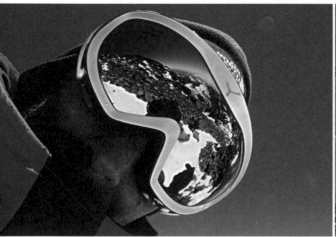

Well, almost anyone. Whereas most mountaineering requires years of apprenticeship – starting on small hills, learning rope work and rock-climbing techniques, graduating from the Highlands to the Alps, and so on – Aconcagua is an anomaly. Despite its fearsome size, it is what is known as a 'trekking peak': you can walk to the top without ropes, and in good weather you don't even need crampons.

The result is that it's an amazing challenge for anyone who is fit and wants a taste of high-altitude mountaineering, but doesn't have years to devote themselves to studying the sport. Purists may scoff, but for others it's the chance of having an incredible climbing adventure, summiting a major mountain on the other side of the world, while taking only three weeks off work.

The usual season is late December to February, the southern-hemisphere summer. Most people fly into Mendoza, in the heart of the Argentinean wine lands, meet up with their guide and drive the 70 miles to Penitentes, a village close to the foot of the mountain. Then the long trek begins.

Aconcagua may not be a technically difficult mountain, but that doesn't mean it's easy or even safe. Deaths are not unknown, sometimes from acute altitude sickness or because of accidents involving climbers who deliberately seek out the more challenging routes up. The 'normal' route, by contrast, should pose few difficulties, snaking up from the south in the valley beside the Rio Horcones, passing to the west of the mountain's huge bulk, then circling round to approach the summit from the north.

Acclimatization is crucial to success. The norm is to stop at five camps on the way to the summit, but spend at least fifteen days doing so, having rest days, or climbing smaller peaks along the way, in order to get used to the thin air.

Altitude sickness can start to affect humans at relatively modest heights, but begins to get more serious above 2,400 metres. The low air pressure means the body doesn't get the oxygen it needs, and so sufferers can feel nauseous, have headaches and be unable to think clearly. There's no way of telling when or who it will strike. Fitness makes no difference, and those who've suffered no ill-effects on previous climbs can suddenly succumb. In more extreme cases, fluid can build up in the lungs or brain and rapidly lead to death.

In practice, on Aconcagua good acclimatization usually means the difference is less between life and death, and more between struggling step by step up the mountain with a terrible cough and splitting headache, and breezing up it. If you do start to suffer altitude sickness, the solution is simple – stop and rest, or descend. The biggest danger is of people becoming so obsessed with reaching the summit that they ignore the warning signs and drive themselves on until a minor problem grows into a life-threatening condition.

But with proper acclimatization, and attention to the weather, chances of success are good. The mountain has been climbed by people aged from ten to eighty-seven, but that doesn't dull the sense of achievement of those getting to the top. As they look down over the Chilean deserts to the Pacific, and across the peaks and glaciers of the Andes, most summiteers will realize that this is the highest point of their lives.

On tough adventures, be careful not to fall out with your team mates.

Getting close to the earth is what it's all about.

Now do it . . .
One of the UK's leading adventure travel tour operators, KE Adventure Travel, offers a 21-day climb on Aconcagua. For more information visit www.keadventure.com

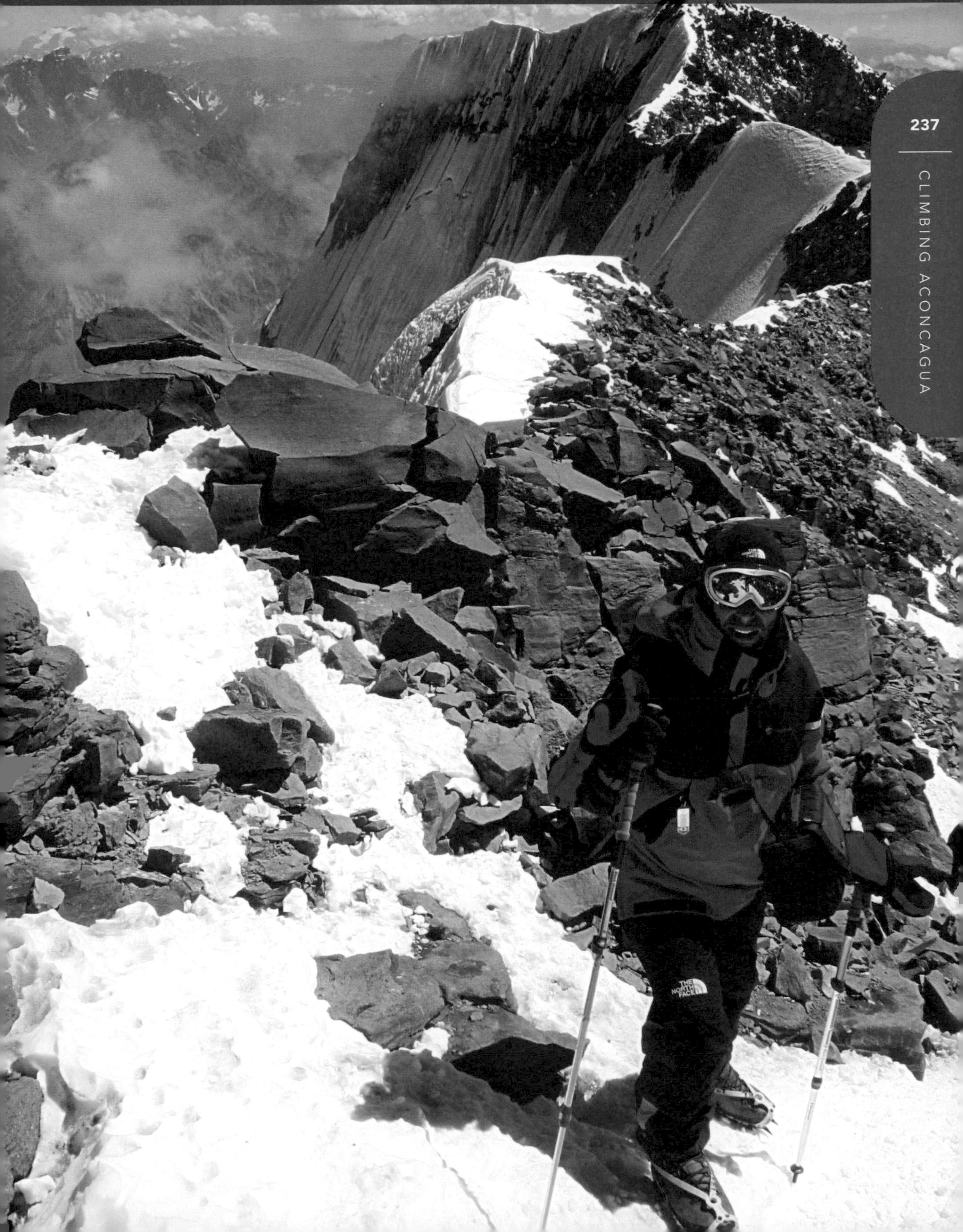

73

Kite-surfing in the Sahara

Why	For an opportunity to ride the waves in a desert
Where	Western Sahara	**Duration**	One day

TWO WEEKS OFF WORK

The Western Sahara is an inhospitable place. A disputed territory, with no internationally recognized ruling government, it has for years been off-limits to all but the most adventurous travellers. Even today, the Foreign Office warns those who do go that there is a high risk from terrorism and unexploded mines.

There's not a great deal to see either. Its 100,000 square miles are almost entirely desert and the population numbers only 500,000. The few towns feel lonely and remote, windswept and sandblasted. The Spanish government, who ruled it as a colony for much of the nineteenth century, decided that one town here, Dakhla, was the perfect place to set up a jail where political prisoners could be sent to be forgotten by the rest of the world.

Spain withdrew in 1975, and a long guerrilla war ensued. Troops from Morocco and Mauritania

Harnessing the power of the wind is one of the biggest adrenaline rushes.

Now do it . . .
To experience kite-surfing for yourself, visit Waveriders (www.waveriders.co.uk) for your own tailor-made kite- or wind-surfing adventure.

both fought for control of the land against the Polisario Front, representing the local Sahrawi people who want independence. The dispute remains unresolved, but a UN-brokered ceasefire has held since the early 1990s.

Now, though, a new group of people are arriving in Dakhla, not soldiers or prisoners of war, but thrill-seekers who've come of their own volition. While it may not have much else going for it, this scrappy little town on the edge of the Sahara is the best place in the world to learn to kite-surf. It doesn't have smart hotels, beach bars or nightclubs, but Dakhla does have a 16-mile-long saltwater lagoon, connected to the Atlantic at one end and surrounded on all sides by dunes. The water is flat, the temperatures warm all year round, and, most importantly of all, there is a constant wind.

Wind is the big problem with kite-surfing. You need a decent wind to power the kites, but the gusts and changes of wind direction you find in many parts of the world can be a nightmare for beginners. Here, the wind is strong and steady, allowing beginners to quickly master flying the kite, then combine this with getting up on the board. Progress at Dakhla is usually far more rapid than elsewhere, and in a couple of days complete beginners can be ripping across the water.

The tricky thing about kite-surfing is that you're doing two things at once, controlling the kite with your arms while riding the waves with your legs. At first it can be frustrating, but when it finally clicks, most people are hooked for life. You have the speed of windsurfing, but also the feel of surfing on the waves, and you can use the kite to perform amazing stunts, launching yourself off a crest and flying up into the air. Few sports come close for adrenalin.

At Dakhla, a kite-surfers' camp has grown up beside the lagoon, a few miles outside the town.

Accommodation is mainly quite basic: there's a campsite and bungalows for rent. In the constant wind, the sand and salt get everywhere – even the sheets on the beds have a granular feel. The water is drawn from a well and filtered through a sulphurous layer in the rocks, so turn on the tap in your basin and a rotten-egg smell fills the room. Persevere – you do get used to it.

There's little to do at night; most people just chill out with a beer, watching the amazingly starry sky. But what the camp lacks in creature comforts, it makes up for with a good friendly vibe and excellent instructors, and you can hire all the equipment you need there. Plus there's one more major advantage. At other kite-surfing meccas – Tarifa in Spain, Essaouira in Morocco, Poole Harbour in England – the sea can be crowded with kites, making surfing a constant struggle to dodge others' lines. Here, there are only ever a handful of people, spread out on the vast lagoon, their luminous kites darting around on the sparkling water like a mirage in the desert.

Make sure you're fit enough to keep yourself out of danger.

74

Wolf-watching in Sweden

Why	To explore wild animals among beautiful scenery
Where	Sweden	**Duration**	Two days

LONG WEEKEND

If you want to see Swedish wolves in the wild, you'd better bring some warm socks. The best time to see the animals is in the middle of winter and in the hours just before dawn – so you will be spending a lot of time sitting, waiting and watching by moonlight in dark, cold, snowy forests.

There is something appropriate about searching for wolves in the eerie hours just before dawn. After all, the wolf seems to belong to the twilight world of nightmares and nursery rhymes, of myth and legend. From 'The Three Little Pigs' and 'Little Red Riding Hood' to the countless werewolf movies, we are so used to thinking of them as demonic embodiments of evil that it feels rather odd to be reminded that they are actually just animals, and even weirder to learn that you can still see them, in the wild, in modern Europe.

There are significant populations in eastern Europe, but it's also possible to see them in Scandinavia, where they were reintroduced in the 1970s after having been hunted to the brink of extinction. Today around two hundred wolves roam free in Sweden, and one of the best places to see them is Bergslagen, a forest two hours' north of Stockholm near the small town of Skinnskatteberg.

It isn't an easy task. Notoriously shy, they are easier to spot between January and March when the ground is covered in snow – their paw marks are then visible, making tracking much simpler.

You can stay at one of several small guesthouses in the area, heading out with a guide long before dawn each morning to search for the wolves. This area is dotted with lakes, frozen in winter, and often the best chance of seeing the wolves is to hide near the banks of a lake and wait for a wolf to break out of the thick forest and run across it.

Any adventure involving wildlife is extremely rewarding.

After a few hours of waiting and watching, you can return to a hearty breakfast at the guesthouse, then spend the day visiting the Grimsö Wildlife Research Station, where conservationists monitor the local packs of wolf and lynx. The researchers will talk about the animals' behaviour and explain

A strange team mate!

about the problems of reintroducing the wolf into the wild in Sweden. Then, after dinner, you head out again into the forest, to listen for the howls and look for paw prints.

After a weekend of the same routine, you might imagine you'd be getting sick of the early starts and late nights, but the scenery is so beautiful that taking some time to sit still and admire it is a wonderfully relaxing experience in itself. And if you are lucky enough to come face to face with a wolf as it saunters across a frozen lake in the moonlight, it will be an encounter you'll never forget.

RECEPTION

Now do it . . .

This trip is operated by Wild Sweden (www.wildsweden.com) and can be booked online through adventure travel specialists Tour Dust (www.tourdust.com). Go to Visit Sweden (www.visitsweden.com) for all you need to know about Sweden.

Competing in the Dakar Rally

Why	To tackle the world's most dangerous motor event
Where	Europe and Africa	**Duration**	Two weeks

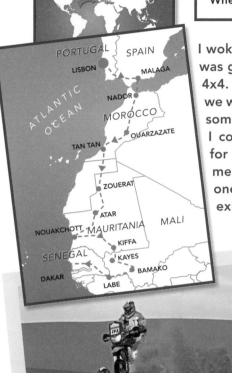

I woke with a start and, for a moment, couldn't work out what was going on. It was night-time and I was in the back seat of a 4x4. The headlights were on and the engine was running, but we weren't moving. The car was sitting motionless on the sand, somewhere in the Sahara, and in the light of the headlamps I could see nothing but dunes. We were the support crew for a three-man bike team which we had entered. Around me in the car were three others, all in a deep sleep. One by one, including the driver, we'd simply succumbed to sheer exhaustion and the car had ground to a halt.

Exploring the outer reaches of fatigue is what the Dakar is all about. 'The aim is to push to the absolute limits of endurance, then push some more,' said Thierry Sabine, the founder of what is the most dangerous and gruelling adventure in this book. In fact, it is one of the most difficult, crazy, life-threatening challenges you can take on anywhere in the world. It's not a question of if you'll get hurt, but when, and how badly.

The event began on Boxing Day 1978, when 170 competitors set off from the Place du Trocadéro in Paris. It was the brainchild of French biker Sabine, who had got lost in the Libyan desert during another rally a few years earlier. Enchanted by the scenery and the feeling of riding over the sand dunes, he decided to create a new annual event, starting in the French capital and ending, 6,250 miles and two weeks later, in the capital of Senegal, Dakar.

It was a big success, and it grew and grew, and today between four hundred and five hundred competitors set off each year, eager to test themselves against what is becoming recognized as motorsport's biggest challenge. The route has changed frequently over the years – since 2009 it has been run in South America, following terrorist threats in North Africa – but the format remains the same. Competitors must complete timed daily stages of up to 600 miles, much of it off-road, over sand, gravel and rocks.

This is the most dangerous race in the world.

Staying on schedule? Ha ha.

One of the great things about the race is that, unlike most other forms of motorsport, the event has always seen a mix of professionals and amateurs. Somehow that helps generate a sense of real adventure and camaraderie. The professional teams backed by the big car manufacturers have huge back-up crews and star drivers – previous entrants have included Formula One drivers and World Rally champions such as Colin McRae and Carlos Sainz. But alongside them are complete amateurs – anyone who can raise the €14,400 entry fee can take part, and there's no need to prove your experience or qualifications. Some of these so-called 'privateers' have support teams, while others do it solo, relying on the race organizers to transport their trunk of spares and supplies between each night's stop.

In a typical year there might be 200 motorbikes, 200 cars and about 75 huge trucks, but it's hardest and most dangerous for the bikers – they are the real gladiators of the Dakar. They ride flat out over terrain it would be hard to walk over. I really don't know how they do it.

We'd put together a team of three bikers – Charley Boorman, Matt Hall and Simon Pavey – and were filming our efforts for the series *Race to Dakar*. I was driving the support vehicle, together with a cameraman and two mechanics. The year we took part, in 2006, the

rally began in Lisbon. Seeing our three riders roll over the start line was the realization of a dream for all of us. None of us could quite believe we were taking part in this legendary event, alongside all the professional teams and star riders. After months of frantic organization, we were elated to be on the road.

The elation didn't last long. We were in trouble before we even left Spain – Charley's bike was having mechanical problems and our 4x4 kept breaking down. The days were chaos – constant, rapid-fire problem solving. At one point our rear wishbone cracked in the middle of the Sahara and we were being left behind by the rally. With assistance from Lucy, my production manager, in London, I had an epic overnight journey in the back of a truck to source the wishbone which we needed to carry on.

The rally doesn't wait – you have to keep up with the ever-ticking clock. There are set start times every morning and if you don't meet them, you're disqualified. You might have had mechanical problems and have finished the previous day's stage at 4 a.m., but your 7 a.m.

Anyone can enter the Dakar Rally, but be prepared.

start time can't be postponed. That means you have three hours to eat, prepare your bike and, if there's any time left, grab a few minutes' sleep.

After the panics of each day's stage, and the hours of driving through the heat and the dust, arriving at the night's bivouac could hardly be more welcome. The race's organizational crew fly between each bivouac in big Hercules transport planes, carrying the supplies for the privateers, plus all the food, medical gear, press tent and so on. Each night they set up a vast U-shaped tent, with the floor at each end covered in Bedouin rugs and a restaurant area at the centre.

This being a French-run event, there is no skimping on the food. In fact, every night there is a five-course meal, with fresh fruit, cheese, and even wine if you want it. After the meal you find a spot on the rugs, lay out your sleeping bag and get some sleep. Soon we were in a routine: the stress of the day, then the reward of the meal, and the camaraderie of the bivouac.

On day five, Charley fell while driving down a sand dune in Morocco, breaking one thumb and spraining the other. He managed to keep going, in ever-worsening pain, for another 250 miles to the bivouac, but his race was over.

Matt made it to day ten, then collapsed with exhaustion in the desert. He'd fallen thirty or forty times already that day and just couldn't lift his bike up out of the sand one more time. He was picked up by an ambulance, but when it came across another rider in a life-threatening condition, Matt had to give up his space. He spent the night sleeping in the dunes, then eventually was picked up by the support team. For sixteen hours he bounced along in a sweltering box on the back of a lorry, then had to take a series of taxis for another twenty hours to catch up with the rest of us.

Others had it far worse. Driving from Kiffa in Mauritania to Bamako in Mali, the tenth and eleventh of the fifteen stages, we passed what seemed like a constant stream of abandoned vehicles

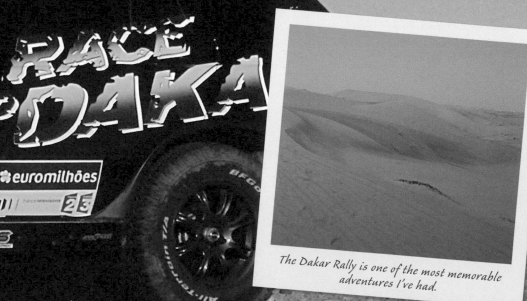

The Dakar Rally is one of the most memorable adventures I've had.

Charley and I felt like winners.

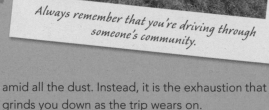

Always remember that you're driving through someone's community.

by the roadside. That year, only 93 of the 240 motorbikes that started made it to the end, along with 66 of the 188 cars and 35 of the 80 trucks. One competitor, Andy Caldecott, died in a crash, and two spectators were killed.

Fatalities are not uncommon. On average there are nearly two deaths per year and in 1986 this included Sabine, the father of the event, who died in a helicopter crash. It's a shocking statistic, and everyone who takes part must do so with their eyes open, knowing that the race has its dark side.

And yet for many who do take part, the race becomes an obsession. Most people who start fail to finish, but a huge proportion of them come back year after year, desperate to get to Dakar and claim their finishers' medal.

The biggest danger isn't the sandstorms, the clumps of camel grass that can throw you from your bike, the huge dunes or the chance of being hit by a thundering truck that hasn't seen you amid all the dust. Instead, it is the exhaustion that grinds you down as the trip wears on.

By the time we reached Dakar, we had nothing left to give. Charley and Matt were out, but we still had one rider, Simon, in the rally. And when we saw him racing across the sand, then crossing the finish line, it felt like a triumph. Against all the odds, we'd managed to get a rider to the end of the toughest off-road race of them all. He may have only come eighty-sixth out of the ninety-three finishers, but we celebrated as if we'd won the bloody thing.

Now do it . . .

Amaury Sport Organisation (www.aso.fr) can organize most of the major sport competitions of the world, including the Dakar Challenge, for you.

Wilderness swimming in Iceland

76

LONG WEEKEND

Why	For a unique volcanic landscape seen from the water
Where	Iceland	**Duration**	Two days

With its icecaps and volcanic lava fields, Iceland's barren interior is hardly the most obvious destination for a swimming holiday. But spend a weekend here and, as well as travelling through jaw-dropping scenery, you can try out two unique swimming experiences.

After spending a night in Reykjavik, Iceland's small but buzzing capital, start by driving for an hour or so north-east to Þingvellir national park. Þingvellir is famous as the original site of Iceland's parliament, arguably the world's first. Clan chiefs met here from 930 AD until 1789, with the speaker standing on a rocky outcrop and his audience gathered on the grass below. It's worthwhile climbing up to the speaker's rock and looking out over the vast empty plain beneath you, but then it's time to get swimming.

Running through the area is the Silfra fissure. From the surface, it doesn't look much – like a river with rocky banks, 5 or 6 metres wide. But this is the spot where the North American and Eurasian tectonic plates meet. For most of its distance, the meeting point between these plates, the so-called Mid Atlantic Ridge, runs along the sea floor, but it also passes right through Iceland – the reason the country has so much volcanic activity. The Silfra fissure has been created by the plates pulling apart in opposite directions, leaving a trench up

to 40 metres deep and anywhere from 2 to over 100 metres wide, which is filled with water. With a few flipper-strokes, swimmers in the trench can go between Europe and North America (from a geological perspective at least!).

Be prepared for the cold – the water stays between 2°C and 4°C all year round. You'll need a full drysuit to snorkel or scuba-dive here (numerous tour operators in Reykjavik or abroad will provide them, along with a guide).

It's only when you jump in that you really appreciate this place – the water is so crystal clear that you feel as if you're weightless, floating in air. Partly the clarity is because this is a mix of glacial meltwater and rain that has been filtered through miles of volcanic rocks then risen here as a spring. Partly it's because it's simply too cold for most flora or fauna to survive.

You probably won't see any fish, you certainly won't see any coral, but it will be one of the most beautiful and fascinating swims of your life. The water is so pure you can take off your snorkel and drink it, and so clear you can see for more than 100 metres, letting you marvel at the rock formations and the way the shafts of sunlight sparkle down through the water. It's like hovering over the surface of an alien planet.

Once you're out, and warmed up with a cup of hot chocolate, you hop into a 4x4 for the 140-mile drive past the huge waterfall of Gulfoss, then on over rough tracks through lava fields and into the remote, mountainous heart of the country, to the refuge at Landmannalaugar, where you spend the night. It will be dark by the time you get there, so there's little to do but get inside, have dinner and get an early night – you'll need it.

Long before sunrise the next morning, you must force yourself to leave the warmth of your bed and go back outside into the cold. After a short walk, and though the temperature might be as low as –10°C, it's time to get undressed for another swim.

Landmannalaugar means 'the people's pools' – hidden in this cold, desolate mountain valley is a series of steaming natural hot springs. As the wind howls around, you can strip off, dive in and sit there, completely toasty and warm while you wait for the sunrise. There's something wonderfully bizarre about lounging in bath-temperature water in the middle of the dark Icelandic wilderness, but things are about to get even more spectacular. As dawn slowly breaks, the colours of the volcanic rocks surrounding the pools gradually reveal themselves – black, purple, yellow, blue, green, brown and pink, the result of the different minerals they contain. The longer you lie in the water, and the stronger the sun's rays, the more vivid the colours become, until it's as if you are part of a surrealist painting.

One weekend, two amazing swims.

Now do it . . .

Go into the wild with Arctic Adventures (www.adventures. is) on a super jeep safari. Snorkelling at Þingvellir and swimming at Landmannlaugar can be combined with a weekend of glacier hiking, ice climbing on Sólheimajökull Glacier and caving in the lava tubes. While in Reykjavik, we recommend you stay at comfortable Reykjavik Backpackers (www.reykjavikbackpackers.com). Iceland Air (www.icelandair.com) can fly you to Iceland from Europe or the US.

77

Camping at the Gate of Hell

Why	To marvel at an unusual man-made accident
Where	Turkmenistan	**Duration**	One night

In 1971 Derweze was an unremarkable village in Turkmenistan's Karakum desert, about 160 miles, or a four-hour drive, north of the capital Ashgabat. The desert surrounding the village is rich in natural gas, and that year geologists from the state energy company were drilling for gas when they accidentally bored into a vast underground gas-filled cavern.

The cavern collapsed, sending the drilling rig tumbling down into a huge new crater, 75 metres wide. Aware that the gas pouring out of the crater was poisonous, the geologists decided to set it on fire, so it would flare off. They expected it to burn out after six days. Forty years later, it's still burning.

At night the flaming crater, which quickly became known locally as the Gate of Hell, can be seen from 25 miles away, and the hiss of the gas heard from several hundred yards. It's an incredible sight, a yawning opening in the flat desert floor with a large flame right at the bottom and hundreds of smaller flames licking the rocky ground on the crater's sloping sides. It has been called the world's most beautiful ecological disaster.

Turkmenistan is still well off the tourist trail and there's little infrastructure at Derweze. The 350 residents are mainly members of the semi-nomadic Teke tribe, who live in houses but set up traditional yurts in front of them to give more space and to preserve their traditions.

Of course you could bring your own tent and camp on the warm sands close to the crater, but it's also possible to stay in one of the yurts with the Teke and sample the local cuisine (typically lamb or mutton, rice, carrots and dumplings) and the famous Turkmen drink, chal, made from fermented camel's milk.

If you are planning to make a trip to the Gate of Hell, don't leave it too long – the Turkmen government has suggested the crater be closed so it doesn't interfere with further natural gas exploration in the area.

Sometimes it's hard to take on board everything you see.

Now do it . . .

For more on this 'hellish' adventure, contact Advantour (www.advantour.com), who specialize in tours in Central Asia and Russia.

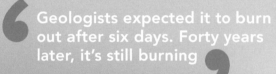

'Geologists expected it to burn out after six days. Forty years later, it's still burning'

78

Northern lights and the Sami

| Why | To witness the magical lights while getting back to basics |
| **Where** | Lapland | **Duration** | Two days + |

Understanding the scientific explanation for the northern lights is fiendishly complicated. It involves solar wind, photons, ionized nitrogen atoms and magnetic field lines. Appreciating the result is rather more straightforward. 'It was the most beautiful thing I had ever seen,' said the travel writer Bill Bryson.

The lights can be capricious, sometimes putting on lavish displays of multi-coloured swirling luminescence night after night, at other times refusing to show themselves at all. For the best chance to see them, you need to be between the latitudes of 65 and 72 degrees either north or south, and to have a cloudless sky.

You could do what Bryson did and go to a hotel in a northern Norwegian town and kick your heels until the lights choose to play ball. But for those with less time, it's far better to combine your hunt for the lights with an adventure through the Arctic, guided by members of the region's indigenous Sami tribe.

The Sami's homeland, which they call Sampi, is an area of forest and tundra that straddles Sweden, Norway, Russia and Finland. Traditionally the tribe are nomadic reindeer herders, fishermen and hunters, and though today many have settled in towns and taken jobs in the urban economy, others continue to live as nomads. Some combine the two worlds, owning flats with all mod cons in town, but still heading out to herd reindeer and to camp in the wilderness for weeks at a time.

There's something very cosy about cabins in the snow.

Start by flying to Kiruna, 90 miles north of the Arctic Circle in Swedish Lapland. From here it's about 10 miles to the village of Jukkasjärvi, the location of the famous Ice Hotel which is built every winter entirely from ice, and a good starting point for expeditions heading north. You can take day trips on horseback through the forest, seeking out elk as well as the northern lights, or rent snowmobiles. You can also enjoy a week-long trip with a Sami guide, travelling on wooden sleds pulled by reindeer and sleeping at night in Sami Lavvu, traditional teepees. Days are spent travelling through the forests of birch, pine and willow, stopping to fish through holes cut into frozen lakes.

Could you live here?

The peace of Lapland is worth all the effort.

Getting around the indigenous way...

It's great to listen to other people's views on the world.

... and the fast way.

Travelling and living with the Sami, you get an insight into their distinct culture that has grown over the last 11,000 years. They have their own language and beliefs, including many about the northern lights. Traditionally they believed the lights were linked to departed souls and that they possessed great powers. Mocking the lights, or waving at them, was thought to be dangerous, but when the lights are dancing, the Sami believe it is a good time to resolve disputes and restore harmony.

Whether caused by departed souls or solar wind, if you're lucky enough to see them, it's a sight you won't forget.

Far from the madding crowd.

Now do it . . .

For eco-adventures with the Sami and reindeer sleigh experiences, visit www.nutti.se. We recommend you stay at the Reindeer Lodge or Ice Hotel (www.icehotel. com), where they can organize incredible adventures in Lapland's big outdoor playground. Visit Ofelas (www.ofelas.se) to book your horse and northern lights adventures.

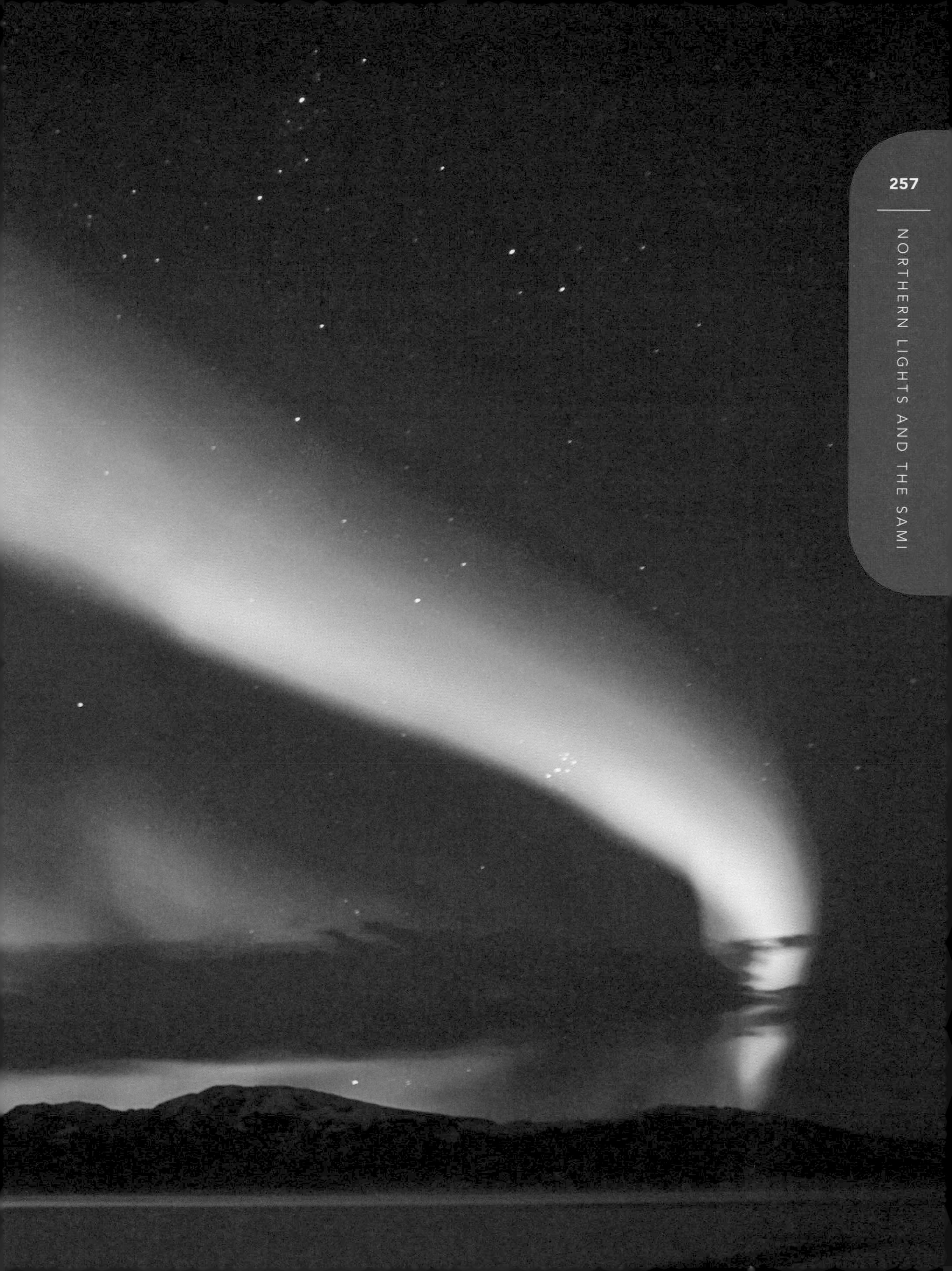

79

The Darien Gap

Why	To confront one of the most dangerous crossings
Where	Panama and Colombia	**Duration**	Two months +

Once in a Lifetime

Running from Prudhoe Bay, Alaska, to Ushuaia at the southernmost point of Argentina, the Pan-American Highway is an amazing engineering achievement – 29,800 miles of road stretching the length of the Americas. Yet there's a problem: the greatest road in the world has a gap in the middle, a 100-mile section of dense rainforest and swamp, where Indian tribes and paramilitary forces roam, and no road has ever been built.

This is the Darien Gap. Not just a barrier to the continuation of the Pan-American Highway, it sits between Colombia and Panama, effectively cutting off South and Central America. Travellers who want to complete a journey between the two continents have to fly over the gap or take a boat around it, but very few adventurers do go through it.

The first was the Trans-Darien expedition of 1959, in which a Land Rover and a Jeep spent 136 days travelling from Chepo in Panama to Quibdó in Colombia. Their average speed was just 201 metres per hour.

That expedition, like several more since, used boats to travel some of the distance, but the first entirely land-based crossing was by the British cyclist Ian Hibbell as part of a ride from Cape Horn to Alaska. Honours for the first all-land car crossing went to American couple Loren Upton and Patty Mercier in the mid-1980s. They took 741 days. Upton went back a few years later to claim the first land-only motorbike crossing, this time managing it in just 49 days.

Normally, once the pioneers have proved an adventure is possible, more and more people come to try it, and eventually it becomes easier and more commercial until the original sense of adventure has almost disappeared: not so with the Darien Gap.

During the 1990s, a small number of travellers made the crossing, usually either on foot or by motorbike, often paying the local Kuna Indians to help them travel sections in dugout canoes. But since then the Gap has become increasingly dangerous – even Upton currently advises against attempting it.

In 1993 three missionaries were kidnapped and killed. In 2000 the orchid hunter Tom Hart Dyke was captured in Darien by guerrillas fighting the Colombian government, and was held for nine months before being released. Three years later, American journalist Robert Pelton was ambushed and held captive for ten days by another Colombian rebel group.

At least three guerrilla groups are thought to be active in the area, as well as bandits who simply want to steal from travellers. Oh yes, and it goes without saying that there are numerous deadly snakes and spiders, not to mention crocodiles.

It is possible that the political violence in Colombia will die down and the Darien will become safer once more. This is certainly a great adventure, but it isn't one to be undertaken lightly.

Now do it . . .
Out Back Of Beyond (www.outbackofbeyond.com) is a
great website set up by people who have completed the
treacherous journey – a great source of information for
your own adventure.

80

Surfing the Galapagos

Why	To form a connection with the birthplace of evolution
Where	Galapagos Islands	**Duration**	Two days +

When Charles Darwin came to the Galapagos islands in 1835, he rode on the back of the giant tortoises. Today, a handful of adventurers come to the islands, not to ride the animals, but the waves.

Scattered close to the equator, 600 miles off the coast of Ecuador, the Galapagos get swells from both the north and south Pacific, creating world-class surfing conditions. Since almost all the visitors to the islands are there to see the famous animals, if you come to surf you'll probably have the waves to yourselves.

There are waves all year round, but the best conditions are usually between January and May. Of the eighteen islands, the best for surfing is San Cristobal, where the waves usually reach 5 feet, and can reach up to 10 feet.

As well as the lack of fellow surfers, one of the key attractions is the consistency of the waves, helped by the volcanic rock ridges on the seabed. Of course there can be calm days, but you can use these to explore the islands. Around 97 per cent of the islands' land mass is national park, and access is heavily restricted. The only real way to get around is by boat, but rather than join one of the large cruise ships it's possible to join a trip on a small sailing boat, or even sea kayak around the coastline.

The volcanic Galapagos aren't immediately attractive. 'Nothing could be less inviting than the first appearance,' wrote Darwin. 'A broken field of black basaltic lava is everywhere covered by a stunted brushwood, which shows little sign of life.'

Of course, he soon discovered he was wrong about the life. Here you can see flightless cormorants, sea lions, flamingos, penguins, iguanas, seals, giant tortoises (which, on average, live to 150 years old), frigate birds, albatrosses, gulls, boobies, pelicans – the list goes on and on. Better still, because of their isolation and the lack of natural predators, many of the animals are incredibly tame. The sea lions lounging on the beach will stay there and allow you to walk right up to them. And, if it weren't strictly forbidden these days, you could even ride on the back of the giant tortoises.

And when you've spent enough time playing Dr Dolittle, you can get back into the water and enjoy some of the best, and least busy, waves on the planet.

Now do it . . .
Ecuador Adventure (www.opuntiagalapagoshotels.com) can arrange your unique surfing adventure.

Why	To achieve what many before have tried and failed
Where	Arctic Circle	**Duration**	Two months +

Once in a Lifetime

For British explorers of the nineteenth century, finding the Northwest Passage was an obsession. A long-dreamed-of sea route around the north of Canada, its discovery could have revolutionized trade between Europe and Asia by creating a shortcut between the Atlantic and the Pacific. By using the Northwest Passage, ships would no longer need to sail all the way round the bottom of South America, a route that was long, passed through dangerous waters and ran the gauntlet of attack from rival nations.

In fact, the British had been trying to locate the passage since as early as 1497, when Henry VII sent the explorer John Cabot to search for a direct route to Asia. In 1775 the British Admiralty offered the considerable sum of £20,000 to anyone who could discover it, and Captain James Cook set off on an unsuccessful attempt the following year. The search reached fever pitch in the mid-nineteenth century when Sir John Franklin launched several expeditions. His third, a two-ship expedition that was lavishly equipped with all the latest technological advances, departed in 1845 but never returned. More than forty expeditions were sent to find him, but the ships were never found and all 129 crew were presumed dead. Worse still, one of the search parties brought back stories

If you get through the passage you will be one of an élite few

from the local Inuit that they had witnessed Franklin's starving crew turning to cannibalism in order to survive.

The problem was the ice that blocked the sea every winter, meaning that the expeditions typically lasted for several years, the boats frozen solid in the ice until spring. Even in summer the ships would have to pick their way carefully through channels in the ice or around icebergs.

In the end, a Norwegian beat the British to it. In 1906 Roald Amundsen completed the journey, taking three years to do so. (If that wasn't humiliation enough, five years later Amundsen beat Scott to the South Pole, too.)

Despite the anticipation, the great breakthrough didn't revolutionize world trade as had once been hoped. Thanks to the ice, the passage took too long and was too dangerous to be commercially viable, so in the last century, only around 150 boats repeated the feat.

Now though, things are changing. Global warming has dramatically reduced the amount of ice in the Arctic sea during summer, and in 2007, satellite imagery showed that the Northwest Passage was completely clear of ice for the first time since records began. That year Sébastien Roubinet, a French sailor, completed the passage in a lightweight catamaran, becoming the first to do so in a single season in a boat with no engine. Subsequent summers have seen similarly small amounts of ice, allowing more and ever smaller boats to attempt the route. What was once a challenge for big military expedition vessels and icebreakers is now being attempted by ordinary sailing boats and recreational sailors looking for adventure. In August 2010, Bear Grylls and a crew of five became the first to complete the crossing in an 11-metre rigid inflatable boat (or RIB), open to the elements except for a small cover over the driver's seat.

There may now be little ice, but the trip remains dangerous. Boats must be constantly on the lookout for icebergs lurking just below the surface of the water, the temperature can drop rapidly, and if camping on shore at night, there is the risk of attack by bears.

How can you set about doing it yourself? If you don't have your own boat, the ideal option is to search the web for other sailors looking for crew – there are several such trips each summer. The alternatives are to pay for a place on a commercial cruise (there are now several planned per summer and they tend to be in large ships with hulls reinforced against the ice) or to pay to join a small sailing boat being operated as a commercial venture.

With less ice the route may eventually become a common commercial shipping lane, but disputes over which country has territorial rights to the water may delay this. For the next few years at least, it looks like crossing the Northwest Passage will be the domain of the amateur adventurer.

Now do it . . .
To experience this unique area, Sim Expeditions (www.simexpeditions.com) offer a cruise through the Northwest Passage.

| Why | To indulge in Africa with just your bike and the road |
| Where | Egypt to South Africa | **Duration** | Five months |

Once in a Lifetime

The Tour de France may be the world's most celebrated bike race, but when it comes to distance, it's really something of a minnow. Le Tour covers around 2,200 miles in a circle around France. The Tour d'Afrique, by contrast, covers at least 7,500 miles, starting in Cairo and finishing in Cape Town – and it's open to absolutely everyone.

Admittedly the pace is rather slower than the pros in France – it takes about four months, including twenty rest days – but the Tour d'Afrique is a major challenge of endurance, both mental and physical. The event takes place every year, starting in mid-January. The route can vary slightly, but usually runs from Egypt to Sudan, Ethiopia, Kenya, Tanzania, Malawi, Zambia, Botswana, Namibia, then South Africa.

Like the Tour de France, it is divided into daily stages of set distances, ranging from 50 to 110 miles. First run in 2003, around fifty people complete the journey each year. Most are amateur adventurers rather than competitive cyclists, and the Tour has been completed by riders aged from eighteen to seventy-one, not to mention a blind rider and a

double amputee. Riders must bring their bikes, and camping equipment, but food is provided by the organizers and the equipment is transported by truck between each night's rest stop.

Such a long race might sound monotonous, but the reality is that there is great variety – from the pyramids and ancient temples of Egypt, to the flat Sudanese desert, the green and lush Simien mountains of Ethiopia, Kilimanjaro, Lake Malawi, Victoria Falls, and so on. In Sudan you might be dodging camel trains on the road, in Botswana you learn that elephants have right of way. The frequent rest days also allow the riders to meet local people and explore the sights, rather than simply focusing on the riding.

If bikes break down, or riders succumb to

illness or exhaustion, they can ride in one of the support trucks for that day. Those who never have to do so are considered members of the EFI club, standing for 'every fabulous inch' (though some say the 'f' stands for something else . . .). By Cape Town, the EFI club has usually dwindled to ten riders or even fewer.

One other tradition that has grown up is the 'naked mile' – somewhere in the remotest and emptiest part of Namibia, cyclists strip off their Lycra for a celebratory streak. You certainly don't get that on the Tour de France.

Always take time to stop and look around you.

Now do it . . .
To embark on your own cross-continent cycling adventure, contact Tour d'Afrique (www.tourdafrique.com).

Why	To uncover the hidden relics of Mayan history
Where	Belize	**Duration**	One day

We'd been deep underground for more than an hour when the beam of my head-torch flashed across something white. I stopped and turned back to look closer, then quickly wished I hadn't. There, lit up by my torchlight, was a human skull, resting on the ground and looking straight back at me.

Casting my light left and right, I could see we had entered a huge subterranean chamber, 350 metres long, 50 metres wide and perhaps 25 metres high. Scattered on the floor were the broken remains of several huge ceramic urns, and bones, lots of bones. Our guide explained that the remains of fourteen people have been discovered here, most of them only teenagers, offered as sacrifices by the Mayans more than a thousand years ago.

The Mayan civilization extended through much of what is now southern Mexico, Guatemala and Belize, as well as northern El Salvador and western Honduras, and throughout the region are caves that were once used for ceremonial purposes. The Mayans believed they were entrances to the underworld, Xibalba (which literally means 'place

of fright'), home of the 'death gods'. Priests and members of the ruling families would descend into the caves to take hallucinogens and bleed themselves with obsidian knives, in order to try to speak to the gods. They would make offerings too – of grain and other food (hence the urns in the cave), and also humans. One theory is that a drought in the ninth century left the Mayans desperately pleading with the gods for a change of fortune. They offered ever-greater sacrifices, until they were placing still-beating hearts on the underground altars.

As our guide explained all this, you could feel the tension rising in our group, a strange mix of claustrophobia and sympathy for the victims whose remains lay scattered around us. It's hard to

feel any connection with ancient skeletons when you see them in museum cases, but here there were no 'do not touch' signs, roped-off areas or anything else to distance you. More than that – here we were seeing the victims' bones in the place they were actually killed.

We were in a cave called Actun Tunichil Muknal, in the Cayo district of western Belize. We'd started that morning from the town of San Ignacio and driven for 45 minutes into the jungle. Next came an hour's walk through pristine rainforest, crossing three streams along the way, before we arrived at the cave mouth. A narrow opening in a rocky cliff wall, it is surrounded by creepers, ferns and moss and filled with a pool of turquoise water. It looks idyllic – and gives no hint of what lies inside . . .

To enter the cave, you have to swim through the pool, wearing trainers to avoid cutting your feet on the rough rocks. Helmets and head-torches are essential and you have to go with a government-licensed guide. To prevent looting, only these guides are allowed to take people in.

If you are at all claustrophobic, forget it. As you press deeper into the cave, the walls narrow until you are forced to turn your body side on to squeeze through. In some places you have to get back in the water and walk along with your head in the confined space between the water's surface and the cave roof.

The sacrificial chamber is, ironically perhaps, known as the 'cathedral'. There are beautiful formations of stalagmites and stalactites, and huge columns where they've joined together. At one side there is a flat stone slab, believed to have been used as an altar, though for the most ungodly of purposes.

After the cathedral, we moved on and up a rope ladder to a smaller chamber. In it was the skeleton of another teenager, the only girl found in the cave. Her skeleton is spread-eagled on the floor, and complete, except for some missing vertebrae. Archaeologists believe she was killed with a blow to the spine. It's macabre stuff. Stranger still is that the bones seem to sparkle. At first I thought this was my imagination running wild, but it is actually the result of natural calcification in the cave's atmosphere. As a result, she has become known as the 'crystal maiden'.

We continued, swimming, scrambling and clambering through the cave towards a different exit. Finally, after four hours underground, we saw a shaft of natural light. It had been an incredible adventure – real Indiana Jones stuff – but stepping out of the darkness into the warm afternoon sun was absolutely wonderful – like leaving Xibalba and returning to the land of the living.

Now do it . . .

Contact Chaa Creek Belize Resort (www.chaacreek.
com) or www.thebelizecollection.com to book your
Mayan adventure. For more information, contact

Journey Latin America (www.journeylatinamerica.
co.uk) or go to www.visitcentroamerica.com

Riding the TT

Why	To experience an iconic motorcycle race
Where	Isle of Man	**Duration**	One day

LONG WEEKEND

Ever since I started riding motorbikes at the age of seventeen, I dreamt of visiting the Isle of Man for the TT races. The TT, which stands for Tourist Trophy, has run since 1907 and is the most revered of motorbike races; perhaps because of the beauty of the course, perhaps because of its history, but probably because of the danger.

The event came about because in 1903 the authorities in Britain introduced a 20mph speed limit, making road-racing impossible. Pioneering car racers moved their attention to the Isle of Man, where the authorities took a more relaxed view, and they were soon followed by the early bikers. At first the course went through the mountains on what were little more than farm tracks – the first rider of the day had to open the gates, the last had to close them again.

Today, the race still takes place on public roads rather than a race track, though the tarmac is in rather better condition and riders now reach speeds of up to 200mph. The best bikers maintain an average of up to 130mph over the 37-mile course as it snakes through villages, over the Snaefell mountains, through narrow lanes flanked by dry stone walls and back to the starting point in Douglas. The late, great Barry Sheene rode in the event only once, and had a succinct description. It was, he said, 'a suicide mission'. To date there have been 231 recorded deaths.

This sounds crazy enough, but there's more. The races are spread over two weeks, but on the middle Sunday – 'Mad Sunday' – anyone can go out and ride the course themselves. You don't need a special licence, or any training, and there's no speed limit. To the health and safety lobby it's the ultimate nightmare; to bikers it is the stuff of fantasy, the chance to test your bike and yourself against the world's most famous course.

The adventure begins at home as you prepare your bike and decide who to ride with. Then you head for Liverpool, where you catch the Steam Packet Company ferry over to Douglas. There must be a thousand bikes at a time on the ferry. Moto Guzzis, Nortons, Triumphs, Kawasakis, Hondas –

An adventure with the family is always rewarding: here with my dad and brothers.

they're all there, and the camaraderie between the bikers as everyone goes round checking out the machines is tremendous. Once you dock, there's a frenzy of engines starting up, then you ride out into Douglas which is teeming with tens of thousands of bikes. You won't see as many anywhere else in the world.

Watching the race is thrilling in itself. You drive off up a country lane, then come to a T-junction blocked by a rope and a marshal. It looks like any other B road, but it's actually the track. You get off and wait, listening to the birds twittering, the breeze rustling in the trees, and then you hear this little high-pitched whine somewhere in the

> To the health and safety lobby it's the ultimate nightmare; to bikers it is the stuff of fantasy

distance. It gets louder and louder then suddenly this bike doing 200mph comes rushing past you, wiggling like crazy. You feel a surge of respect for the man on that bike. He's a god.

Then Sunday comes and it's your turn. When I finally made it over to the Isle of Man in 1999 for my first 'Mad Sunday' I got up at 6 a.m. to set off. It was misty and I had the entire track to myself. I passed the legendary spots – Ballaugh Bridge, Cronky-y-Voddy, The Bungalow – places that I had known so well, for so long, from watching the races on TV. I was there, riding it for real. There was something quite spiritual about it.

Later in the afternoon I couldn't resist going out again. This time there were huge numbers of bikes riding together. The more nervous would stick to the left, bolder people would ride in the middle at 70 or 80mph, then the complete nutters would come screaming past on the right doing 160mph on Yamaha R1s and other superbikes. Coming off at that speed doesn't bear thinking about. The course is lined with pillar boxes, telegraph poles, houses and stone walls. There's some padding, straw bales and mattresses tied to walls, but if you're doing 160mph a mattress isn't really going to help very much . . .

So there is danger, but also an unbelievable thrill. It's like a football fan being allowed to play at Wembley, or a tennis player getting the chance to have a game at Wimbledon. Without a doubt, it's one of the top ten adventures I've ever had.

If you fancy it, go soon, before the safety lobby succeed in closing it down for ever.

Now do it . . .

Visit the official Isle of Man TT website for information on the race (www.iomtt.com). For information on ferries to and from the Isle of Man, visit Steam Packet Company (www.steam-packet.com). A great place to stay during your trip is the 4-star Sefton Hotel (www.seftonhotel.co.im).

Why	For freedom and fun in the Outback, Oz-style
Where	Australia	**Duration**	One week +

If you want to see the Australian Outback in style, you should catch the luxurious and super-expensive Ghan train, which takes three days to travel across the country from Adelaide to Darwin, and boasts double beds, en suite bathrooms and a gourmet restaurant. But if you want adventure, sleeping under the stars and a lot of laughs on the way, go for a Wicked Camper.

Wicked takes old vans that are possibly a bit past their sell-by date, makes them perfectly road legal and safe, then gives them crazy graffiti paint jobs, each one unique. Some seat and sleep just two, with a kitchen in the back that converts to a double bed at night, while others seat up to five, with a kitchen and storage for tents and sleeping bags, so you can set up camp wherever you like.

We picked up a van from Darwin, on Australia's north coast, and headed due south towards Alice Springs, 950 miles of desert-driving away. The van was all a bit loose, the gearbox crunched sometimes, but it worked fine. There were four of us in the van and we had a right old laugh – iPod on, singing along, cruising down the dead straight road with the sun shining.

Soon out of Darwin, the palm trees and tropical greenery changed into full-on desert. We passed incredible red rock formations, kangaroos skipping alongside the road, mile after mile of sand and scrub, and all beneath the biggest skies I've ever seen.

A railway line ran alongside the road, and we watched the trains come past, some of them up to two miles long. At first we tried to race them, but we couldn't really win, so we parked up, took some pictures of each other lying on the track, and waited for the next to come right past us. It was an amazing sight, the driver blasting his horn as he went, and this colossal beast that took twenty minutes just to pass by.

Instead of tents we slept in swags, an Australian bush tradition. These are basically a large canvas envelope that buttons up down the side, with a real duvet, mattress and pillow inside. It means you can have all the comfort of a bed but sleep out in the open. We'd cook round an open fire, have a few beers, shoot the breeze, then lay out our swags around the fire and stare at the stars, the meteorites coming in and the satellites going round. You'd think in Australia there'd be loads of bugs and animals but there was nothing – no sound at all.

We stopped to fill up in the little town of Daly Waters. There was no one at the petrol station, so we went over to the pub to ask how we should pay. 'Just fill her up and come over to tell us how much it was,' said the barmaid. That kind of laid-back attitude summed up the trip perfectly.

Now do it . . .

Wicked Campers (www.wickedcampers.com.au) can help you with your wicked adventure. There are 16 depots around Australia which all offer one-way rentals, making any road-trip itinerary possible.
For accommodation and travel information visit Tourism Australia (www.australia.com).

RAILWAY CROSSING

STOP

LOOK FOR TRAINS

" We passed incredible red rock formations, kangaroos skipping alongside the road ... and all beneath the biggest skies I've ever seen "

| **Why** | To slow down and absorb the breathtaking canyon |
| **Where** | USA | **Duration** | One day + |

To get to the lookout point above the San Juan River in Utah, you drive 10 miles north of a village called Mexican Hat, park up, then walk for a few minutes over rocky ground. There are no gift shops, guardrails or souvenir stalls, but after passing through a few scrubby bushes, you suddenly find yourself standing on a cliff, with one of the planet's most bizarre landscapes stretched out before you.

Hundreds of metres below the lookout, the San Juan River runs through the deep canyon it has cut into the rocky desert floor. But rather than travelling in a straight line, the river bends back on itself in a series of U-shaped meanders that give the area its name: 'Goosenecks'. The river's route is so circuitous that to cover one mile as the crow flies, it must travel six.

Aside from the sense of wonder at the geological formations, as you stand there you can't help but think about how remote and inaccessible the river is, hidden away in canyons with 300-metre-high rock walls, the patches of grass and pebble beaches on its banks unreachable by any path, let alone road.

Rafting can be peaceful ... and then it can be upside-down.

If you want to get down there, into the canyon, there is only one way – on the water. You can canoe, but going by raft makes it easier to take all the provisions needed for a self-sufficient multi-day expedition, and there are several local rafting companies who can organize one.

In recent years, white-water rafting has become hugely popular around the world and in many places it's offered to tourists as a fun activity lasting a couple of hours, more of an 'experience' than a real adventure. Here it's different – you are using the raft as a way of travelling through areas that would otherwise be off-limits.

There are numerous possibilities for rafting expeditions in Utah and Arizona. Many people start at Moab and travel down the Green or Colorado rivers through Cataract Canyon, to Hite Marina on Lake Powell, a journey that covers 112 miles, passes twenty-six rapids and typically takes six days. Alternatively, you can raft down the Grand Canyon itself, starting at Lee's Ferry and ending on Lake Mead, a 225-mile trip that usually takes two weeks. Both are excellent adventures, but if you want to raft through the Goosenecks you should start at Bluff in Utah, and finish on Lake Powell, spending a week or more on the journey.

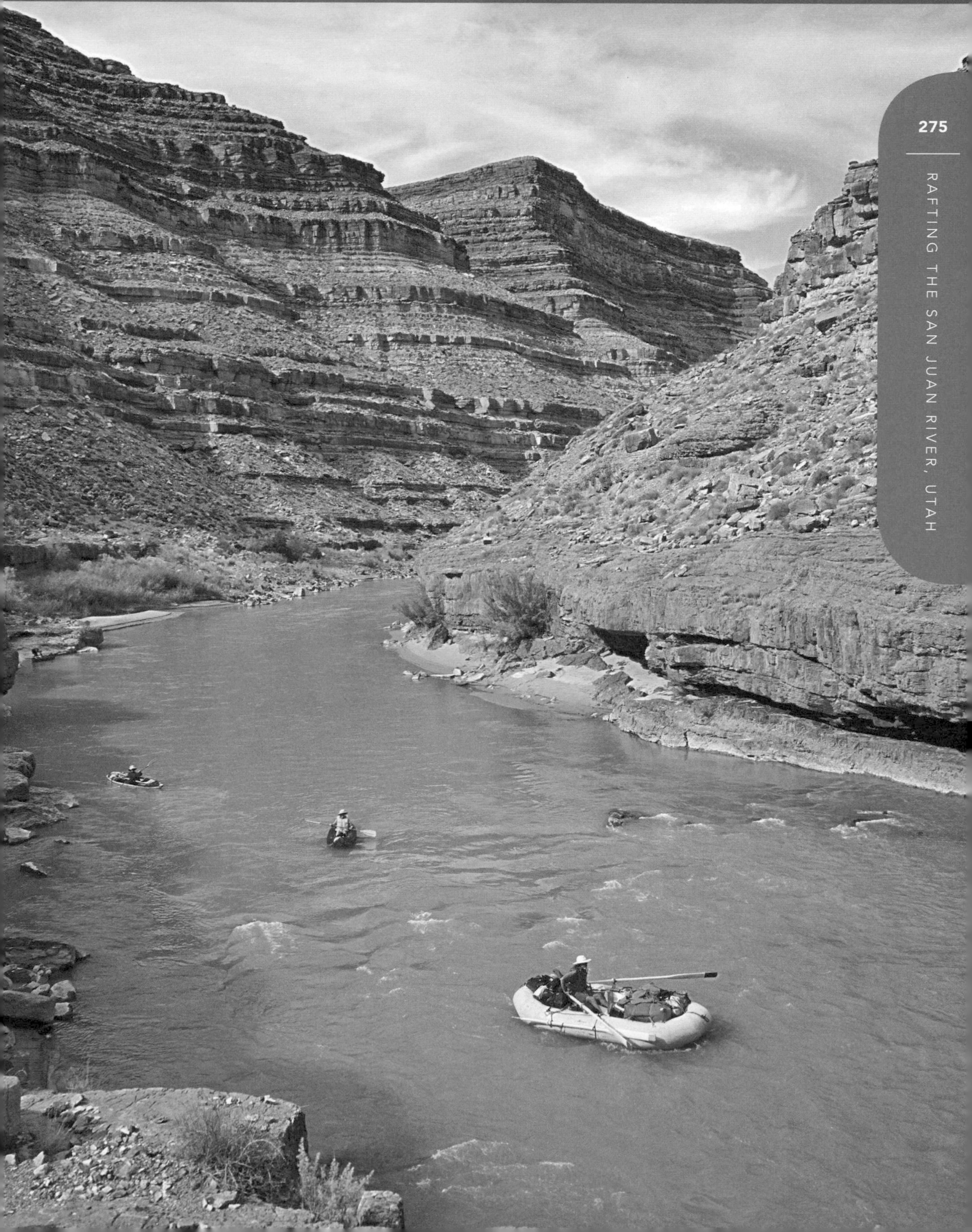

Some rafting companies offer faster versions, using powered 'jet' boats to cover the areas of flat water between the more exciting rapids. But these miss the point – the whole adventure is about submitting to the rhythm of the river over a long period of time. At some points, you float at a snail's pace, drifting along the calm water with nothing to do but stare up at the canyon walls and the clouds as they pass over the strip of blue sky above, or spot the Big Horn sheep that scrabble about on impossibly steep rock faces. At others you are paddling in a frenzy as the raft is thrown around in the white water.

There are a couple of access points in case of emergency, but for much of the trip down the San Juan River you are on your own. Even in places where there are no cliffs beside the river, you are likely to be surrounded by nothing but miles of empty desert. Obviously this means you have to carry all your food and other supplies, but it also means the trip is more committing. If you decide you don't like the others in the group, or you're desperate for a proper shower, you can't slope off to a hotel. So you are forced to bond with your teammates, to give in to the pace of the river.

How many people you travel with depends on which rafting operator you use and how you set up your trip. Wild Rivers Expeditions, for example, asks for a minimum group size of four people before it will organize a multi-day trip down the San Juan. Its rafts carry up to eight, plus the guide, so with four you'd have plenty of room. If you are alone or travelling with fewer than three others, you can get in touch to see if there are any scheduled expeditions you can join.

The more you slow down, the more you find

there is to do and see. In numerous places it's possible to moor the rafts and hike into side canyons to see rock drawings and fossils, even the remains of ancient dwellings. Some of the side canyons, like Slickhorn Gulch, are worth hiking purely for their beauty. In Slickhorn, the limestone has been sculpted by water to form a series of pools and waterfalls where you can swim, interspersed with small 'gardens' of vegetation, atmospheric places to simply stop and read a book in.

Popping out of the canyons on to Lake Powell is another surreal experience. This is where the opening scenes of *Planet of the Apes* were filmed, a huge, perfectly blue expanse of water surrounded by sun-blasted white rock formations, like a thousand mirages melted into one.

Powell is a popular destination for tourists and as you paddle down into the lake, you'll probably pass huge rented houseboats. Their opulence – complete with water slides, sundecks, wine coolers, TVs and sound systems – comes as a bit of a shock after a week in the silence of the canyons. For a second you might look across enviously at them, but then you'll remember that while they've been bobbing about drinking beer, you've had a far more memorable experience, escaping into the wilderness, bonding with your teammates and exploring a landscape that remains remote and little visited, even today.

Now do it . . .

For rafting on the San Juan visit www.riversandruins. com, or for rafting the Grand Canyon visit www.azraft. com

Long skating in Sweden

Why	To take a favourite pastime back to where it began
Where	Sweden	**Duration**	Two days +

LONG WEEKEND

The skater in front of me was flying across the frozen lake when he seemed to stumble on the ice and his foot broke through the surface. He managed to pull it out and keep gliding forward, but then the other foot crashed through and suddenly the ice had collapsed around him, sending him crashing into the freezing water.

We were on a day's 'long skating' tour, travelling around the lakes in Sörmland, 45 miles south-west of Stockholm. In Sweden, skating is a national obsession, and entirely different to the sport as we know it in Britain. Rather than being confined to going in circles around ice-rinks, here skating is a means of escaping the cities and travelling out into the wilderness.

Sweden is a land of forests and lakes – there are 97,500 lakes larger than 2 acres – and as soon as winter freezes them and the waterways that connect them, enthusiasts head out on their skates. Dotted about beside the lakes and rivers are thousands of log cabins, both privately owned and belonging to clubs. You can either base yourself in one of them and make day trips on the ice from there, or make multi-day excursions, staying at a different cabin each night.

In the same way that skiers obsessively seek out perfect powder snow, for Swedish skaters it's all about finding the smoothest ice. There are countless websites on which they post reports and chat about ice conditions around the country.

Having the right kit is essential. The skates themselves are about six inches longer than conventional ones, enabling easier gliding, and the runners are wider and more stable. Some skaters carry a long pole to test the ice thickness, but all carry a rope, two small claws (like miniature ice axes that hang on a rope round your neck) and a spare set of clothes, sealed inside waterproof bags in a rucksack. If you break through the ice and get wet, you only have minutes to change before the onset of hypothermia.

Which brings us back to my friend. 'Stop right there!' he yelled as soon as he had broken through. I was following about 30 metres behind – it's vital

You wear small hooks around your neck in case you fall into the ice.

everyone keeps some distance, to spread the weight on the ice, and to give you a chance to stop if the person in front breaks through. If that happens, you have to fight the natural instinct to rush forward to help – you'll only make the hole bigger and the situation worse. So my friend set about hauling himself out. First, he turned round. The only ice you know is thick enough to carry you is the stuff you've already skated over. Then he took the two claws on the rope round his neck, one in each hand, and drove them into the ice. Though they looked small and flimsy, they gave him just enough purchase to scrabble out of the freezing water.

Thankfully, we were only a few minutes from our cabin, so rather than change, we sped back across the ice to the warmth of the cabin and got straight into the sauna (considered a necessity by the Swedes, even in the most basic and remote hut). After a couple of minutes my friend was fully warmed up and laughing about the incident. The occasional dunk in freezing water is an accepted part of being a keen long skater.

I'd gone out with some Swedish friends, but there are several tour companies who can arrange three- or four-day skating itineraries. And skating on the inland lakes and along the rivers isn't the only adventure to be had.

In the Baltic Sea around Stockholm is an archipelago of some 24,000 islands and islets. Some are uninhabited, others have nothing but a couple of log cabins, some have small hotels or restaurants. In summer there's a buzzing scene as people cruise between them in small boats, stopping for meals or to sunbathe on deserted islands, and you can wild camp where you want as long as you're out of sight of the local houses. In winter, they are mainly shut up and inaccessible, but after a few weeks of bitterly cold weather, the sea sometimes freezes over. Then the skaters can head out from the lakes and rivers and on to the open water, gliding across the sea and staying overnight in cabins on the islands. It's a whole new type of island-hopping.

Now do it . . .

Nature Travels (www.naturetravels.co.uk) are experts in outdoor and adventure travel and can organize your long skating adventure. See Visit Sweden (www.visitsweden.com) for all you need to know about Sweden.

| **Why** | For an exhilarating twist on a popular activity |
| **Where** | Brazil | **Duration** | Two days + |

Where do you find the world's longest wave? Hawaii perhaps, Tahiti or Australia's Gold Coast? In fact, for the ultimate surfing experience, you need to look to Brazil – not to any of its sun-kissed beaches, but to a river that runs through the Amazon jungle.

Several times a year, usually between February and March, the Pororoca comes to the Amazon. In the Tupi language of the local indigenous tribes, the word means 'great destructive noise', and it describes the tidal wave that rushes from the sea up the rivers of the Amazon basin. In places the wave can last more than half an hour, travel for 16 miles inland and stand 4 metres high. It must be a terrifying sight for local fishermen in their dugout canoes, but for surfers it's the stuff of fantasy. Even the biggest sea waves only break for a matter of seconds. By comparison, this seems almost never-ending.

Technically, the wave is known as a 'tidal bore', created when a particularly big tide comes in from the sea and meets the water flowing in the opposite direction down the river. They occur in a small number of locations around the world, usually where there's a wide range between water levels at low and high tide, and where the incoming tide is funnelled along the coastline towards the mouth of the river. Britain has a famous one on the River Severn, where the tide coming up the Bristol Channel washes down the river, but the world's biggest bore is on the Qiantang River in China. That wave, known locally as the Silver Dragon, can reach 9 metres high, though it doesn't last as long as the Pororoca.

Brazil's epic wave only began to attract significant worldwide interest when Jacques Cousteau, the marine biologist, encountered it on an expedition in 1984. He wrote of the wall of water that hurtled towards his research boat, capsizing it and damaging his equipment. Growing numbers of surfers have travelled to Brazil in search of the wave ever since.

The Pororoca occurs on the Amazon itself and numerous smaller rivers in the area, but the consensus is that the best place to experience it is the Rio Araguari, just north of the Amazon. The closest airport, and major town, is

Learn to surf before you go.

Macapá, from where it's a four-hour drive north on rough roads to the river. Most people hire a boat to stay on, mooring up close to the mouth of the river to await the wave.

When it does come, you hear it before you see it, a low growl gradually getting louder. Then, what looks like a blur on the horizon as you look out to sea starts kicking up into a rush of white water, stretching for more than half a mile across the mouth of the river. You really need a small, manoeuvrable boat with an outboard motor, so it can position you just in front of the Pororoca, where you jump into the chocolate-brown water and swim like mad to catch the wave. Some pro-surfers come with jet skis, so that if they miss the wave, they can be picked up behind it and towed back in front of it. Otherwise you only have one shot.

A 4-metre wave rushing towards you is intimidating enough, but the force of the water isn't the only danger. As the water rushes upstream, it rakes along the banks, washing logs and dead branches into the water, along with snakes and alligators. There are stories of sharks lurking behind the wave, ready to pick off anything it has swept up. Plus, of course, there are piranhas, and the threat of the candiru fish, a tiny parasite that attaches itself to fish gills, or, in the case of humans, swims up into the urethra, with agonizing consequences.

But the difficulties and dangers only add to the challenge, and the sense of achievement if you do manage to get up on your board. Do that and you're in for the ride of your life – speeding upriver through the jungle on a frothing wall of water, watching the birds fly up from the trees as the wave's noise disturbs them, and surfing longer than you've ever done in your life, until your legs are burning so much you can go no further.

Now do it . . .
Visit Wanna Surf (www.wannasurf.com) for information on surfing the Pororoca wave, and also on other amazing surfs of the world.

| **Why** | To push yourself to the ultimate height…literally |
| **Where** | Nepal | **Duration** | One month |

When we were in Nepal making *By Any Means*, Charley and I travelled by helicopter from Kathmandu into the mountains, so we could get a look at Mount Everest. Our destination was Tengboche, a village in the Khumbu Valley which is home to an important monastery, and from where you get a panoramic view of the high Himalayan peaks, including Nuptse, Lhotse, Ama Dablam and, of course, Everest.

Approaching the village in the helicopter, we were met with a view I'll never forget – the beautiful monastery set above the village, trains of yaks carrying loads, sherpas in their traditional robes tending crops in the fields and, rising above them all, the huge white peaks, the ice of their glaciers sparkling in the morning sun. But as I looked closer, something odd caught my eye. On one of the paths leading across the hillside towards the village, I saw a man in shorts and a T-shirt, running. He soon disappeared from view but then I saw another, clearly a Westerner, and looking for all the world as if he'd gone for a jog in Hyde Park but got lost and ended up on the flanks of the world's highest mountain. Then came a great cluster of runners and I could see all were wearing race numbers. Charley and I looked at each other in bemusement.

We later found out that our visit had just happened to coincide with one of the most bonkers sporting events on the planet, the Tenzing-Hillary

Everest Marathon, an annual race that starts at Everest base camp and finishes, 26.2 miles later, at the town of Namche Bazaar, the Sherpa capital.

Anyone who has ever done any trekking, skiing or climbing in the high mountains knows how significant the effects of altitude can be. Just walking up the stairs in a hotel can leave you panting for air, and the higher you are, the worse it gets. Everest base camp is at 5,356 metres – more than 500 metres higher than the summit of Mont Blanc, western Europe's highest peak, and more than double the altitude of Europe's highest ski resort.

For most people, the idea of running a marathon at such altitude must seem utterly crazy, but for some runners, the Everest marathon is the ultimate challenge. In fact, such is the demand from participants that there are now two Everest marathons: the Tenzing-Hillary, which was first run in 2003 and takes place in May, and the original Everest Marathon, which takes place in November or early December and began in 1987. The event had been the idea of Jan Turner and Tony Hunt, two Britons who were trekking to Everest base camp in 1985 and decided to have an impromptu race along the way. Apparently the idea took off after newspaper reports condemned the event and warned it risked lives – demand for places surged.

Making our breakfast.

Even getting to the start line is a slog. Participants must hike up to base camp, typically taking at least two weeks. This time is crucial for acclimatization and for getting to know the route. With the hike out after the race, usually to Lukla airstrip where you can catch a small plane back to Kathmandu, the whole adventure takes about twenty-six days.

As well as the altitude, the other difficulty is that the path is narrow and uneven, there can be snow, ice and scree, and it is used by yaks, farmers and other trekkers, whom you have to dodge as you run. It's a world away from running a conventional city-centre marathon, and anyone taking part must have experience of other fell-running races.

There is one piece of good news, though. Namche Bazaar is at 3,446 metres, so despite about 1,000 metres of climbing along the way, overall the course is downhill.

Given the terrain and the altitude, the times are incredibly fast. The record for the original event (which starts just below base camp at Gorak Shep) stands at three hours fifty minutes, with nine of the top ten finishes going to local Nepalis. Whatever their time, though, runners who make it to the end can expect to feel on top of the world.

Learning other people's cultures is essential.

Now do it . . .

For more information on the Everest Marathon which takes place in November and December, visit www.everestmarathon.org.uk. For more information on the Tenzing–Hillary Everest Marathon in May, visit www.everestmarathon.com

Why	For the scariest leap of faith you will ever experience
Where	USA	**Duration**	One week

In 1978, Carl Boenish filmed his wife and two friends jumping off the top of El Capitan, a mountain in Yosemite National Park, California, and in doing so, created one of the world's most extreme sports. People had occasionally jumped from buildings or bridges before, saving themselves by opening parachutes on the way down, but Boenish's film is seen as the turning point when such one-off stunts became formalized into a sport. He even came up with a name for it: BASE jumping.

BASE stands for buildings, antennae, spans (meaning bridges) and earth (meaning cliffs). Soon more and more skydivers were trying out the new sport, looking for a new thrill that could recapture the adrenalin rush of their first jump from a plane. Headline moments followed (including the time a man jumped from the Whispering Gallery inside St Paul's Cathedral), and in 1985 a BASE jump from the Eiffel Tower in the James Bond film *A View to a Kill* ensured mainstream attention. Anyone who completes a jump in each of the four categories qualifies for a BASE number – Boenish and his wife became BASE3 and BASE4, and by November 2010, there were around 1,400 BASE numbers issued worldwide.

But with growing popularity came growing numbers of accidents. At least 147 people have been killed in the last twenty-two years, including Boenish himself, who died after leaping from a cliff in Norway in 1984. Then there's the issue of legality. While most countries don't have laws explicitly prohibiting the sport, the owners of buildings and bridges usually do not want people jumping off them, forcing BASE jumpers to trespass, often disguising themselves as workmen or breaking in at night. There are numerous cases of jumpers being carted off by police when they land, helping the sport to acquire a shadowy, subversive image.

If you value your life, and your freedom, you should never attempt this unsupervised.

But there is one place where would-be jumpers are welcomed with open arms, and where there's even a BASE jump 'school'. Just outside the small town of Twin Falls, Idaho is the Snake River canyon, and the Perrine Bridge that crosses it is one of the few places in the world where BASE jumping is explicitly permitted. Other bridges in the US have annual days when jumping is legal, or they allow jumpers who have special permits, but the Perrine Bridge is open year round to all-comers.

This is also the perfect location for it. The main danger in BASE jumping is in hitting the object you're leaping from, but the Perrine Bridge is

> When you clamber over the handrail, and stand on the edge of the bridge looking down, you are on your own

There are several courses operating at Perrine, including Snake River Base Academy and Apex Base, and they typically offer three- or four-day courses. You must already be a proficient sky-diver, and the courses stress that they are there to help make your first jump as safe as possible, rather than to turn you into a fully fledged BASE jumper. As with so many extreme sports, the key to success is having an obsessive, even nerdy, level of attention to detail, and on these courses you'll spend a long time focusing on correctly packing the parachutes, and the safety routines for checking harnesses and other kit.

Of course, BASE jumping remains dangerous, but an organized jump like this, led by experienced instructors, is probably its safest guise. Even so, when you clamber over the handrail, and stand on the edge of the bridge looking down, you are on your own.

one simple wide span, rather than being held up by a series of columns, so if you leap from the centre, there's nothing to hit. It's also high, 148 metres above the river below, plus there's a wide, flat, grassy field beneath it that makes the ideal landing zone.

Now do it . . .

For more information on BASE jumping, visit Snake River Base (www.snakeriverbase.com) and Apex Base (www. apexbase.com).

91

Charity trekking in Morocco

Why	For challenging trekking which changes lives
Where	Morocco	**Duration**	Two weeks

With all of the Big Earth trips over the years, the philosophy has been to travel the world but to try to do some good at the same time, and we've always worked with UNICEF, the United Nations Children's Fund, visiting their projects around the globe to raise awareness of children's rights and to raise money for vulnerable children. And you can pick any charity you want and combine your adventures with fundraising for them.

So-called 'charity challenges' have grown from almost nothing twenty years ago into a key way for charities to make money. Some big charities run their own adventurous events, but if your chosen charity doesn't, you can still get sponsorship for whichever challenge or adventure you're doing and donate the money to them independently. Websites like www.justgiving.com have made this even easier to do.

I joined my first organized charity event in November 2010, a UNICEF trek in Morocco. They run several treks a year, and while the destinations vary – in 2011 they are to Jordan and Namibia – the style of the trip, the atmosphere and the goals are broadly similar.

For me the big shock was that I was going away without my team of friends and colleagues. Instead, it was me and forty complete strangers. At first I felt some trepidation about that – you inevitably wonder if you'll get on with people – but almost immediately I found it a complete delight. It was like I was leaving behind my ordinary life, leaving behind the stress of work, stepping outside the framework of friends and relationships and, in a small way, starting again. It was as if all the white noise of daily life had vanished.

The other key difference from normal adventures is that everything is arranged for you. There are pre-departure notes about training and packing, the itinerary is already mapped out, and when you get to your destination there's a support crew to set up the

Travel the world and do some good.

> While the destinations vary ... the style of the trip, the atmosphere and the goals are broadly similar

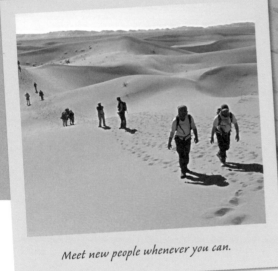

Meet new people whenever you can.

tents every night and so on. The idea is that this leaves you free to concentrate on raising the sponsorship required (£2,600 for this trip), but the reality is that it also means those with busy working lives can tackle some fascinating adventures they'd never have the time or confidence to arrange themselves.

We flew to Ouarzazate, a city on the south side of the Atlas mountains that is the gateway to the Sahara desert. From there we had a two-hour transfer by minibus to the village of Tazzarine, where we swapped into the back of open trucks. They were the kind of vehicle you'd expect to see cattle transported in, and were bumpy, dusty and offered no shade. But as soon as we were sitting inside them, everyone started talking to each other. Riding in the minibuses had felt mundane and so the normal social barriers remained in place, but as soon as we were taken outside our comfort zone, and our ordinary lives, the barriers came down. By the time we reached our destination, Oum Jrane, four hours later, we were already starting to feel like a group with some shared experience.

For four days we walked through the desert. We rose early and were walking by 8 a.m., covering fifteen to sixteen miles a day before stopping for dinner round the camp fire and retiring to the big canvas tents where six or seven of us slept side by side. We only carried daypacks (our kitbags, tents and sleeping bags were transferred to the next campsite by truck), but even so, it was gruelling at times, particularly when we were climbing up sandy dunes where for every six feet you walked up, you slid back five. One problem was how hot your feet got in walking boots – by the final day I was walking barefoot. Another was the flies. As you walked you could see hundreds of them sitting on the rucksack of the person in front; then, when he stopped, they would fly up around his face. My dad, as a joke, had given me an old Australian-style bush hat before I left, complete with corks on strings hanging from the brim. It actually worked really well, even if I did look ridiculous.

At first there was lots of chatter as the group got to know each other, but gradually this died away as attention turned to discovering the desert around us. In some parts the Sahara is exactly like the deserts of popular imagination, rolling orange dunes as far as the eye can see. This is known as *erg*, but it is only a tiny part of the story. In fact, the desert is hugely varied – we walked over rocky plains, flat as far as the horizon (known as *reg* in the Sahara, or 'desert pavement' in the US), then areas of bare rock (or *hamada*) and cracked parched mud, but also mountains and fields of rough desert grass.

On the third day we started off from our camp near Jbel Zireg and climbed all morning up a steep ridge, which gave fabulous views for

Falling down the dunes in style!

miles across the desert. We walked along the narrow rocky ridge until we reached a sand dune, perhaps 200 metres high, which led down to the flat plain below. We looked at each other, then just ran forward, slipping and sliding down the sandy slope and laughing like kids. After crossing the plain, we spent a couple of hours walking down a dried-out riverbed, then turned a corner to find an idyllic oasis, its green palm trees a shock to the eyes after hours of nothing but rock and sand. It was a fabulous day.

As well as tackling an adventure, all the trips it organizes visit UNICEF projects so you can see first-hand the work they carry out for children. The idea is not so much that you help out on the ground (much of the work is highly skilled, after all), but that in seeing the work in action, participants become life-long supporters and advocates for the cause.

On this trip we saw two projects. The first was a maternity 'waiting house' at Taznakhte. Deaths during childbirth, of both mothers and babies, are still common here, largely because many women live so far from any medical care that by the time they go into labour, it's too late to think about getting there. Now, pregnant mothers approaching full term can travel from their remote farms and villages to this centre, which is close to the hospital, where they can wait until they go into labour.

Deep in thought as we walk.

At Timjijte we saw a primary school and a pre-school centre. In this area a high proportion of kids don't go to school, because suitable facilities are just not available. Parents tend to keep the children at home, helping with chores or working on the land. This not only stops them from attending school later, it can also keep their older siblings out of school too, as they are needed to help care for the little ones whilst the adults do the bulk of the work. Pre-school helps on both counts. Firstly, the children can get access to toys and materials to stimulate their curiosity and help them develop their motor skills and hand-eye co-ordination, which will mean that they are much better prepared when they reach primary school level. Secondly, now that the little ones are safe and cared for at pre-school, the older kids are able to leave the home and go back to school themselves. This is vital to reduce the incredible 38 per cent drop-out rate of kids in school in Morocco, and therefore enable every child to gain the skills and education to make the very best of their lives.

Seeing both the happy, safe, expectant mothers and the kids who were clearly so enthusiastic about learning added an extra dimension to the trip.

On the final night, eleven of us spontaneously decided we should sleep outside. As we lay there on the sand dune, looking at the stars and spotting satellites as they moved overhead, I felt a deep sense of how fulfilling the trip had been. Beyond the stunning scenery and the camaraderie, the trip had the perfect balance – deeply rewarding on a personal level, but also, far more importantly, rewarding for those who really need help.

Working with UNICEF has been one of the most important parts of our adventures.

Now do it . . .

For a chance to participate in one of UNICEF's fundraising treks, visit the official UNICEF website at www.unicef.org

92

A Journey of the spirit

| **Why** | To connect with your tranquil inner self |
| **Where** | India | **Duration** | Two days + |

Many of the trips in this book are all about adrenalin, about physical challenges, danger and excitement. But adventures can also be about taking time out from the stress of living a fast-paced modern life, and having space to think. In my experience, having an adventure is certainly about exploring the world and learning from other people's cultures, but it is also about learning more about yourself.

If you really want to slow things down, Rishikesh in northern India is the ideal place. It's often called the 'birthplace of yoga', though the practice is so ancient that it's hard to say for sure where it began. But Rishikesh's claim to be the world capital of yoga is undoubtedly true – this small town in the foothills of the Himalayas is packed with scores of ashrams where Indians and foreigners come to meditate and practise yoga, and every March it hosts the International Yoga Festival, drawing thousands of devotees. Even if you've no direct interest in yoga, this holy city (where meat and alcohol are banned) is a peaceful and spiritual place in which to unwind.

You reach Rishikesh by taking a train from Delhi to Haridwar (a four-hour trip), then a rickshaw the final 14 miles from there. Rishikesh is on the banks of the Ganges, and the bustling main part of the city lies on the western bank. Swarg Ashram and Lakshman Jhula, where many of the ashrams and

An inward journey is more important than you may think.

temples are clustered together, are on the east bank, and to get across you have to walk over one of two huge pedestrian suspension bridges, the Ram Jhula and the Lakshman Jhula. Walking across them, you can't help but feel you're leaving the frantic chaos of the journey behind.

There are a huge number of ashrams to choose from, and which one you go for depends on the style of yoga you're interested in. Some come with meals (vegetarian) and accommodation attached, others offer only classes. Some teach for free, others charge, although the fee is usually very small. Among the best known are the Parmarth Niketan Ashram, the Shivananda Ashram, the Yoga Study Centre, Yoga Niketan and Ved Niketan. Perhaps the most famous ashram of all is that of the Maharishi Mahesh Yogi, which sits among forest above the river but is currently not operational. It was there that The Beatles came in 1968, spending several weeks writing songs and learning about meditation. It was a pivotal moment, when interest in Eastern beliefs and yoga hit the mainstream in the Western world.

The good thing about the city is that you can take things entirely at your own pace. You can sign up for a week of complete detox and hours of yoga classes per day, or you can drop by for the odd class, then relax by the river or visit the ancient temples. If you want a more luxurious experience, check into the Ananda Spa, high on a hill above the town, where yoga is offered alongside decadent spa treatments, five-star rooms and a golf course.

Part of the reason Rishikesh is so relaxing is its setting, surrounded by forest-covered hills. You can walk up into the hills directly behind Swarg Ashram (spotting monkeys and possibly elephants along the way), or you can take a bus or taxi a few miles upstream from the city, where the Ganges cuts through a beautiful steep-sided, wooded gorge. Here, on a beach beside the river, is the Leopard Camp, where you can stay in a spacious safari tent, enjoy good food, walk in the hills and swim in the river. The name isn't fanciful: you may well see leopard paw prints in the sand on the riverbanks. There's even the option of abseiling, kayaking and rafting – just in case you find you're missing the adrenalin after all . . .

Yoga gives a different perspective on the world.

Now do it . . .

Indian Experiences (www.indianexperiences.com) is the first step on your spiritual adventure. Incredible India (www.incredibleindia.org) can provide all the information you need on India.

93

Around the UK in a Black Cab

Why	For weirdness and fun combined in your own mission
Where	Great Britain	**Duration**	One week

There's one obvious question: why? Well, quite simply, because it's fun. Three of us had a week to spare, we wanted to see a bit more of our own country and we wanted an adventure – so we set off for the longest taxi ride of our lives.

Old taxis are cheap and easy to pick up. In 2001 a new rule came in requiring all London black cabs to have wheelchair ramps. Retro-fitting these to old vehicles would cost several thousand pounds, so many drivers decided it would be better to buy a new cab, which in turn meant numerous old taxis hit the second-hand market.

My friend Steve Hubbard picked up his for £250. Admittedly it wasn't in the first flush of youth. In fact, it had more than a million miles on the clock, but it seemed to run fine and we set off from London heading for John O'Groats, the farthest tip of Scotland.

As silly as it might seem to go around Britain in a taxi, they do have practical plus points. The two people in the back can stretch right out with their feet on the fold-down seats, cover themselves in their duvets and take in the view from the wide rear windows. We took turns to drive, starting at about 9 a.m. and continuing till about 7 p.m. each day, then finding a bed and breakfast for the night.

We got to John O'Groats about 8 p.m. on day three, spent a few hours gazing at the North Sea, then set off for our next objective – Land's End. We didn't get far. About 10 p.m., with Steve at the wheel, we ran out of diesel in the middle of nowhere.

The old taxi that was our home for a week before her demise.

It looked like a bit of a dire situation. But when you're travelling and find yourself in trouble, luck often seems to come to the rescue in one guise or another. By absolute fluke, only minutes after we'd broken down, a breakdown truck happened to pass, going in the other direction. We flagged him down, he towed us to his garage, cleaned the injectors and refuelled the cab for us, all at about 11.30 p.m. at night. I guess he just took pity on us and wanted to help us on our bonkers mission.

Later, I was at the wheel and speeding south to try to make up time. I knew I was going too fast when I looked in the rear-view mirror and saw the whites of the other two's eyes. And then I lost it on a corner, slipped off the road and hit a rock, which somehow managed to knock us back on to the

> For one week only, while everyone else is going through the grind of their daily business, you are doing something fun and silly

road. I just kept going, and about 2 a.m. we finally reached our B'n'B in Lairg.

The next morning I looked at the wheel and saw a huge gash in the tyre, through which the inner tube was protruding, ballooning out like a football. It was a miracle we hadn't had a blow-out, which, at the speed I'd been going, would have led to a serious crash. We really had been lucky that night.

The week continued with similar scrapes and mishaps and lots of laughs along the way. When you have an adventure in Britain, rather than on the other side of the world, you get this delicious sense of stepping outside the normal run of life. For one week only, while everyone else is going through the grind of their daily business, you are doing something fun and silly. Driving in our cab past office blocks where everyone was at work, we couldn't help but be conscious of how fortunate we were.

As we approached Land's End a policeman stopped us because one of our lights

wasn't working. But when we told him how far we'd come and that we were rushing to get to Land's End before sunset, he just laughed and waved us on our way. When we finally got there, we cheered and toasted our success with champagne. It may not be a particularly picturesque place, but for British people, travelling from John O'Groats to Land's End is a special journey, not quite a pilgrimage, but something deeply ingrained in our national psyche.

On the way back to London, the taxi's rumbling exhaust pipe finally ruptured, and diesel fumes started leaking into the cabin. There was nothing we could do but put all our clothes on and drive with the windows open, shivering all the way along the A303.

When we reached London and stepped out of the cab, we were feeling light-headed and nauseous from the fumes. But there was a sense of elation too, partly because we were so pleased to be in the fresh air again but mainly because we'd accomplished our mission. For the cab, it really was the end of the road. Our 1,720-mile trip had finished it off. But after years of trundling around the narrow streets of London, at least we'd given it one glorious swansong!

Now do it . . .

This trip is not commercially available. You will need to do all the planning, buying and preparation yourself. Used black cabs can be found on many internet websites such as eBay (www.ebay.co.uk) or Auto Trader (www.autotrader.co.uk).

94

Kayaking and hiking in Tortuguero

| **Why** | To explore peaceful rivers and to trek through the jungle |
| **Where** | Costa Rica | **Duration** | Two days + |

From tiny, brightly coloured tree frogs to giant turtles, Tortuguero National Park is teeming with wildlife. On the north-eastern coast of Costa Rica, the park can only be reached by light aircraft or boat. Within its 120 square miles are eleven distinct habitats, which help it to host a vast array of flora and fauna – more than 600 species of animal and 2,200 species of plant.

Most people come here to see the turtles ('tortuga' means turtle in Spanish). At night, you can watch hawksbill, loggerhead, green and leatherback turtles heave their way up the beach and lay their eggs in the sand. But behind the beaches is a huge network of waterways which go deep into the jungle, and the best way to explore these is by kayak.

From your boat you can see the monkeys playing in the trees, the toucans flying overhead and listen to the hum of the insects, all the while feeling relaxed and serene as you float along. We set off for a couple of hours' paddle up the River Penitencia, but you could mount a far longer expedition through these channels, camping on the banks at night. After our kayaking trip, a guide from the hotel took us out for a circular night-time hike of a few miles through the forest. The plan was to see the animals that come out after dark, then to end up on the beach.

Striking out into the jungle at night is exciting, but your mind does start thinking about the possible dangers lurking in the trees. Of those 600-odd species of animal in this area, more than a hundred are reptiles, and there are scorpions and spiders, not to mention jaguar. Even for a short walk, it's worth taking a few precautions. Always wear proper walking boots, long sleeves and trousers, and use mosquito repellent.

Thankfully, though we saw plenty of monkeys and some big armadillos scuttling along the path, we managed to avoid all of the nastier species on the list. Nevertheless, it was something of a relief to break out from the pitch-black bush on to the beach and see the surf glinting silver under a big tropical moon. And if you are lucky you may see a giant green turtle, slowly lumbering back down to the sea.

The kayaking is unbelievably peaceful.

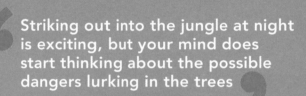

> Striking out into the jungle at night is exciting, but your mind does start thinking about the possible dangers lurking in the trees

Now do it . . .

Saint Germain Tours (www.saintgermaintours.com) can help organize your adventure in Costa Rica. We recommend you stay at the Manatus Lodge (www. manatuscostarica.com) while visiting Tortuguero

National Park, or visit Enchanting Hotels (www. enchanting-hotels.com) for other options around Costa Rica. For information on Central America visit www.visitcentroamerica.com

95

Camping with the Inuit

Once in a Lifetime

Why	To immerse yourself in a wilderness and culture
Where	Canada	**Duration**	Two days +

Nunavut is vast, wild and empty. It's the largest territory in Canada, making up a fifth of the country's landmass, and is eight times bigger than the UK. If Nunavut were a country, it would be the fifteenth largest on the planet, but in all that space, there is a population of just 33,000.

Almost all of these are Inuit, the indigenous people of the high Arctic. There's very little tourism infrastructure and few roads, but making the effort to travel to Nunavut and learn about Inuit culture is an amazing experience.

A good place to start is Cape Dorset, a village on a small island where archaeological remains show Inuit people lived as long ago as 1100 BC. It's a long way from anywhere but it bills itself as the 'capital of Inuit art'. Cape Dorset is also the base for Huit Huit Tours, an Inuit-owned company which will take you out into the wilderness to camp, fish, watch wildlife or dog-sled. For what on the surface appears like a region of barren nothingness, there is a surprising amount to see and do. You can share a traditional dinner in an Inuit home, listen to a performance of 'throat singing', and talk to elders about their lives and art. After that, you can leave Cape Dorset and head out by open boat to visit remote archaeological sites or fishing camps.

As you travel along the empty coastline, past glaciers and soaring cliffs, you'll start to make out eerie figures looking out to sea from the shore. These are the inukshuk, piles of rocks which resemble people with arms outstretched, created for thousands of years as markers to guide boats or indicate good fishing spots or campsites.

Huit Huit's itineraries usually involve several nights' camping in different locations. Polar bears can be a danger, so a husky will often be brought along as protection. You camp together in big canvas tents, set up in the traditional Inuit way. Keen fishermen can set up camp on the banks of pristine rivers and spend days catching abundant arctic char. But for others, the expansive views and the sense of peace are reward enough.

About a hundred miles west of Cape Dorset, you reach Inukaugasait, meaning 'the place of many inukshuk'. There are more than a hundred of the figures, clustered together on the rocks like an Arctic version of Stonehenge or Easter Island. It's a deeply atmospheric place, and one thing's for sure – as with pretty much everything in Nunavut, you won't have to share it with another soul.

Now do it . . .
Huit Huit Tours (www.capedorsettours.com) has the knowledge of the locals behind them and can organize various eco-culture tours in the Northern Territories.

Why	To feel the need…the need for speed
Where	USA	**Duration**	One day +

You are pulling a steep banked turn over the Pacific Ocean when you spot your enemy, far below. Pushing the stick forward, you put the plane into a fast dive until you come up into position behind him, and squeeze the trigger. The noise of the guns rings in your ears and up ahead, smoke pours from the enemy plane. 'Good job,' says your instructor, and orders you to return to base for a debrief.

It could be a scene from *Top Gun*, or a sequence of a video game, but all of this is real. Though at first it seems hard to believe, at Air Combat USA, a flight school in Fullerton, California, complete novices are trained in air-to-air combat by former members of the US Air Force and Navy. Many of the instructors have flown combat missions in Vietnam and Iraq, and some are former instructors with the Navy Fighter Weapons School (the very establishment on which the movie *Top Gun* was based).

The courses typically last for a full or half day, and start in the classroom, where you learn vital

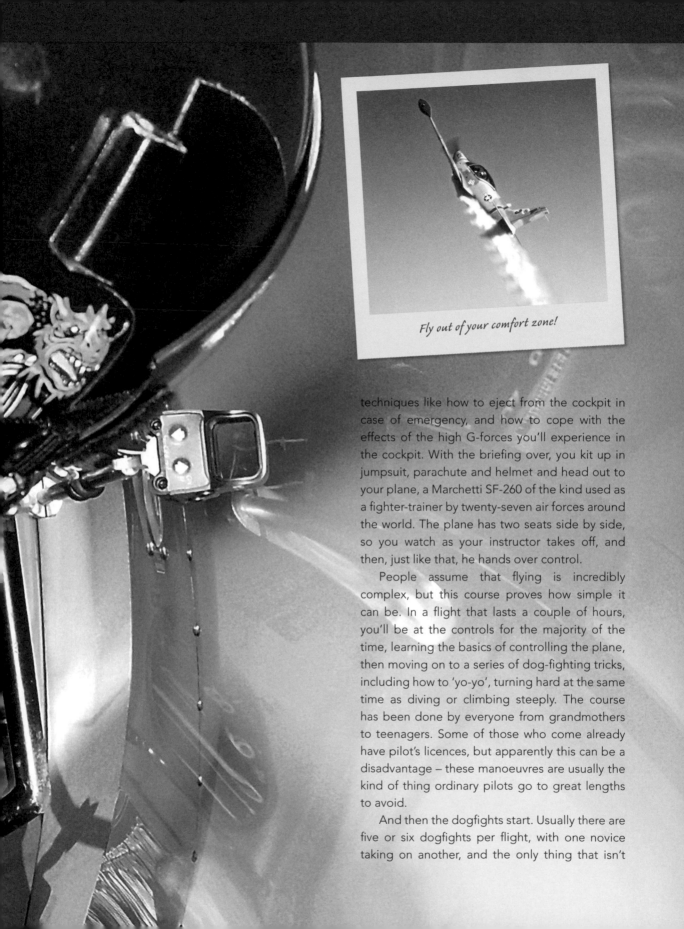

Fly out of your comfort zone!

techniques like how to eject from the cockpit in case of emergency, and how to cope with the effects of the high G-forces you'll experience in the cockpit. With the briefing over, you kit up in jumpsuit, parachute and helmet and head out to your plane, a Marchetti SF-260 of the kind used as a fighter-trainer by twenty-seven air forces around the world. The plane has two seats side by side, so you watch as your instructor takes off, and then, just like that, he hands over control.

People assume that flying is incredibly complex, but this course proves how simple it can be. In a flight that lasts a couple of hours, you'll be at the controls for the majority of the time, learning the basics of controlling the plane, then moving on to a series of dog-fighting tricks, including how to 'yo-yo', turning hard at the same time as diving or climbing steeply. The course has been done by everyone from grandmothers to teenagers. Some of those who come already have pilot's licences, but apparently this can be a disadvantage – these manoeuvres are usually the kind of thing ordinary pilots go to great lengths to avoid.

And then the dogfights start. Usually there are five or six dogfights per flight, with one novice taking on another, and the only thing that isn't real is the bullets. Instead the planes send out an electronic signal, which, if it hits the receiver on the rival aircraft, triggers a smoke canister.

Even if the bullets are imaginary, letting absolute novices battle it out at high speed and in mid-air might sound dangerous enough, but there are strict safety procedures and the whole thing is approved by the Federal Aviation Authority. The planes are not allowed to fly below a 'hard deck', a minimum altitude (typically set at 3,500 feet), so the instructors have time to rectify a novice's mistakes. They must stay within a block of airspace reserved for the course, and must not come within 500 feet of each other. Of course, this level of instruction and equipment isn't cheap – a one-flight 'basic air combat manoeuvres' course currently costs $1,395, a two-flight 'fighter lead-in program' costs $2,095.

The mission over, you return to base for a debrief and to watch video footage of the engagements. As you climb out of the cockpit, pull off your helmet and walk back across the tarmac to the hangar, you might find it hard to resist adopting the swagger of a fighter pilot. Make sure you keep a photo – otherwise no one will ever believe you.

> As you climb out of the cockpit ... you might find it hard to resist adopting the swagger of a fighter pilot

Now do it . . .
To become a fighter pilot for the day, visit Air Combat USA (www.aircombat.com) to get your wings.

97

Crewing a yacht and crossing the line

Why	To cross between hemispheres the old-fashioned way
Where	The ocean	**Duration**	One week +

There's something very special about being in a small boat in the middle of the ocean, out of sight of land for four or five days at a time. Your universe is stripped back to the daily routines of the yacht, the state of the sea and the weather. For hours on end you can find yourself watching dolphins play in the waves beside the bow, or staring at stars that are brighter than any you've seen, because you are so far from any other source of light.

Once in a Lifetime

Unfortunately, today it's an experience very few people get to share. While crossing continents by plane has become an everyday occurrence, long sea voyages are being consigned to history. But there is a way of getting out on to the high seas, and without having to spend thousands on your own yacht.

Owners often want their yachts to be moved around the world. Typically they might want their boat in the Mediterranean in summer and the Caribbean in winter. And whether they do it themselves or hire a professional captain, they will usually need some crew to help with the sailing, the cleaning and anything else that needs doing.

Experienced sailors are in high demand for this kind of thing, but complete novices do get taken on too. A typical 40-foot yacht might carry four people: a captain and two experienced crew plus one eager first-timer who can pick up skills as

*You only cross the line for the first time once —
make it special.*

> If you've crossed the equator on the way, you'll also have undergone a bizarre ceremony

they go. Normally there's no pay, but food is often provided.

The tricky bit is finding a boat in need of crew. Traditionally this was done by heading down to the docks and asking around, and this can still work. But while it's fine if you live near a port on the Med, if you live inland or in a landlocked country you can hardly keep travelling down to the coast on the off-chance. Thankfully the internet has revolutionized the whole procedure and there are now numerous websites that put yacht owners and crew in touch with each other. Often they charge a small registration fee, but since you might end up with a free trip around the world on a millionaire's yacht, it's probably worth it.

Once you're on board, don't think it will be like going on a cruise. You'll be expected to work the watch system, with four hours on and eight hours off, and could be hauling ropes, at the helm, cleaning the galley or, the old favourite, scrubbing the decks.

By the time you come into port after a long journey, you'll feel as if you don't really belong on land and that your home is the boat. And if you've crossed the equator on the way, you'll also have undergone a bizarre ceremony that's a rite of passage for sailors.

I experienced the 'crossing the line' initiation while I was spending three months crewing a 142-foot yacht around Indonesia, stopping at East Timor, Sulawesi and countless other islands along the way. Crossing the line is an old seafaring tradition, the origins of which remain obscure. Some think it was a pagan ritual designed to appease the gods and monsters of the deep, others that it was a test to see if novice sailors were tough enough to handle life at sea. But it was also a day of officially permitted anarchy, when the strict hierarchy and rules of the ship could be ignored. Over the years there have been numerous reports of events getting out of hand on some naval ships, but many still do observe the tradition, albeit in a strictly controlled manner.

I'd heard some of the nastier stories, so I was a little apprehensive when, with the other 'slimy pollywogs' (people who had never sailed across the equator before), I was told to put on a grass skirt and coconut-shell bra, then kneel on deck. Next, the rest of the crew came out and daubed us in slops from the galley – melted chocolate, ketchup and honey. Someone force-fed me a load of cheese, they threw flour all over us, then at last we were ready for the appearance of the captain, now dressed up as King Neptune. He laid a sword on our shoulders and whispered some ancient poem, and then we were thrown overboard to clean off.

Back on board, we may still have had some ketchup in our hair, but now we were considered pollywogs no more. Instead we had become 'trusty shellbacks' and 'sons of Neptune'. We were fully fledged sailors at last.

Now do it . . .
Crew Seekers (www.crewseekers.net) is a great place to find out information about possible crewing opportunities for your own sea adventure.

98

Norfolk's secret beach

| **Why** | To escape the rat-race, into the wild |
| **Where** | England | **Duration** | Two days |

LONG WEEKEND

I thought long and hard about whether to include this in the book, because it's one of those very special places you want to keep to yourself. But it's such a great adventure, and such a favourite of mine, I decided I couldn't leave it out.

Wells-next-the-Sea is a well-known Norfolk seaside village, with fish and chip shops, brightly painted beach huts, crazy golf, ice-cream vans and a miniature railway. Nice as it is, in mid-summer it can be impossible to find a parking space and the beach is teeming with people.

But separated from the main beach and the village by a channel of deep water is a large area of salt marsh. It's completely ignored by the crowds, and it's here, only a stone's throw from the chip shops, that you can have a great adventure.

The first thing you must do is check the tide tables – success here is all about timing. We hired a small boat with an outboard motor, packed our supplies, then set off about 8 a.m., heading not out to sea, but into the salt marsh. As we motored up the creeks of the marsh, they grew narrower and narrower, the long grasses on the banks getting close enough to touch. It reminded me a little of the Pantanal or the Okavango Delta, but where they flood in the rainy season, this marshland floods at every high tide, then the water gradually flows out, back down the channels and out to sea. We were heading up the channels as the water was flowing in the opposite direction, in a race against time to reach our destination.

Soon the boat was hitting the bottom, and the propeller spinning in mud. We all leapt out, then heaved the boat forward until we found another stretch deep enough to motor forward again. And so we carried on, jumping in and out of the boat, falling about laughing and having a great time.

Eventually we could go no further so we heaved the boat on to the bank, anchored it, picked up our things and set off on foot. The marshy grassland turned into heather and big dunes, and then, after perhaps half an hour, we broke out of the dunes on to the biggest beach I've ever seen. Between the dunes and the sea was more than a mile of perfect white sand, and it must be five miles wide. And there was not a soul on it.

In the distance, across the channel, we could see the crowds on the main beach, but this one, Bob Hall Sands, was all ours. We swam, then came back, built a fire, cooked some sausages, told ghost stories and slept out in our sleeping bags staring up at the stars.

Next morning, we explored the creeks some more, almost getting stuck again, but making it in the nick of time back to the deep channel and Wells. As silly as it sounds, though we'd only been a couple of miles from the crazy golf and caravan park, we'd had a genuine wilderness experience.

Now do it . . .

For information on Wells-next-the-Sea, visit Wells Guide (www.wells-guide.co.uk).

Maggie May

| **Why** | To spend a day achieving something great |
| **Where** | USA | **Duration** | One day |

LONG WEEKEND

Driving down into Death Valley, it's hard not to feel a sense of foreboding. The area got its name when a group of travellers heading west in the gold rush of 1849 became lost and were trapped here. One of them died before they were rescued and shown the route out. But it's not just the name that's intimidating. It's the way that as the road descends for mile after mile, the mirages that lie across it become more and more regular, and the temperature creeps relentlessly upwards.

Death Valley is the hottest, driest and lowest place in North America. It's more or less the shape of a huge bath – a flat valley about 140 miles long, encircled by mountains. At its lowest point it is 282 feet below sea level, and this unusual topography means hot air becomes trapped in the valley and circulates around it like a natural convection oven, creating extremely high temperatures. The highest recorded here was 56.7°C, second only in the record books to Al 'Aziziyah, Libya, where the mercury once hit 57.8°C. On

average, there are less than two inches of rain a year, and in some years it doesn't rain at all. So how do you fancy coming here for a 200-mile bike ride?

For one day every spring and autumn, Death Valley is filled with cyclists. They come to take part in the Death Valley Century, Ultra Century and Double Century, courses which cover 108, 144 and 197 miles respectively. The events start and finish at the Furnace Creek Resort in the centre of the valley, with riders starting in waves from just after 6 a.m. The organizers insist it isn't a race and that everyone who finishes within the maximum time limits – 10, 12 and 17 hours, dependent on the distance – is a winner.

And though it may sound like submitting to a day in purgatory, this event is always oversubscribed. Eager cyclists make sure they log on to the organizer's website as soon as registration opens in the hope of getting a place.

It's not just that they are masochists. As well as being a place of extreme heat, Death Valley has a unique beauty. The cyclists will pass sand dunes that look like they should be in the Sahara, parched salt pans like those of the Chilean desert, and areas where mineral deposits have turned the rocks into a rainbow of colours. The route includes a loop up to the top of the mountains that surround the valley, so there are great views too, and those doing the Double will also have the pleasure of riding through the desert by moonlight. They also get to ride on roads with very little traffic and with regular food and water posts, plus support cars that roam the course and can help with mechanical problems.

It's a tough day, but certainly one you'll never forget. It's also one of the few cycling adventures where you really don't need to bother bringing waterproofs.

Now do it . . .

To embark on this marathon adventure in one of the toughest climates, visit AdventureCORPS (www.adventurecorps.com).

The Yukon Ultra Race

Once in a Lifetime

Why | For an endurance test and satisfaction at the finish line

Where | Canada | **Duration** | Nine to twelve days

For more than twenty-five years, the annual Yukon Quest has been seen as the ultimate dog-sled race. Each competitor rides across Canada's Yukon province on a sled pulled by between six and fourteen dogs, battling temperatures that regularly fall as low as –50°C. It's a gruelling endurance challenge, but in 2004, someone came up with the idea for an even tougher race. It would follow much of the same course, but have one vital twist – there would be no dogs.

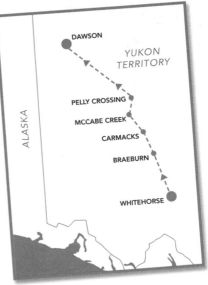

This then is the Yukon Arctic Ultra, in which competitors run for up to 430 miles, dragging the sleds themselves. Running that kind of distance would be a major undertaking anywhere in the world, but in the remote Yukon, in the middle of winter, it borders on crazy. Snow can be so deep on the course that competitors sink to their knees, and there is a constant risk of frostbite. The 2007 race was called off when temperatures hit –61°C, and it wasn't until 2009 that anyone managed to complete the whole course. When the organizers call it 'the world's toughest and coldest race', they are not exaggerating.

It's not taken in stages either – the clock starts counting when the runners leave Whitehorse, the capital of the Yukon, and stops when they reach the finish line in Dawson City. They must decide when to get out their bivvy bags and grab a few hours' sleep. And it's a routine they need to get used to – the race can take anything from nine to twelve days. If you are not back in thirteen days, you are disqualified – and they come searching for you.

As well as the 430-mile race, there are also races over 100 and 300 miles, which take between one and two and a half days, and between five and seven days respectively.

Competitors say that despite the conditions, and the danger of attack from wolves or moose, the real battle is a mental one. The runners quickly become separated, so for much of the time they are completely alone in the wilderness, battling to stay motivated while suffering from the hallucinations caused by sleep deprivation.

Entry costs, in euros, 850, 1,350 and 2,050 for the 100, 300 and 430 miles respectively, and first-timers must take a two-day course before they start, in order to learn the basics of extreme cold weather survival.

There has been a surge of interest in these 'ultra' marathons in recent years, including the 156-mile Marathon des Sables in Morocco, the 153-mile Spartathlon in Greece and the 103-mile Ultra Trail du Mont Blanc, which circles around western Europe's highest peak. But while more than 100,000 people apply to compete in the London Marathon each year, and the Marathon des Sables had more than 1,000 competitors in 2010, the Yukon Arctic Ultra is so tough that it remains a very small and low-key event. It wasn't held in 2010, but the previous year saw a total of 39 runners in the three distance categories, plus three competitors on cross-country skis and one on a converted mountain bike.

Of those 39, only 22 reached the finish. It may be the world's toughest race, but for the winner there is no prize money and no trophy, just a massive sense of achievement, and the prospect of a very well-earned bath.

Now do it . . .
Yukon Arctic Ultra (www.arcticultra.de) can provide you with all the details you need to complete this epic challenge.

Why	To reach a place very few have ever seen
Where	Antarctica	**Duration**	Two days to two months

'Great God! This is an awful place,' wrote Captain Robert Falcon Scott when he finally reached the South Pole on 17 January 1912. He had spent seventy-eight days trudging across more than 800 miles of snow and ice to get there, but all he found waiting for him was bitter disappointment. Amid the great expanse of white was an empty tent flapping in the wind and inside that was a note, in which Scott's Norwegian rival Roald Amundsen announced he had got there first. With his quest for polar glory thus thwarted, all that remained for Scott was the long march back to the coast, a journey neither he nor any of his team would live to complete.

Despite the terrible fate that befell Scott and his men, getting to that 'awful place', at the centre of the coldest and windiest of all the continents, remains a burning ambition for thousands of adventurers around the world. Perhaps it is because the South Pole is a symbol of inaccessibility, the extreme opposite of our modern urban world, sitting on an ice sheet several miles thick and surrounded by five million square miles of nothingness. But perhaps it is also partly because Scott's doomed expedition has become the most famous adventure story of them all.

Today, though, reaching the Pole doesn't necessarily require months of hardship, and the chances of making it back alive are much higher. In fact, if you have $40,000 to spare, you can get to the Pole with almost no physical effort at all, and do the round trip in a week. Several tour companies offer these trips to the Pole, flying visits in every sense. You set out from either Punta Arenas, in southern Chile, or Cape Town, South Africa, fly to a base camp in Antarctica where you spend the night, then fly on to the Pole where you typically might stay for four hours before starting your return. It must be a thrilling experience, but with every lunch stop carefully pre-planned, and the biggest challenge being how to deal with cramp from spending so long sitting in planes, it's hardly a real polar adventure.

Thankfully, there are other, more fulfilling options. One is to 'ski the last degree', an expedition that gives you a taste of genuine polar exploration, but within a two-to-three-week trip. These trips are run by Adventure Network International (ANI), Antarctica's leading expedition-organizing company. You fly from Punta Arenas to their tented base camp at Patriot Hills, at the foot of the Ellsworth Mountains, some 670 miles from the Pole.

There you spend several days with a guide making final preparations and practising dragging the sleds, known as pulks, in which you carry your equipment. When the team is ready, and there's a sufficient weather window, you fly south to a latitude of 89 degrees, landing on the ice in a ski-equipped plane. From here, you travel under your own steam, walking on cross-country skis and dragging your pulk, across the final degree of latitude – 69 miles – to reach the Pole.

That might not sound a great distance, but the going is not easy here. The Pole is at an altitude of 2,835 metres, and the shortage of oxygen in the air makes breathing harder. The wind can blow the snow and ice into 'sastrugi', wave-like formations you have to clamber over. These expeditions only take place in December and January, during the Antarctic summer when there is 24-hour sunlight, but even so, storms can blow in, taking the temperature as low as –30°C. (In winter, temperatures in Antarctica have fallen as low as –89°C.) Taking all that into consideration, even with eight hours' walking you can expect to cover only 6 to 10 miles a day, so it will take nine or ten days to reach the Pole.

But if you really want to live out the full South Pole adventure, ANI also offers a 'ski all the way' expedition. For this you need to set aside two months (not to mention the best part of a year to train). The trip starts in the same way as the 'last degree' expedition, but rather than fly south, the ski-equipped plane from Patriot Hills makes a short hop back to the Antarctic coast at Hercules Inlet, where the long trek begins. From there, it's 730 miles to the Pole, a journey that will take fifty to sixty days. For up to nine hours a day you'll haul your 50-kilo pulk over snow and ice, crossing glaciers and crevasses and sastrugi up to 8 feet high.

The route climbs up from the coast at Hercules Inlet (where there is solid year-round ice, as opposed to open water), then passes Patriot Hills, where you rest for a day and can drop off kit or pick up items you've forgotten. From there you climb

up on to the icecap, a vast white plain dotted by occasional rocky peaks or 'nunataks', the summits of mountains submerged under hundreds of metres of ice. The scenery is beautiful, but absolutely stark and elemental – for the duration you will see nothing but ice, snow, rock and the blue sky above. In such surroundings, trekking for hour after hour takes on a meditative quality.

The logistics of expeditions like this mean they don't come cheap. Flying to Antarctica, and within it, is hugely expensive, and the flights between Patriot Hills and the South Pole have to stop for fuel on the way – fuel which itself has had to be previously flown in and cached. The 'ski all the way' expedition costs around $64,000; the 'last degree' trip costs $50,000: the much longer

trip costs only slightly more because it involves less flying. For both trips you can sign up as an individual or with friends. For the 'last degree', there needs to be a minimum of four people, plus the guide, for the trip to operate, and there's a maximum group size of five. The 'ski all the way' expeditions operate with groups of between one and five people, plus the guide.

But whether it comes after two weeks or two months, when you finally see a dot on the white horizon, and watch as it grows to form the US South Pole research station, the end of your epic journey, you may well find yourself disagreeing with Scott's verdict. In fact, you might feel you've reached the most wonderful place in the world.

'The South Pole is a symbol of inaccessibility, the extreme opposite of our modern urban world'

Now do it . . .
For information on various adventures you can achieve on the South Pole, visit Adventure Network International (www.adventure-network.com).

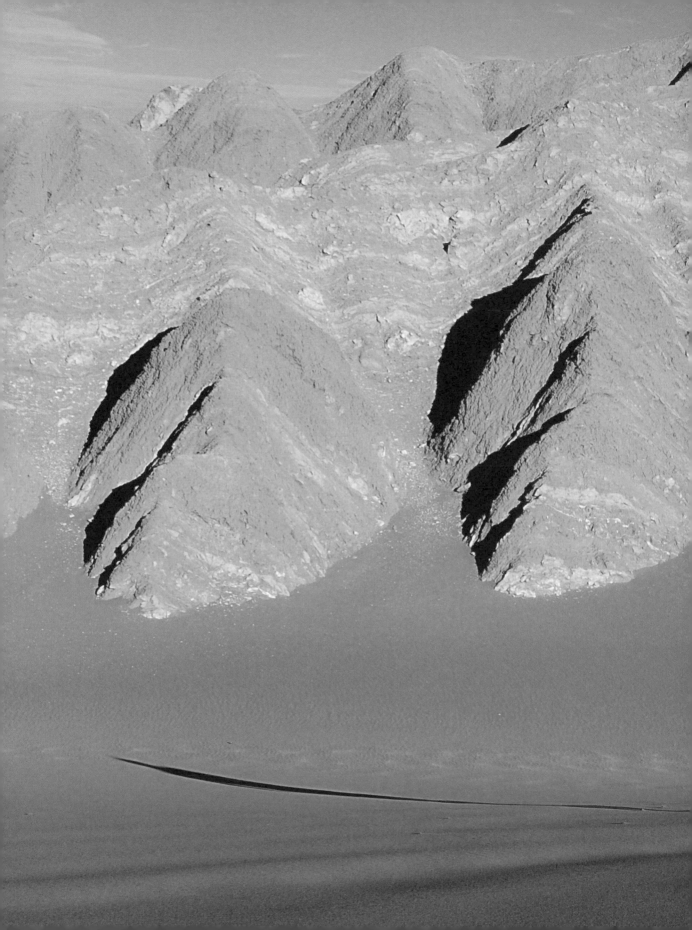

Enjoy your adventure

A very big thank-you to my daughter Emily, for photographing and supporting me on our expeditions.

A big thank-you to Mum and Dad, without whom none of this would have been possible.

Thank you also to Vics, my girlfriend and stalwart supporter, for keeping me in check.

I would like to say a very big thank-you to Tom Robbins, who helped to write the book and whose hard work helped to bring all of these adventures together.

Thank you to Robert Kirby, my agent, for introducing me to the team at Transworld, including my editor Sarah Emsley, project editor Kate Tolley, Lynsey Dalladay and Claire Evans. Thanks also to designer Bobby Birchall.

Airlines Fact Files
Cathay Pacific: all Hong Kong and New Zealand adventures (www.cathaypacific.co.uk); TACA: all Central America adventures (www.taca.com); Iberia: all Central America adventures (www.iberia.com); SAS: all Sweden adventures (www.flysas.com)

Head Researchers
Louisa Edwards, Lisa Downs

Contributors
Peter Harmer, Michael Cotton

Thank Yous
Anna Westall, Hire-a-Camera, Christian Lopez, Sibella Argnello, Small World Marketing, Patrick Weston, Amber Laree, Jimmy Simak, Marcello Meneses, Ecuador Adventure, Hills Balfour Synergy PR, Claire Antell, Paul Bondsfield, Joanne Cheok, Ian Hutchinson, Hotel Monasterio, Peru, Las Castias del Colca, Peru, Anna Nash, Orient Express Hotels, and to all those at Tru who helped with the communications for our adventures.

Photo Credits

With exceptions as listed below: journeys 4, 5, 21, 23, 26, 35, 36, 38, 39, 46, 48, 56, 62, 75, 82, 85, 89, 97 © Big Earth Ltd; journeys 2, 3, 20, 30, 57 © Long Way Round Ltd; journey 91 © Russ Malkin and Jeanie Davidson; journeys 1, 6, 8, 14, 22, 27, 31, 32, 37, 42, 44, 45, 51, 53, 54, 63, 64, 67, 83, 94 © Russ Malkin and Victoria Morton; journeys 18, 28, 61, 98 © Russ and Emily Malkin; journeys 41, 50, 68, 69 © Russ Malkin; journeys 9, 11, 15, 40, 49, 59, 65 © Russ and Emily Malkin and Victoria Morton; p. 2-3: footprints in the snow © Marcus Peel; p. 16-17: world map © Fotolia; p. 21: Abismo Anhumas cavern © Marcelo Krause; p. 21 diver in cavern © Marcelo Krause; p.24: rusting boats on desert © Michael Runkel/Alamy; p. 40: both images © Scott Markewitz/Getty Images; p. 43: starry sky © Photolibrary; p. 44: clam © Aitutaki Marine Research Centre; p. 48-9: motorbikers © Jason Baxter/Alamy; p. 50-1: Route 66 © Maik Blume/Getty Images, motorbike © blickwinkel/Alamy; p. 54: both images © Borneoguide.com; p. 55-7: all images © World of Greenland; p. 59: the Wild Bunch © Getty Images; p. 61: film still © Alamy; p. 67: both images © National Geographic/Getty Images; p. 68-9: all images © Aquamarine Santo; p. 70: wreck dive © National Geographic/Getty Images; p. 71: Cresta Run © Leo Mason/Alamy; p. 72: historic image © Getty Images; p. 92-6: all images © Wilderness Journeys; p. 109: Leptis Magna © imagebroker/Alamy; p. 110: arch © imagebroker/Alamy; p. 111: latrine © Martin Beddall/Alamy, ruins © Getty Images; p. 112-3 © Panoramic Journeys; p. 120: two men climbing © LOOK Die Bildagentur der Fotografen GmbH/Alamy; p. 122: Tiger Moth © Antony Nettle/Alamy; p. 123: historic image © Mary Evans Picture Library/Alamy; p. 124: view of Tiblisi © Michael Runkel/Getty Images; p. 144: Fox Glacier © Frans Lemmens/Getty Images; p. 154: both images © Habitat for Humanity; p. 163-5: all images ©Hadrian's Wall Country; p. 178: Okavango Delta and lion kill © Helge Pedersen/Alamy; p. 179: hippo © Gary Dublanko/Alamy; p. 180-1: Okavango Delta © Helge Pedersen/Alamy, hyena attack © Beverly Joubert/Getty Images; p. 186: historic image © Illustrated London News Ltd/Mary Evans; p. 187: Orient Express © Peter Jordan/Alamy; p. 193: ship on shore © Chris Howes/Wild Places Photography/Alamy, sand dunes © George Silk/Getty Images; p. 194: ski shop © Christophe Archambault/Getty Images; p. 195 skiing ©Lonely Planet Images/Alamy; p. 202: steam train © John White Photos/Alamy; p. 207: man in tunnels © Alamy; p. 219: two divers © Stuart Westmorland/Getty Images, snorkelling © Norbert Wu/Getty Images; p. 220: two divers © Stuart Westmorland/Getty Images; p. 226: rock church at Lalibela © Helen Edwards; p. 229: man with load © National Geographic/Getty Images, man walking © Slow Images/Getty Images; p. 230-1: boy on ice © Slow Images/Getty Images, walkers on frozen river © National Geographic/Getty Images; p. 235-7: all images © Ben Walker/KE Adventure Travel, except p. 236 bottom Polaroid © Steve Jeffrey/KE Adventure Travel; p. 238-8: all images © Wave Riders; p. 240-2: all images © Marcus Peel; p. 247-9: all images © Lisa Downs; p. 250-1: all images © Norma Downs; p. 252-5: all images © Marcus Peel; p. 256-7 Northern lights © Lars Thulin/Getty Images; p. 258: end of the road © Richard Wareham Fotografie/Alamy; p. 259: jungle © National Geographic/Getty Images; p. 261: boat through ice © National Geographic/Getty Images; p. 262: Northwest Passage © Mary Evans Picture Library/Alamy; p. 263-4: all images © Tour d'Afrique; p. 274: front of dinghy © Whit Richardson/Alamy; p. 275: rafting © imagebroker/Alamy; p. 276-7: Goosenecks © imagebroker/Alamy; p. 278: lone skater © Johan Klovsjö/Getty Images; p. 279: sunrise skating © David Thyberg/Getty Images; p. 280: skating © David Thyberg/Alamy; p. 281: both images © Globo via Getty Images; p. 286-7: BASE jumpers © Chris Bazil/Alamy; p. 292: Rishikesh © Roman Soumar/Corbis; p. 293: yoga © Chris Fredriksson/Alamy; p. 295: black cab © Martyn Vickery/Alamy; p. 298: top image © Jeremy Williams/Alamy, bottom image © First Light/Alamy; p. 299-301: all images © Air Combat USA; p. 306: cyclists © Peter Burian/Alamy; road through Death Valley © Reg Garner/Alamy; p. 309: Yukon Quest © imagebroker/Alamy; p. 311: ice and sky © B&C Alexander/ArcticPhoto; p. 312-3: image © Alamy

TRANSWORLD PUBLISHERS
61–63 Uxbridge Road, London W5 5SA
A Random House Group Company
www.rbooks.co.uk

First published in Great Britain
in 2011 by Bantam Press
an imprint of Transworld Publishers

A CIP catalogue record for this book
is available from the British Library.

ISBN 9780593066119

Addresses for Random House Group Ltd companies outside the UK can be found at: www.randomhouse.co.uk
The Random House Group Ltd Reg. No. 954009

The Random House Group Ltd supports the Forest Stewardship Council (FSC), the leading international forest-certification organization. All our titles that are printed on Greenpeace-approved FSC-certified paper carry the FSC logo. Our paper procurement policy can be found at www.rbooks.co.uk/environment

Designed by Bobby Birchall; Bobby&Co.
Journey maps by Tom Coulson at Encompass Graphics
Typeset in Avenir
Printed and bound in Great Britain by
Butler Tanner & Dennis Ltd

2 4 6 8 10 9 7 5 3 1